ON DURKHEIM'S *ELEMENTARY FORMS OF RELIGIOUS LIFE*

This is the first collection of essays to be published on Durkheim's master-piece, *The Elementary Forms of Religious Life*. A classic of sociology and the study of religion, and one of his most important and influential works, *The Elementary Forms* is currently enjoying a renaissance in other, related disciplines.

This collection represents the work of the most important, international Durkheim scholars from the fields of anthropology, philosophy and sociology. From these diverse viewpoints, the contributors examine Durkheim's perspective on the role of religion and social life. The essays focus on key issues, for example, the method Durkheim adopted in his study; the role of ritual and belief in society; the nature of contemporary religion, as well as on debates on the notion of the soul and contemporary collective civic rituals. This collection fills a major gap in studies on Durkheim, and will be a vital resource for students and researchers in anthropology, sociology and philosophy and religious studies.

The contributors N. J. Allen, Werner Gephart, Terry F. Godlove, Jr., Robert Alun Jones, Dominique Merllié, Howard Morphy, Dénes Némedi, Giovanni Paoletti, William Ramp, Malcolm Ruel, Warren Schmaus, Sue Stedman Jones, Ivan Strenski, Kenneth Thompson, W. Watts Miller.

The editors N. J. Allen is Reader in the Social Anthropology of South Asia at Oxford University and specialist in the work of Marcel Mauss. W. S. F. Pickering helped to found the British Centre for Durkheimian Studies in the Institute of Social and Cultural Anthropology in Oxford in 1991. He has written on Durkheim's sociology of religion and, more recently, was joint editor of *Debating Durkheim*, published by Routledge. W. Watts Miller is editor of *Durkheim Studies/Études durkheimiennes*, and the author of *Durkheim, Morals and Modernity* (1996). He lectures in the Departments of Sociology and Philosophy at the University of Bristol.

ROUTLEDGE STUDIES IN SOCIAL AND POLITICAL THOUGHT

ON DURKHEIM'S
ELEMENTARY FORMS OF RELIGIOUS LIFE

Edited by N. J. Allen,
W. S. F. Pickering and W. Watts Miller

Published in conjunction with the British Centre
for Durkheimian Studies

London and New York

First published 1998
by Routledge
11 New Fetter Lane, London EC4P 4EE

Simultaneously published in the USA and Canada
by Routledge
29 West 35th Street, New York, NY 10001

Reprinted 2001

Routledge is an imprint of the Taylor & Francis Group

© 1998 Edited by N. J. Allen, W. S. F. Pickering and
W. Watts Miller
Typeset in Baskerville by
Florencetype Limited, Stoodleigh, Devon
Printed and bound in Great Britain by
Selwood Printing Ltd, Burgess Hill, West Sussex

Transferred to Digital Printing 2003

British Library Cataloguing in Publication Data
A catalogue record for this book is available
from the British Library

Library of Congress Cataloguing in Publication Data
On Durkheim's Elementary Forms of Religious Life / edited by
N. J. Allen, W. S. F Pickering and W. Watts Miller.
p.   cm. – (Routledge studies in social and political thought)
(hc : alk. paper)
1. Durkheim, Emile, 1858–1917. Formes élémentaires de la vie
religieuse. 2. Religion. 3. Totemism. I. Allen, N. J. II. Pickering,
W. S. F. III. Watts Miller, William, 1944–
IV. Series
GN470.D83069   1998
306.6–dc21   97–29595
CIP
AC

ISBN 0–415–16286–6

CONTENTS

CONTRIBUTORS

N. J. Allen won a scholarship in classics to New College, Oxford, in 1957. He studied medicine there and later in London. He returned to Oxford to study social anthropology, basing his D.Phil. on fieldwork in Nepal. He lectured in Durham from 1972 to 1976. Since then he has been Lecturer and Reader in the Social Anthropology of South Asia in Oxford. His forty main publications focus on the Himalayas, kinship theory, the history of French anthropology and Indo-European comparativism with special reference to Hinduism.

Werner Gephart has been Professor of Sociology at the University of Bonn since 1992. He was Alfred Grosser Guest Professor at the Institut d'Etudes Politiques in Paris. His main interests are in the sociology of law, sociological theory, symbolism, culture and religion, on all of which he has written various articles. He is to be the editor of a critical edition of Max Weber's sociology of law.

Terry Godlove, Jr., is Associate Professor of Philosophy and Chair at Hofstra University, New York. His research interests include epistemology and interpretation theory. In 1989 he published *Religion, Interpretation and Diversity of Belief: The Framework Model from Kant to Durkheim to Davidson*. His articles are on epistemology and the category of space in Durkheim.

Robert Alun Jones is Professor of Religious Studies, History and Sociology at the University of Illinois, Urbana. His major research interests include Durkheim and his intellectual context, the methodology of the history of ideas, and the scholarly use of electronic documents and networked information systems. He is the author of *Emile Durkheim: an Introduction to Four Major Works* (1986) as well as numerous journal articles on Durkheim. He has been editor of *Etudes durkheimiennes*, and is also responsible for the Durkheim site on the Internet. He is writing a book on Durkheim's social realism.

Dominique Merllié teaches sociology at the University of Saint-Denis in Paris. He is a member of the Centre de Sociologie de l'Education et de la Culture (EHESS and CNRS, Paris). His research fields include social mobility and the uses of statistical categories. Among his publications are: *Initiation à la pratique sociologique* (with P. Champagne, R. Lenoir and

L. Pinto (1996), and *La mobilité sociale* (1994). He was the editor of a special issue of the *Revue philosophique* (1989, 4) about L. Lévy-Bruhl, which includes some of his publications on this author.

Howard Morphy is Professor of Anthropology at University College London. He has conducted fieldwork in Arnhem Land, Northern Australia, and has collaborated on many films with Ian Dunlop of Film Australia. His most recent books are *Ancestral Connections* (1991) and *Rethinking Visual Anthropology* (edited with Marcus Banks, 1977). With John Mulvaney and Alison Petch he has recently completed an edited edition of Gillen's letters to Spencer (1997). He has twice been awarded the Stanner Prize for Aboriginal studies.

Dénes Némedi studied history in Debrecen in Hungary and is now Assistant Professor of Sociology at the Eötvös University of Budapest. He has written on social research in Hungary in the inter-war period, on modern German sociology and on Durkheim. He has recently published in Hungarian, *Durkheim: Knowledge and Society*.

Giovanni Paoletti studied philosophy at the Scuola Normale of Pisa. He is at present preparing a doctoral dissertation. He is the author of articles on the history of sociology and Durkheim's sociology of religion, including 'Durkheim à l'Ecole Normale Supérieure: lectures de jeunesse', *Etudes durkheimiennes/Durkheim Studies*, IV, 1992; 'Les *Règles en France*, du vivant de Durkheim' in M. Borlandi and L. Mucchielli (eds) *La Sociologie et sa méthode; 'Les 'Règles de Durkheim un siècle après'* (1995).

W. S. F. Pickering was a lecturer in social studies at the University of Newcastle upon Tyne until he retired in 1987. In 1991 he helped to found the British Centre for Durkheimian Studies in the Institute of Social and Cultural Anthropology, Oxford. He has written and edited books on Durkheim and published articles on him and members of the Année Sociologique group.

William Ramp is Assistant Professor of Sociology at the University of Lethbridge, Alberta, Canada, where he teaches classical sociological theory. He is the author of 'Durkheim and Foucault on the Genesis of the Disciplinary Society', forthcoming in M. S. Cladis (ed.) *Durkheim and Foucault: Punishment and the School* (British Centre for Durkheimian Studies, 1997). His interests include sociological theories of identity and subjectivity as applied to religion and social movements.

Malcolm Ruel, D.Phil. (Oxon. 1959), is a Fellow of Clare College, Cambridge, and until his retirement was a University Lecturer in the Department of Social Anthropology. He has conducted fieldwork in West and East Africa. His most recent publication, *Belief, Ritual and the Securing of Life: Reflexive Essays on a Bantu Religion* (1997), matches the role of 'belief' in Christianity against that of 'ritual' (*inyangi*) for the Kuria people of East Africa.

Warren Schmaus is the author of *Durkheim's Philosophy of Science and the Sociology of Knowledge* (1994), as well as numerous articles in the history and philosophy of the social sciences and on issues of science and values. He is Professor of Philosophy at the Illinois Institute of Technology in Chicago and a fellow of the Center of the Philosophy of Science at the University of Pittsburgh.

Sue Stedman Jones studied philosophy and completed a London doctorate titled 'From Kant to Durkheim'. She formerly taught social philosophy and the philosophy of the social sciences at Goldsmith's College, London. She is now pursuing independent research and is currently working on a book, *Durkheim Re-considered*, dividing her time between London and Paris.

Ivan Strenski is Holstein Family Community Professor of Religious Studies at the University of California, Riverside. He is author of *Four Theories of Myth in Twentieth Century History* (1987), *Religion in Relation* (1993), and *Durkheim and the Jews of France* (1997). He has also published an edition of Malinowski's writing on myth (1992). His articles include ones on Durkheim and the Durkheimians, Henri Hubert and Marcel Mauss, on questions of race, historiography, political mythology, the rise of ritualism and on the sacred.

Kenneth Thompson is Professor of Sociology at the Open University, UK. Educated at Leicester and Oxford universities, he has held teaching appointments at the University of California, Los Angeles, Rutgers University and Smith College. His books include *Bureaucracy and Church Reform* (1970), *Auguste Comte: The Foundation of Sociology* (1975), *Emile Durkheim* (1982), *Sartre: Life and Works* (1984), *Beliefs and Ideology* (1986) and *Moral Panics* (1997). His most recent edited book is *Media and Cultural Regulation* (1997). His current ESRC-funded research project is on 'Moral Regulation and Television'.

Willie Watts Miller is editor of *Durkheim Studies / Etudes durkheimiennes*. His publications include *Durkheim, Morals and Modernity* (1996) and a critical edition and translation of Durkheim's Latin thesis on Montesquieu. He is a member of the Centre for Durkheimian Studies, Oxford, and of the Departments of Sociology and Philosophy in the University of Bristol.

ACKNOWLEDGEMENTS

First and foremost the authors wish to express their appreciation for the help they received in the organization of the conference which gave rise to the papers constituting the basis of this book. In particular, they thank Jean-Claude Vatin, Director of the Maison Française, Oxford, for encouraging us to hold the conference there, and for the assistance of its administrative staff.

Financial assistance came by way of a seminar award of the Economic and Social Research Council. Without it the conference would not have been as large as it was and many people could not have come from various parts of the world to present papers. For the administration of the grant we appreciate the work of Isabella Birkin of the Institute of Social and Cultural Anthropology, Oxford.

For the preparation of the book, we should above all thank the contributors themselves, who had to provide chapters in accordance with stringent technical instructions. Without willing authors there would indeed be no book. But we should also show our appreciation to those who gave papers which, for various reasons, we have not been able to include but who all made a positive contribution to the conference.

We are also grateful to certain members of staff of the Computing Service of Oxford University for helping us in technical matters, to Chris Holdsworth for assisting in the preparation of the bibliography, to Miriam Kochan for translating one of the papers and to Carol Pickering who undertook a great deal of typing and sub-editing.

EXPLANATORY NOTE

It is necessary to forewarn readers of some technical points in the format of this book.

Lukes' dating-enumeration has been followed throughout (see Bibliography). Since the book is a commentary on another book, references to the latter are inevitably numerous. Instead of continually referring to *Les Formes élémentaires* as 1912a, the dating-enumeration '1912a' is omitted. In many cases a bracket contains two numbers, e.g. (589/412). This means that the quotation or reference is to be found on page 589 of *Les Formes élémentaires* and on page 412 of Swain's translation, perhaps corrected (see below). Where only one number appears, e.g. (133), this relates to page 133 of the French text. If the quotation from *Les Formes élémentaires* is in English with no translation dating-enumeration, it is assumed that the translation has been made by the author. Further, unless otherwise stated, English translations of pieces in Italian or German have also been made by the author of the chapter. If the reference is of the kind (1968c/1975b 2:18–19), it means that it is located by referring to Durkheim 1968c in the Bibliography, but the reference is also to be found, reprinted, in Durkheim 1975b, volume 2, with the page numbers 18–19, also located in the Bibliography.

Where contributors have used an English translation of passages in *Les Formes élémentaires*, they have nearly all drawn on Swain's translation of 1915. As is well known, it is often inaccurate. Unfortunately the new translation by Karen Fields did not appear until 1995, just before the conference, and the editors decided against the wholesale changes that would have been involved in adopting it throughout. Instead, quotations using the Swain translation have been retained, and where necessary corrected. At least, giving the page number in Swain's translation allows the reader to see the context of the reference in English. We have followed Fields' translation of the title of Durkheim's book however, by omitting the word 'the' before 'Religious Life'.

It is the common practice in writing on Durkheim and Année Sociologique group to keep certain terms in French since there is no satisfactory equivalent in English. The practice is followed here, as with the words, *conscience* and *représentation*. The first of these means either consciousness or conscience; the second, image, reflection, idea. The reader has to judge the meaning from the context.

INTRODUCTION

The object of the following essays is certainly not a collective plea, an apologia, for people to read *The Elementary Forms of Religious Life*. Suffice it to say that it was Durkheim's most powerful book – his most demanding and exciting. As readers may know, it has become a classic in the realm of sociology and the study of religion. Further, its importance has become increasingly recognized, not least by the demands made in the production of a new, commendable English translation which appeared in 1995. Whether Durkheim's book on ethics which was planned to follow *The Elementary Forms*, but of which only the opening sections were written, would have been more outstanding is anyone's guess. To be sure, ethics was his overriding concern, more so perhaps than religion, though for him the two had a common origin and were very closely intertwined.

But if this book does not go out of its way to 'sell' *The Elementary Forms*, neither is it an exposition of the book viewed as a whole – a book that has so many themes relating to sociology, anthropology and the 'scientific' study of religion. Anyone wishing to be convinced of the importance today of Durkheim's book should consult the introduction in Karen Fields' new translation mentioned above (1995:xvii–lxxiii). For a more general appreciation, the reader's attention is drawn to the relevant sections in Steven Lukes' unique intellectual biography of Durkheim, published in 1973.

If *The Elementary Forms* is not systematically treated here as a whole, neither are all its main academic issues. Rather, this book forms an occasion for scholars of various disciplines, who would call themselves serious students of Durkheim, to reflect on key issues which have been the subject of debate over the years, such as the method Durkheim adopted in his study, the role of ritual and belief in society, and the nature of contemporary religion. In one or two cases, relatively less-discussed problems are analysed which are beginning to come to the fore, such as the notion of the soul and collective effervescence.

Where well-known issues are raised, the intention is not simply to rehearse them according to the inclination of individual writers but to bring to them new light and insights. Before these are mentioned in more detail, something of the origins and the internal problems of the book might be mentioned.

The reader has gleaned enough already to realize that the book is the product of a conference. It took place over three days in July 1995 and was organised by the British Centre for Durkheimian Studies in Oxford. The year 1995 was in fact the centenary of the 'revelation' which came to Durkheim when he read the work of Robertson Smith: it consequently made him take seriously the sociological study of religion (Durkheim 1907b:613). *Les Formes élémentaires de la vie religieuse* published in 1912 was in fact the culmination of that 'revelation'.

As mentioned, a large number of subjects is covered in the book. This gives rise to many possibilities in the presentation of papers at a conference where the participants have freedom in the choice of topics. Whilst a certain openness might be acceptable for a conference, a book based on its papers is a different matter. Publishers rightly make certain demands about uniformity, coherence and length. For such reasons not all the 28 papers given at the Oxford conference could be accepted for this book. The editors were faced with the unenviable problem of choosing some and eliminating others, and the even more exacting task of arranging in a coherent order the papers which had been selected. The structure finally adopted was that used by Durkheim in his book. Thus, the papers here included fall into four sections – methodology, belief, ritual and epistemology. Not surprisingly some of the papers cross the rigidity of such boundaries.

Where is the contemporary interest in issues raised by *Les Formes élémentaires*? The response of scholars to the internationally advertised conference provides some, albeit limited, indication of this. In terms of reinterpretation or criticism nothing was offered with regard to defining religion or to overall theories about religion *per se*, such as functionalism and structuralism (but see Chapters 7 and 13). Issues relating to belief and ritual received approximately equal attention. But popular areas proved to be epistemology; the sociology of knowledge; and the cult of individual, seen as the religion of today's western world. Many of the contributions of this kind were made by those who would call themselves philosophers rather than sociologists or anthropologists. A narrower issue which appeared in many of the papers, irrespective of their titles, was collective effervescence or effervescent assembly (see Pickering 1984:Chs 21 and 22). Although this is a phenomenon which has usually been kept in the background in Durkheimian studies, it appeared in many papers across the board. For many years it was not discussed in any systematic or comprehensive way and little was done to develop the idea. In part this may have been because it was thought that such a phenomenon could not be fitted into a scientific approach to social change in society as well as to religion.

Another observation arising from the conference was the relatively large number of American participants who attended it and a corresponding lack of those from France. This, it might be argued, is a reflection of the place of *Les Formes élémentaires* within Durkheimian studies, not least perhaps in the teaching of undergraduates. It is probably not far wrong to say that in France, of all Durkheim's works published in his lifetime and most frequently referred to in books and articles, relatively few citations consider in detail the classic which is the subject of this book. Preference is for issues raised by *De la Division du travail social* (1893b), *Les Règles* (1895a) and

Le Suicide (1897a). This is reflected in the fact that in France, of these four books, *Les Formes élémentaires* is the one that has sold the fewest copies. Nor are epistemological issues relating to the sociology of knowledge as prominent in France as they seem to be amongst American and English scholars. Again, it might be argued that the relative popularity of *Les Formes élémentaires* in the United States reflects the fact that the United States still considers itself to be a religious or Christian country and that in the academic world issues of religion are still prominently debated. Might one be so bold as to say this is in stark contrast to the position in the academic world in France?

Now to a brief examination of the issues raised by this book.

I

Since Durkheim made the claim that sociology was in some sense a scientific study and that truth comes from science, his approach to religion was one that inevitably meant it had to comply with the canons of the natural sciences – at least to the degree that this was possible and in accordance with the canons of science as they were seen in his day (see 1895a). In *Les Formes élémentaires* he asserted that all that was required scientifically was 'one well carried out experiment' to prove his conclusions (593/415).[1] The 'experiment' written up in the book was based on a study of what he along with others held to be one of the most primitive and simple of all societies then known to scholars, the Arunta of Australia which had been so well described by ethnographers (1/1). In such a society, he assumed, it was possible to see religion in its most basic form, to observe how it functioned and its place in social behaviour.

These methodological axioms have not been without their opponents. Criticism was levelled against his definition of religion, which was based on the notion of the sacred as a universal concept (49–65/36–42). More basic questions centred on the validity of studying religion by the method of the natural sciences. These two issues, which were once so prominent, have receded into the background as being either irresolvable or of little practical merit, seen against the development of the sociology of religion. Most anthropologists and sociologists now side with Durkheim on these well-worn matters, not with his opponents. The word scientific has become more flexible with the growth of the philosophy of science. The notion of the sacred as being at the heart of religion is no longer openly rejected: it is a matter for refinement. The area, however, which has from time to time been raised concerns the 'material' used in the 'experiment'. How well did Durkheim carry out his work? Was the 'material' adequate to make generalizations which, once formulated, would apply without reference to culture or time?

With the exception of Mauss, Durkheim was probably one of the last, if not the last, great armchair anthropologist. It seems generally agreed that his knowledge of Australian ethnography proved to be quite outstanding, and Evans-Pritchard certainly thought so (1960:24). In his task Durkheim was aided by Mauss' extensive reading of the data. Nevertheless, Durkheim may well have made mistakes in detail and his assumptions may have been wrong. The fact that he chose preliterate groups based on totemism, which he held to be the most primitive form of social organization, and through which every society had passed, is a case in point. But there is the question of the interpretation of what the ethnographers wrote, especially Spencer and Gillen. Did he read too much into them? Did he overlook important material?

To a limited extent these issues have been raised before, though infrequently by anthropologists specializing in the Arunta. One post-war exception was W. E. H. Stanner, who worked in the 1950s and '60s amongst the Aborigines of northern and central Australia (see also Hiatt 1996). Howard Morphy, a younger scholar in Australian ethnography, raises the question of ethnography and theory in Durkheim's approach to the data he had available (see Chapter 1). It is not so much a matter of error or false deduction that distances the theorist from the ethnographers, Spencer and Gillen, as one of emphasis. For example, Durkheim saw totemism and religion as being more important than magic for the upholding of social solidarity. In his concept of religion he made a clear differentiation between the sacred and the profane, and indeed postulates them as a universal socio-religious characteristic. Not so for Spencer and Gillen. They accepted the notion of the sacred and the profane but held that it had great variations and related to a person's life-cycle and to seasonal activities. The older a man, the more sacred he was seen to be. Nor is the separation between the sacred and the profane as rigid in Spencer and Gillen as it was in Durkheim. Durkheim associated totemism with social organization: the clan was seen as a socially tight group, something Spencer and Gillen did not suggest. They showed a more complex relation between the clan and social organization. Totems went across territorial organization. Durkheim reified the clan in the way the ethnographers did not. Further, his lack of attention to Aboriginal myths, songs and dances excluded a fruitful area which became overlooked by scholars (see also Chapter 13).

Do these and other criticisms of a similar ilk nullify the 'experiment'? Here scholars remain divided. No one would see *The Elementary Forms* fit only for the wastepaper basket. The book remains a classic, not so much on account of the rigour of its scientific method but because of the imaginative and penetrating ideas it contained, and which were later verified. Morphy argues that *The Elementary Forms* is not dependent on the ethnography for its merits.

Arising from the publication of *Les Formes élémentaires* and also within a somewhat wider debate, was the question of whether 'primitive peoples', as they were then termed, exhibited a mentality far from that of modern, western man, which might be called 'prelogical'. If it could be demonstrated that those tribes to which Durkheim referred had a mentality that both preceded and was radically different from that of modern, rational man, then doubts might be raised about our understanding of the religion of man in preliterate societies. If early man possessed quite a different mentality, would our established 'scientific' deductions about religion and its evolution, extending to mankind today, be wrong? Hence the debate about the mentality of preliterate man was, in at least one respect, of considerable importance to Durkheim's enterprise. His deductions would be invalid if they were held to be inapplicable to modern man. Lévy-Bruhl, standing just outside the Durkheim circle, had in 1911 posited the idea of a prelogical mentality, maintaining a clear distinction between the thinking abilities of primitive man and those of modern man. For various reasons, one of which we have just mentioned, Durkheim attacked this position in a review and opposed the notion of a sharp and distinctive break in the development of man's mentality (1913a(ii)(6) and (7)). Rather than positing discontinuity, Durkheim argued in terms of a gradual evolution. But there was another type of evolution. The nature of religion was such that it gave birth to science. Science gained its autonomy to the degree it was able to sever itself from the religious womb and leave dogma behind. There was, however, no decisive break or sudden emergence, the birth was a long and gradual process.

The debate, heightened by the ideas of Lévy-Bruhl and Durkheim, was to continue, and the outcome has never been clearly resolved, although Lévy-Bruhl supposedly changed his mind. There is little doubt that he did change his mind, the problem is over what? Nomenclature or substance? Certainly Lévy-Bruhl can be applauded for attempting to explore the particular 'logic' of preliterate societies. The contest with Durkheim was far from useless (Merllié in Chapter 2).

Durkheim's commitment to science in terms of its method and its ability to deliver 'truth' – something absent from other human activities – is, hardly surprisingly, not without its problems. When he was at the Ecole Normale Supérieure as a student he was very much the young philosopher who was nicknamed the 'Metaphysician'. To be sure, he quickly asserted that a great deal of the philosophy taught in his days was dilettantism. How, then, did he become so committed to science? In this it would appear that he was much influenced by one of his teachers, Emile Boutroux, a philosopher and especially a philosopher of science, who is not much known in the English-speaking world (Jones in Chapter 3). Two problems engaged the men – the nature of science and whether there can be a science of religion. Durkheim followed Boutroux's thinking in holding that in any science one set of phenomena had to be explained by another set within the orbit of that science; for example, electrical facts are to be explained by electrical facts. But what of social facts? They were to be 'explained' by other social facts. And more pertinently, what of religious facts? Here the two men differed. Surely religious facts would have to be explained by religious facts? Events showed this was not acceptable to Durkheim. Boutroux, a Catholic modernist, felt that a science of religion was a contradiction in terms, because such a science would dissolve the very material the scientist was studying. This point Durkheim never responded to.

II

Every religion contains a belief system – intellectual ideas, a credo or a set of doctrines. They may not be coherent or systematized in the eyes of modern, western thinkers but they exist, and it is impossible to imagine a religion without them. To rational-minded thinkers beliefs are usually held to be the most important element of a religion. It is argued that action emerges from thought, and so thought is prior. Belief is the means by which a religion is communicated to others. Through it religion is comprehensible to an observer.

The prime issue which faced rationalists, and amongst them one would initially place Durkheim, was that of the truth of religious beliefs. No thorough-going rationalist could accept the proclaimed truth of any religion, let alone that in which they found themselves, namely Christianity. They were atheists or agnostics and that was certainly Durkheim's position religiously speaking. But for him, and here he differed from other rationalists, it did not mean that religious beliefs were illusory. He calmly proclaimed 'there are no false religions' (3/3). If they were completely false, they would quickly dissolve. Truth persists: the lie disappears. Durkheim holds that the 'truth' of religious beliefs is that they are socially effective and constitute part of the social reality that is the subject matter of sociology. There is a parallel here in the approach of William James to religion – a parallel however which also has sharp divergences (Stedman Jones in Chapter 4). Durkheim went beyond James' pragmatism (Durkheim 1955a). It was not just a question of their being *'true practically'* (113/80. Durkheim's emphasis), but that religious beliefs, even of preliterate peoples, revealed in their own way certain truths about the human condition in its social and individual modes.

But the question arises, what exactly did Durkheim mean by religious belief and how was it to be distinguished from other beliefs? Religious belief relates to the 'otherworldly', to God or the gods, and is deemed to be sacred but is expressed in terms of this world. In order to explore the idea what Durkheim emphasized was not so much individual beliefs but collective beliefs. Many of these ideas can be traced back to Kant, who held that religious belief was not of the order of pure reason but of practical reason, that is, while failing to satisfy the canons of logic, it is necessary for human living. But Durkheim goes further and asserts that gods and the sacred are not only the objects of belief but that they become such through belief. Some support for this comes from Renouvier, whom Durkheim recognized as an influence on his own thinking. Renouvier, while praising Kant for his analysis of religious belief, criticized him for leaving belief suspended in a void. Durkheim would seem to provide an answer in positing that beliefs spring from the community and through individuals return to the community by which they are reinforced.

There has been widespread neglect of Durkheim's discussion of ideas of the soul. Perhaps this is because the subject seems of purely academic interest, with little bearing on contemporary issues. But his treatment of the idea of the soul has recently been explored by Karen Fields (1995; 1996; and see Chapter 7 of this book). Watts Miller also enters this deserted area in examining Durkheim's general interpretative strategy in dealing with particular religious beliefs and in considering their modern secular substitutes (see Chapter 5). Durkheim opposes the view that ideas of the soul are nonsense and illusion. He first tries to make sense of them as ritual beliefs and a subsidiary move allows for their metaphorical expression in story-like myths. It is only then that he interprets beliefs as a more or less obscure social symbolism, in which, for example, the idea of the soul represents the individual's membership of an enduring group.

Can modern society dispense with the immortal soul and God? Kant insists it is necessary to believe in them, as postulates required by any coherent understanding of morality. Durkheim, in his engagement with Kant, is more sensitive than philosophers of today are to the dangers of secularization. Watts Miller argues that it is particularly disastrous if, in giving up the soul, we fall back on a highly individualistic idea of the self, so completely annihilated at death that it cannot have post-mortal concerns. We need a Durkheimian 'organic' self to have, as mortality requires, a commitment in our lives to concerns that go beyond us and to ideals that may never be realized until long after death. This is different from abandoning God – the one 'religious' belief so many people in our secular world continue to hold. God might be a Durkheimian symbol of society, man and the moral dualism of duty and the good. This still leaves out a wider cosmological function. But also, Watts Miller argues, it is precisely as a symbol of the good – in the Kantian sense of all the happiness consistent with virtue – that God does not and cannot have a secular substitute.

A set of beliefs may not consist of logically related statements, and indeed beliefs may not be expressed intellectually. Particular beliefs may be held in myths or in physical objects – in short through symbols. Such a position seems most applicable to preliterate societies. Here stands the pioneering work of Durkheim and the claim could well be made for Durkheim as the father of the sociological study of symbolism. His unshakeable stand was that if the literal content of religious beliefs cannot be accepted as 'truth', other truths can be postulated which are hidden or implied, apart from the general assertion that they are part of the social reality. These hidden meanings often relate to things, objects, actions, events, be they sacred or otherwise. The hidden meanings have to be communicated and interpreted.

Probably the most profound and extensively debated part of *Les Formes élémentaires* is Chapter VII of Book II, which is Durkheim's final consideration of the origin of totemic beliefs. In it symbol or image as a key concept stand between knowledge and religion, between intellectual proposition and worship. One of Durkheim's much quoted assertions is that 'social life, in all its aspects and at every moment of its history, is made possible only by a vast symbolism' (331/231). A problem that calls for exploration is why a society needs to have symbols in order to be a society. In trying to answer this question, Durkheim holds that a symbol has properties of materiality and represents a sets of ideas. He points to a flag, but in referring to a flag with contemporary connotations he opened up an area of controversy. In a symbol there exists a relation between reality, image and observer, which in turn is related to the individual and to society. Paoletti argues that rules about symbolic images follow rules about social facts as Durkheim conceived them in *The Rules of Sociological Method* (1895a) (see Chapter 6).

While concentrating on the 'well carried out experiment', and always basing his argument on ethnographic material, Durkheim not only suggests generalizations but links his findings to examples current in his day. If Durkheim did this, it seems legitimate for those who follow him to apply his ideas to the contemporary scene. Thus, it might be argued that the notion of the clan and the soul help us to understand modern social formations, not least in marginal groups, such as ethnic groups and new social movements, whose ideology and practice have certain affinities with early societies. Indeed, Thompson holds that one way of reading *Les Formes élémentaires* is seeing it as a contribution to the theory of ideology. Ideology acts in a such a way as to produce or reproduce social order largely through the agency of symbolic representation (see Chapter 7). Amongst marginal groups in a post-modern setting, as it is called, body-symbolism may well play an important part as an individual appropriates collective symbolism. Once again Durkheim showed himself to be a pioneer in developing a sociology of the body in his analysis of tattooing amongst the Arunta. But tattooing is making its reappearance in today's marginal groups which are highly dependent on symbolism and here Durkheim's analysis is helpful in accounting for such trends.

III

If religious belief is not illusory but is to be regarded in a positive way as being 'true' for society, indeed necessary, then surely the same thing is to be said for the other side of the religious coin, namely ritual. It is indeed the other side of the coin, not least because Durkheim defined religion in terms of 'a unified system of beliefs and practices relative to sacred things' (65/47). The question of the relation of belief and action and their relative importance or primacy, is one of continual debate, as is evident in several of the essays of this book (e.g. Chapter 4). It raises problems of logic, history, and anthropological evidence.

To the observer, ritual *per se* is not causally effective or instrumental, as believers would assert; but neither in Durkheimian thought is it valueless or wasted action. Like belief, its real virtue is perceived by the 'scientist' to be in its value to society. In utilizing the ethnographic material from the Arunta for an analysis of ritual, Durkheim surpassed any other thinker who preceded him. One result was that he created an ideal which others have attempted to follow, if not emulate.

How then is ritual to be studied if scholars either deny its literal virtue as asserted by believers, or assume its irrelevance? We have just said that it is in its relation to the collective. One British anthropologist, Radcliffe-Brown, supposedly basing his reasoning on Durkheim, adopted a functional account, in which ritual was seen to be an expression of the unity of society (Radcliffe-Brown 1933). But not only does it express this unity it helps to create it (Ruel, Chapter 8). The weakness of Radcliffe-Brown's position, which was to become very influential, is that he did not really differentiate ritual from, on the one hand, religion or, on the other, religious belief. Indeed, belief plays a very secondary role in his analysis, which is not the case in Durkheim. Evans-Pritchard, while adopting a symbolic stance, held that one must take into consideration the beliefs of the participants in any interpretation of ritual. The point is that religious action cannot be separated from belief. This is all the more necessary where it is not a question of the analysis of one ritual but of a system of interlocking rituals. Durkheim emphasized that rituals are actions supported by tradition and authority, and therefore by belief. What is of importance is that they exert a force and beyond that, Malcolm Ruel argues, generalizations cannot be made. What is more important is to relate a ritual to its associated objects and to see the place of ritual in particular societies. At least Durkheim stressed one methodological canon – the necessity of focusing on ritual in a specific society or culture.

Amongst religious rituals perhaps none is more complicated or open to different interpretations than sacrifice. It is commonly found in a large number of religions, be the sacrifice a bloody one involving animals or a spiritualized form of sacrifice as in Christianity. Durkheim devoted a whole chapter to the *Intichiuma*, the 'sacrifice' of the Arunta (Book III, Ch.II). It should be noted in passing that many today, such as Testart, the French anthropologist, deny that the Australian ritual is a sacrifice in the true sense of the word. However, the debate which was raging in Durkheim's time was fuelled by what he said about the intention of the sacrifice. Robertson Smith's writing changed Durkheim's attitude towards religion and encouraged him to see it as the *fons et origo* of society (see Pickering 1984:62ff.). Durkheim is also said to have followed Robertson Smith's radical theory of sacrifice in holding that sacrifice is a communal meal at which one eats the deity or with the deity. But also present in *Les Formes élémentaires* is the theory of sacrifice as gift and consecration. Much evidence shows that Durkheim's final theory of sacrifice was influenced by the theories of the Indologist, Sylvain Lévi, a relatively little known scholar in Britain or the United States. Lévi's ideas were taken up by Durkheim through his disciples, Hubert and Mauss (Strenski in Chapter 9).

If a religion needs to recall past events through myth and ritual, so does a society. This is very much the message of *Les Formes élémentaires*, where certain conclusions derived from studying the Arunta may be seen to be applicable to modern, western society – a society no longer based on a religious belief system. As we have noted, Durkheim gave little place to myth in his use of Australian ethnography. With the cult of the individual, which he held was the secular religion of modern society, myth also plays little or no part, and that is what is evident in what Durkheim wrote about the cult of the individual. Indeed, can there be a myth within such a religion? Perhaps it is more fruitful to turn to the notion of social memory, for it stands at the heart of a society's system of rituals. The notion of the social memory is strongly evident in Durkheim and was later developed by his disciple, Maurice Halbwachs. Social memory, it can be argued, is the best way of interpreting Durkheim's social theory (Gephart in Chapter 10). The unity of a society is closely connected with its collective memory which guarantees social identity. But this memory is dependent on organization and on collective symbols which need to be ritualized. One problem of modern, western societies is how to ritualize its changing social memory – changed through historical events. How does one 'successfully' hold a celebratory ritual for, say, the French Revolution, the founding of a city, the end of Communist rule? How is one to recall the Revocation of the Edict of Nantes? Different and perhaps hostile interpretations of great historical events emerge, even in one society. Probably no such attempt is more problematic than in finding an adequate ritual which recalls the Holocaust. It is to be remembered: but how is it to be remembered? Does uncertainty or various readings of past events mean no rituals are possible and therefore the social memory fades?

Much overlooked by traditional commentators is the concept of collective effervescence or collective assembly. It is held to be a *sui generis* experience or event and is analysed in creative and ritualistic terms. The nature of the phenomenon was such that it did not fit into a sociological framework and its 'explanation' was better suited to psychology. But its significance sociologically is now being understood. Excitable gatherings, regularly convened or otherwise, heighten people's passions and energies. Role reversals may take place: moral norms may be deliberately broken. In the delirium unimagined actions may occur and radical ideas emerge. A revolution or a period of revolution, or a national crisis, exemplified in the Dreyfus Affair (Durkheim 1898c), is very much an effervescent occasion. One general appraisal of effervescent assemblies is that of celebration and the creation of social cohesion, but it is also one of violence, suffering and differentiation (Ramp in Chapter 11). Unity and disunity co-exist, as creativity and destruction. There is a parallel with sacrifice in which there is controlled violence, not least in the slaying of the victim. Sometimes difficult to accept by contemporary religious thinkers is the fact that for a very long time there has been a violent side to religion. But it should be noted that the suffering and disunity produced by collective effervescence is never that of social chaos. Great effervescent happenings have to be remembered and this is achieved through ritual re-enactment (see also Chapter 13).

Durkheim held that all institutions stem from religion and in *Les Formes élémentaires* he attempted to analyse and derive the origin of religion itself. It can be argued, as Allen does, that by extension the book can shed light on the origin of society, despite the fact that it was written many years ago and that palaeoanthropology has made great advances since then. If it is held that human societies were originally quadripartite, which is arguably the simplest imaginable kinship-based structure and is exemplified by many Australian tribes, how is it that they have emerged, since such holistic structures are absent among non-human primates? The key is to be found in collective effervescence as the locus *par excellence* of human and social creativity (see Chapter 12).

IV

Durkheim never really lost his love for philosophy, although he distanced his cherished sociology from it in order to give the new discipline its autonomy. His brand of sociology was always close to philosophy, however, in a way that that of Max Weber was not. Removed from it also was the empirical sociology that later developed in the English-speaking world. Durkheim's interest turned full circle, for in *The Elementary Forms* he goes so far as to assert that sociology can solve at least two age-old philosophical problems. One question was concerned with epistemology. From where does man gain knowledge, what are its origins? Here Durkheim established a close link with the social, for knowledge is socially mediated. And in origin, the social was in fact religious, since the two were scarcely separable. Another issue was the problem of categories. From whence come the basic categories – concepts of number, class, space, time? Between the a priori and empiricist arguments, Durkheim postulated that the origin of categories again lay in society, in social causes. Both these solutions implied relativism and a denial of absolutes, since societies vary one from another in the matter of specific categories.

Némedi in seeing a weakness in Durkheim's arguments holds that in searching for the origin of religious categories Durkheim adopted contradictory approaches (see Chapter 13). He first focused on religious institutions as the observable side of religion, but then he had to go beyond practices to an initial state – to an original beginning. Durkheim's epistemological position is unsatisfactory because he sees religion as being at the heart of knowledge and indeed the seed-bed of categories. Earlier, in 1903, Durkheim and Mauss' essay on primitive classification showed the connection between social institutions and classification, but by 1912, it has been argued, Durkheim felt forced to focus on religion by itself as the key to the origin of categories (see also Pickering 1993).

Némedi asserts that Durkheim posited three concepts which had categorical status – sacred–profane, impersonal force (mana) and soul. Was Durkheim not too ambitious in thinking that a study of religion could provide the key to a multitude of social issues? Durkheim's book contained flaws of several kinds, including the assertion that religion is the centre of the understanding of society. He juggled with institutionalization but was forced to turn to creative effervescence, which can in no way be regarded as a theory of change. Indeed, attractive though it may be, collective effervescence has little to commend it in terms of theory or epistemology. Although Némédi's views on collective effervescence may be contrary to those of many Durkheimians, he poses a problem which will not go away. In itself effervescent assembly is difficult to accommodate in a general theory of society, even though it can be classified as a social phenomenon.

Plenty of scholars have turned against Durkheim's relativist sociological solution to the origins of categories. It can be shown in a new analysis that the notion of category in Durkheim's hands contains an ambiguity and assumes an essentialist model of explanation which combines causal and functional accounts and denies the plurality of causes (Schmaus in Chapter 14). What vary with social causes are not categories but classificatory concepts – ways of representing time, space and causality. If categories are necessary for the existence of society they must be the same for all societies. Indeed, all societies have categories of time and space, etc. but each can have different measurements of time and of space. In this way, Durkheim's relativism can be challenged.

If all knowledge is in fact relative and there are no absolutes, no universals, how can one hope to establish universal truths? There are only truths which exist for certain societies and cultures. Is there nothing which can be an exception to this rule? One possibility is the law of non-contradiction or the principle of contradiction in the language of Aristotle. It stands at the heart of all reason and knowledge. Whether Durkheim held that the law of contradiction was subject to relativism is open to debate. One author here considers the possibility that Durkheim is an undaunted relativist and that the basic canon of logic is context-dependent – dependent on social structure (Godlove in Chapter 15). Durkheim's relativism at this point is in terms of a religious person speaking of God as one and many. Godlove relates the problem to several thinkers such as Russell, and Bloor and Barnes and puts forward the thesis that it is useless trying to demonstrate precisely why we must conform to the principle of contradiction.

These chapters provide examples of Durkheim's ideas where in some instances the authors not only revise and go beyond them but show the importance of grappling with his thought at the most fundamental level.

W. S. F. P.

Notes

1 For this type of referencing to *Les Formes élémentaires*, see Explanatory Note on p. xi.

1

SPENCER AND GILLEN IN DURKHEIM

The theoretical constructions of ethnography

Howard Morphy[1]

To an anthropologist, and in particular to one who studies Australian Aborigines, Durkheim's *The Elementary Forms of Religious Life* brings to the fore the issue of the relationship between theory and ethnography in anthropology. *The Elementary Forms* is an avowedly theoretical work yet at the same time it has been described as an ethnographic study (e.g. Lukes 1973). W. E. H. Stanner, whose own work *On Aboriginal Religion* (1966), though relatively unknown outside Australia, has superseded Durkheim's in its influence on contemporary writers on the subject, clearly finds the description of Durkheim as an ethnographer problematic. He writes on Goldenweiser's (1915:719) description of Durkheim as 'a veteran of Australian ethnology': 'He might have said "veteran at a distance". Durkheim of course had never visited Australia' (Stanner 1967:217). However Stanner's implicit association of ethnography with fieldwork and data-gathering oversimplifies the issue. Ethnography as a process has increasingly been recognized as a theoretical enterprise in itself; indeed several people have argued that modern fieldwork has involved the collapsing of the distinction between the data-gatherer and the theorist and their embodiment in the same person (Kuklick 1991; Langham 1981; Urry 1993). Viewed in relation to this process of development in anthropology Durkheim's analysis and reinterpretation of Australian ethnography has a particular character that marks it as a modern ethnography even though he was not himself involved in data gathering. This view poses questions about the relationship between theory and data in ethnographic practice.

If we accept this line of reasoning Spencer and Gillen could be said to have provided Durkheim with data which he then interpreted according to his sociological method, and this fact in turn influenced the development of ethnographic practice and anthropological theory-construction. This is indeed the conventional view and it receives considerable support from Durkheim himself. He argues that some of the deficiencies of Frazer's analysis of totemism can be explained by the fact that, at the time of his writing, a totemic religion had yet to be observed in action.

It is only in very recent years that this serious deficiency has been repaired. Two observers of remarkable ability, discovered in the interior of the Australian continent a considerable number of tribes whose basis and unity was founded in totemic beliefs. The results of their observations have been published in two works, which have given new life to the study of totemism.

(128–9/91)

What was the theoretical construction placed on Spencer and Gillen's data by Durkheim that converts it into modern ethnography? What is present in their ethnography *after* it has been processed by Durkheim that was absent in its original form? Is it simply that Durkheim cast the facts in a new theoretical light, seeing Aboriginal ritual as integral to the unity and solidarity of the clan rather than interpreting it according to the intellectualist paradigm in the mode of Frazer? If we adopt a processual view of the history of anthropology the test must ultimately be 'What new questions were asked? What new kinds of data were obtained by anthropologists after Durkheim's reanalysis?' As a significant figure in anthropological discourse Durkheim has had a continuing influence on field research through prompting questions that either test his specific hypotheses or focus on areas of society, such as symbolism or aesthetics, highlighted by his work.

However, as well as focusing on Durkheim's role in the future development of anthropology, it is also possible to ask a different question: what was it about Spencer and Gillen's ethnographies that enabled Durkheim to develop a new theoretical understanding of the nature of religion in general and Aboriginal religion in particular? The influence of theory on Spencer and Gillen's ethnography may itself have been part of a process that made possible Durkheim's subsequent reformulations. As Durkheim himself recognized:

the works of Spencer and Gillen especially have exercised a considerable influence, not only because they were the oldest, but also because the facts were there presented in a systematic form, which was of a nature at the same time to give a direction to later studies and to stimulate speculation.

(130/93)

The dynamic relationship between theory and data in ethnography thus preceded the structural–functional revolution and was as much part of nineteenth-century as it was of twentieth-century anthropology (see Kuklick 1991 and Kuper 1988). We can challenge the retrospectively-constructed history of anthropology that has given the designated paradigm changers – Durkheim, Malinowski and Radcliffe-Brown – such a determining position in its recent history.

It is of course possible to construct a third argument: that despite his extensive use of Spencer and Gillen's ethnography Durkheim neither altered its construction nor allowed it to influence his argument. Some commentators are of the opinion that the argument of *The Elementary Forms* was developed independent of Aranda ethnography.[2] He 'could have chosen to write [it] without more than a passing reference to Australian or any other primitive people' (Seger 1957:20). The theoretical premises of Durkheim's science, in particular his emphasis on a priorism in argument, could lend weight to such an interpretation (see 526/368). Central Australian ethnography, it could be argued, far from providing the substantive basis for Durkheim's analysis was included merely to illustrate his theory. Spencer and Gillen's ethnography escapes unscathed from its incorporation in *The Elementary Forms* and simply adds the authoritative weight of ethnography to an independently developed argument. 'The imperious quality of *The Elementary Forms* came from the junction of revolutionary theses and apparent factual support at a particular time in the history of anthropology' (Stanner 1967:217). Such a use of ethnography could indeed be justified on the grounds that it validated a priori theory construction. Both Frazer and Durkheim saw Spencer and Gillen's account of the eating of the totemic animal in the Engwurra as a partial vindication of Robertson Smith's theory of a social and territorial basis for totemism. While much of the argument of *The Elementary Forms* was developed earlier in Durkheim's writings, and before the publication of Spencer and Gillen's work, I will argue however, that such an argument is unacceptable. Not only is Spencer and Gillen's ethnography selected, given emphasis and reinterpreted to fit the argument that Durkheim developed, but the ethnography in turn can be shown to have influenced or stimulated the argument of *The Elementary Forms*. Spencer and Gillen can be seen to be participants in a discourse with Durkheim and others which produced a dynamic relationship between data gathering and theory construction.

A quantitative perspective

It is difficult to overestimate the impact of Spencer and Gillen on anthropology at the end of the nineteenth and beginning of the twentieth centuries. In a review of their first major work *The Native Tribes of Central Australia* in *L'Année sociologique*, Mauss (1900a:205) wrote that it was 'one of the most important works of ethnology and descriptive sociology that we know … the picture they have given us of social and religious organisation is one of the most complete that anthropology has provided us'. Thirteen years later in his review of *Across Australia*, Malinowski wrote, 'Since the publication of their first volume half the total production of anthropological literature has been based on their work and nine-tenths affected or modified by it. For theories of kinship and religion, social organization, and primitive belief, the central and northern tribes have proved a mine of valuable facts and information' (Malinowski 1913:278).

Pre-eminent among those influenced by Spencer and Gillen (apart from Malinowski himself) were Frazer and Durkheim. Although Durkheim shows an encyclopedic knowledge of the literature on Aborigines there is no doubting the centrality of Spencer and Gillen's ethnographies in *The Elementary Forms*. While other writers such as Mathews, Howitt and Roth are cited for specific ethnographic details, the long, analysed accounts of Aboriginal ritual come largely from Spencer and Gillen's two monographs on Central Australia. There is scarcely a page in the main body of the text outside the introduction and conclusion without a reference to their writings and whole sections of Book III 'The Principal Ritual Attitudes' consist of summaries of their accounts of Aboriginal ritual. The ethnographic feel of the book is the feel of Spencer and Gillen's descriptive writing.

The positioning of Spencer and Gillen in relation to Durkheim and Frazer

Spencer, Gillen, Frazer and Durkheim form an interesting set. Both Frazer and Durkheim were heavily dependent on Spencer and Gillen's ethnography in their writings on religion, yet Durkheim developed his interpretation partly in opposition to Frazer's. Frazer was the arch-intellectualist against whom Durkheim's sociological explanations were directed. Frazer, Durkheim, Spencer, and Gillen were all close to each other in chronological age, yet they are often seen to represent different eras of anthropological sophistication. In Kuhnian terms, they straddle a period when the paradigm of anthropology was undergoing change, when the evolutionist paradigm of the late nineteenth century was under attack and the functionalist paradigm of the early twentieth century was beginning to develop.[3] Frazer, more a popularizer and compiler of data than an original thinker, remained firmly within the evolutionary paradigm, whereas Durkheim laid the theoretical foundations for the new direction that British anthropology was to take under Radcliffe-Brown and Malinowski. In Frazer's hands Spencer and Gillen's data became fixed in relation to an old agenda; in Durkheim's case it became the inspiration for the new paradigm. But, at the cost of their long-term reputation, their work has tended to be more closely associated with the former than the latter.

Spencer's interest in anthropology was initially stimulated by Tylor. Spencer was a student of biology at Oxford and subsequently a Fellow of Exeter College (for details of his life see Mulvaney and Calaby 1985). While still a student in 1885 he assisted Tylor with the removal and unpacking of the Pitt Rivers collections and attended Tylor's initial lecture course at Oxford. In 1887 he left for Australia where he had been appointed the Foundation Professor of Biology at Melbourne University. In 1894 he took part as zoologist in the Horn Expedition to Central Australia, and it was in Alice Springs on 15 July that his partnership with Frank Gillen began. Gillen was postmaster at Alice Springs, at the time a tiny European settlement in the heart of Australia in the country of the Aranda people. Gillen was interested in the Aboriginal population and began, in good nineteenth-century fashion, to record their customs and collect their artefacts. The collaboration began with Spencer helping Gillen to write up his notes in publishable form, but it soon developed into joint fieldwork and co-authorship. Although Spencer did most of the final writing up, the research itself was truly collaborative with both contributing to the collection and analysis of data (see Morphy, Mulvaney and Petch 1997).

The conventional view of the relationship between Spencer and Gillen on the one hand and Frazer and Tylor on the other is clearly put by Adam Kuper in *The Invention of Primitive Society* (1988). He sees a chain of influence leading from the Metropolitan theorists, such as Frazer and Tylor, to the expatriate academic in the colonial city, to the data-gatherer in the bush. 'Spencer was a trained scholar and an experienced naturalist ... and Gillen was a man of little education ... In consequence, Gillen's ethnography was completely subordinated to Spencer's ideas' (Kuper 1988:101).

Spencer and Gillen were certainly influenced by evolutionary theory and felt an enormous debt of gratitude to Frazer, who greatly facilitated the publication of their first two books and took on board the onerous task of proof-reading the manuscripts. However it would be wrong to overestimate his influence on their content. Spencer had not met Frazer and did not begin corresponding with him until after their main period of fieldwork was over, and until after they had written their first book. Frazer certainly sought to find support for his theories in Spencer and Gillen's ethnographies, but his ideas and interpretations were often challenged by them. Gillen's letters to Spencer show him to be a critical thinker who contributed independently to their research, and who produced interpretations that contradicted Frazer's hypotheses.

Evolutionary theory plays a relatively minor role in Spencer's and Gillen's writing (if not in its intellectual positioning). As I will argue later, it is actually much more prominent in Durkheim's work. Spencer and Gillen's books are written as descriptive ethnographies in which fact is as much as possible kept separate from interpretation. They have been more strongly represented as evolutionist than they deserve for two reasons. First, they accepted the Frazerian sequence of magic, science and religion, and Frazer's positioning of totemism (and hence Aboriginal religion) in the category of magic, even though they rejected many of his arguments for doing so. Durkheim, on the other hand, placed Aborigines at the centre of debates on the origin of religion and dealt them a less crushing evolutionary blow. Second, Spencer and Gillen emphasized the primitive nature of Aboriginal society in the prefaces to their books, drawing analogies with the Stone Age and the exotic nature of Antipodean fauna, and emphasizing the extent to which it could be taken to be representative of early stages of human society. There is some evidence that the tone of the prefaces were directly influenced by Frazer, who wanted to encourage readers to interpret Spencer and Gillen's work in the direction of his theories.

There is no doubt that Spencer himself believed it was important for their work to provide data on societies that were fast disappearing and that gave access to early stages of cultural evolution. Indeed Durkheim was attracted to their ethnographies for precisely this reason and there is no suggestion that Durkheim questioned these views which were general at the time. It was partly as a consequence of the richness of Central Australian ritual, revealed through Spencer and Gillen's ethnographies, that such views came under challenge. Durkheim, while clinging equally strongly to the primitivist assumption, hammered further nails in its coffin precisely by identifying

Aboriginal beliefs as religion. Ironically enough he replaced Frazer's evolutionary sequence with one that went from religion to magic to science (518/362). Thus both Spencer and Gillen's and Durkheim's work show a mixture of influences and ideas typical of a paradigm-breaking stage. Both avow evolutionism but at the same time produce data and theories which begin to undermine the evolutionist paradigm.

The quality of Spencer and Gillen's ethnography

Spencer and Gillen's ethnography was qualitatively different from that which preceded it, because they *were* influenced by the questions posed by evolutionary theorists and partly because they developed methods of enquiry that resulted in richer and more analysable data. They looked for group marriage and tried to discover if there was a relationship between totemic affiliation and patterns of marriage. Their focus on Aboriginal religion was motivated in part by the theoretical significance that had been accorded to totemism. However, although their agenda may have reflected the theoretical concerns of their times, the data that they recorded contradicted the theoretical predictions more often than they confirmed them and, in doing so, moved theoretical debates forward. Not only Durkheim but Tylor and Frazer before him developed 'new' theories of totemism as a result of reading Spencer and Gillen's ethnography.

As fieldworkers Spencer and Gillen spent more time in data collection than any of their predecessors. Their joint fieldwork lasted for nearly a year and a half and for most of that time they lived with Aboriginal people. Moreover Gillen spent much of his free time in Alice Springs as an ethnographer, in continuous correspondence with Spencer. Gillen was able to work in the Aranda language and recent linguistic research has tended to confirm the accuracy of his and Spencer's translations. They were meticulous in cross-checking their data and in seeking clarification of things that they had failed to understand. They pioneered the use of film, photography, and sound recording in the field, and used these to further document ritual performances that they had observed. Their ethnography has stood the test of time and continues to be cited by current researchers to an almost unparalleled extent.

In writing up their material for publication they followed an inductive model in which data was kept separate from theory. Their writings are remarkably free from evolutionary polemics or speculative reconstructions. However, it would be quite misleading to say their publications consisted simply of unanalysed data. Three things give their ethnographies a modern feel compared with the writings of contemporaries such as W. E. Roth: the detailed and extended nature of their descriptions of ritual performance, the informal and documentary nature of their photographs, and the analysed nature of their data. Their analyses of social organization followed the model pioneered by Fison and Howitt (1880), which showed the structural relationship between kin and subsection terminologies. Far from focusing on the evolutionary implications of the systems of kinship and marriage they described, they emphasized the dynamics of relationship systems and the recent history of their diffusion and transformation. As Gillen wrote to Spencer, the most exciting thing that they discovered was that the Aranda were in the very process of changing their sociocentric kin terminology.

In the field of religion they forged an interpretative framework that has formed the basis of most subsequent research. Evolutionary theory is once again remarkably absent from the main text, though the perspective adopted fits in with evolutionist and intellectualist discourse. Spencer and Gillen initially focused on establishing the relationship between totemism and social organization and concluded that the totemic belief system was relatively autonomous from kinship and marriage systems though inevitably articulated with them as part of the historical process. They were also intellectualists by inclination, though they emphasized the reasonableness rather than the false rationality of Aboriginal beliefs. They developed a very abstract and in some respects phenomenological concept of spiritual power which they saw ultimately as located in the concept of ancestral beings and underpinning totemism. Their thought processes come out well in a letter from Gillen in which he writes to Spencer:

> When first of all did the Churinga [sacred objects] come in – that question is a poser but you will find it dealt with in my notes – it dates back, I think, before alcheringa man and I am inclined to think that originally it was meant to express the spiritual part of the alcheringa animal or man, the meaning of the term I take to be 'sacred' – in the sense perhaps that the sacramental wafer is sacred to the Roman Catholic – A thing is Churinga that is everything – (Churinga spelt in cap letters please [sic]) – there can be nothing impossible where Churinga are concerned – Men sprung from Churinga, that is from something sacred in the animal or man, just as the Virgin Mary appears at Lourdes, though unless you want to bring down upon me the anathema of the Holy Church don't quote me as saying so.
>
> (Alice Springs 30 July 1897)[4]

Spencer and Gillen's great contribution to the study of Aboriginal religion was as descriptive ethnographers, but their descriptive ethnography was itself theoretically informed. We have been so used to writing about Aboriginal religion in terms of the Dreaming, totemic cult groups, land-transforming ancestral beings and networks of ancestral tracks that it is often difficult to remember that such concepts were the result of analysis and systematization rather than given features of Aboriginal society. And in the majority of cases it is possible to see the early formulation of those concepts in Spencer and Gillen's work (Wolfe 1991, Maddock 1991).

Their understanding developed during the course of their fieldwork and writings as a result of their analysis and interpretation of their data. The realization that the Central Australian landscape was crossed by a network

of intersecting ancestral tracks, which had to be grasped as a whole before
sense could be made of the parts, came as a revolutionary insight to them.
Gillen wrote to Spencer:

> It was a happy inspiration that caused you to start me working out
> the wanderings of the various totems and much of the information
> now going to you is the outcome of that work, if we had possessed
> this information before the Engwura it would have helped us to a
> better understanding of the various ceremonies but even now it
> throws a flood of light upon them and will help you to write defi-
> nitely as to their import.
>
> (18 June 1897, Letter 29)

And he later affirmed this observation in a characteristically biblical allusion: 'Yes, the wanderings of the totems is startlingly like the wanderings of
the Children of Israel – I am daily expecting to meet with the tablets on
the mount – What does Dr Fison think of the Wanderings? Do they know
of anything similar?' (30 July 1897, Letter 30).

Spencer and Gillen were the first to use the word 'Dreamtime' to describe
the cosmogonic framework of Aboriginal religion although in their early
writings they restricted themselves largely to the use of indigenous terms
such as *Alcheringa* and *churinga*. They have been rather unjustly accused
of inventing the concept of the Dreamtime through mistranslation of the
Aranda concept (Wolfe 1991) and undoubtedly the phrase itself proved
catching. However recent linguistic and anthropological work by David
Wilkins and John Morton have tended to confirm their translations of the
Aranda concepts (personal communication). The success of the term reflects
the fact that their analysis has been reinforced and developed, rather than
contradicted, by subsequent researchers (see Morphy 1995 for a detailed
discussion).

Durkheim's use of Spencer and Gillen's ethnography

Spencer and Durkheim were equally evolutionists and scientists in their self-
conceptions. However, they had very different notions of science and those
differences affected the role that evolutionary theory played in their work.
Spencer was an empirical natural scientist who sought to uncover facts that
would confirm or falsify theories. His distinction between fact and theory,
though in its strongest form ultimately unsupportable, meant that evolutionary arguments were kept to the margins of his books so that the body
of the text consisted largely of inductively derived descriptions. Durkheim's
agenda was to apply scientific principles to the analysis of social phenomena
and to move understanding forward by the application of a priori assumptions to the analysis of data (526/368). Evolution has a significant place
in the arguments that are developed throughout *The Elementary Forms*.
Durkheim's particular version of the evolutionary argument is directed not
against Spencer and Gillen but against Frazer. It is Frazer's framing of their

work that Durkheim criticizes. Spencer and Gillen's analyses emerge largely unscathed; but they go almost unnoticed since their data is re-crafted to fit Durkheim's own ends. The irony is that Durkheim's analysis of Central Australian religion provided a theoretical basis for social science which superseded evolutionism even though it was apparently the product of evolutionary reasoning, whereas Spencer and Gillen's apparent empiricism left them outside the process of theory generation in anthropology and stuck with the evolutionist label. The originality of their analyses is revealed only by problematizing the categories and concepts by which they analysed Aranda religion: that is when their observations are no longer accepted as taken-for-granted ethnographic descriptions.

Durkheim begins *The Elementary Forms* by stating that he intends 'to study the most primitive and simple religion which is at present known' (1/1). Throughout the work his interpretation of Aranda ethnography is partly premised on this fact. He tends to put down any ambiguity or lack of clarity in the data to the primitive state of Aranda society. Kin groups are not well demarcated (156/111–12), thinking is fuzzy (136/96, 280/196) and art designs appear unclear (162/115). It is difficult to say precisely which of Durkheim's formulations were positively influenced by Spencer and Gillen since the currency of ideas was very general. It might appear that Durkheim's thinking on religion developed after reading the Australian literature during the 1890s. It is nevertheless much easier to show areas where his work diverged from Spencer and Gillen's and where he was stimulated by disagreement, than it is to show positive stimuli. I will begin by considering evidence which suggests that particular ideas of Durkheim were influenced by Spencer and Gillen, and I will then discuss key areas in which their interpretations diverge.

Convergent interpretations

While Durkheim's concept of the sacred was clearly stimulated by his reading of Robertson Smith, the context in which it occurs in *The Elementary Forms* also reflects the influence of Spencer and Gillen. The concept of the sacred was central to Spencer and Gillen's writings. Certainly Durkheim's definition of religion changed after he read Spencer and Gillen and the sacred and profane began to emerge as a core distinction in his writing. The most influential passage occurs in the introduction to *The Northern Tribes* where Spencer and Gillen relate the place of the sacred in a man's life-cycle to the rhythm of seasonal activity.

> In concluding these general remarks attention may be drawn to one striking feature of savage life so far as men are concerned. During his early years, up until the age of fourteen, the boy is perfectly free, wandering about the bush, searching for food, playing with his companions during the day time and perhaps spending the evening watching ordinary corrobborees. From the moment of his initiation, however, his life is sharply marked into two parts. He

has first of all what we may speak of as the ordinary life, common
to all men and women, and associated with the procuring of food
and the performance of corrobborees, the peaceful monotony of
this part of life being broken up every now and again by the excitement of a fight. On the other hand, he has what gradually becomes
of greater and greater importance, and that is the portion of his
life devoted to matters of a sacred or secret nature. As he grows
older he takes an increasing share in these, until finally this side of
his life occupies by far the greater part of his thoughts. The sacred
ceremonies, which appear very trivial matters to the white man,
are most serious matters to him. They are all connected with the
great ancestors of the tribe, and he is firmly convinced that when
it comes to his turn to die his spirit part will finally return to his
old *alcheringa* home.

(1904:33–4)

The distinction being made by Spencer and Gillen is clearly reminiscent of that between the sacred and profane, although the emphasis is
different. Spencer and Gillen are more concerned with the increasing role
the sacred takes in a man's life as he grows older rather than with dividing
social life and the annual cycle of activity into two absolutely distinct
phases. Nevertheless the distinction between the sacred and ordinary parts
of an individual's life is strongly drawn. Durkheim cites this passage on two
key occasions (307–8/214–15, 437/306, and also 497/348). On the first
he uses it to introduce his discussion of the generation of excitement in
Aboriginal ritual, the creation of that intoxicating state of effervescence
that becomes projected outside the self and objectified in the totem and
its representations. He emphasizes the division of activity into two phases
that are contrasted with each other in the sharpest way. 'The dispersed
condition in which the society finds itself results in making its life uniform
languishing and dull' and the collective ritual gathering where 'a sort of
electricity is formed by their collecting which quickly transports them
to an extraordinary degree of exaltation' (308/215). On the second occasion he uses it as evidence of the incompatibility of the sacred and the
profane, the fact that these 'two forms of activity mutually exclude and
repel one another' (438–9/306–7). The seasonal ebb and flow of Aboriginal
life has an important role in Durkheim's arguments as the context in
which the 'twin elements of morality: devotion and obligation "become
engraved into the conduct of individual members of the group"' (Giddens
1978:92).

Spencer and Gillen's analysis may have had some influence on the development of Durkheim's argument, but the influence of their ethnographic
descriptions seems to have been far more significant. It was their descriptions of Warramunga rituals in particular that stimulated or gave substance
to the ideas of effervescence and the effect of ritual in reinforcing social
solidarity. The discussion on effervescence is introduced by an extended
summary of the fire ceremony:

the general effervescence was constantly increasing ... twelve assis-
tants each took a great lighted torch in their hands, and one of
them holding his like a bayonet, charged into the group ... A
general mêlée followed. The men leaped and pranced about ...
the burning torches continually came crashing down on the heads
and bodies of men, scattering sparks in every direction.

This description is in fact Durkheim's (312/218) but it could equally be
Spencer and Gillen's, so close is the language. They wrote:

The excitement was growing gradually more and more intense ...
each of the twelve men was handed one of the *wanmanmirri*; fires
were made ... one of the men charging full tilt, holding his *wanman-*
mirri like a bayonet, and driving the blazing end into the midst of
the group ... the signal for the commencement of a general melee,
the men were leaping and prancing about, the burning torches
continually came crashing down upon the heads and bodies of men,
scattering lighted embers all around.

(1904:390ff.)

The descriptions are very alike but most interesting is that the key theoretical idea that Durkheim is introducing at this point appears as a simple
substitution for Spencer and Gillen's descriptive term. Excitement becomes
effervescence. 'The excitement was growing gradually more and more
intense' becomes 'the general effervescence was constantly increasing'. A
close reading of the two texts of the fire ceremony shows overlap in interpretation and in the images evoked.

Not all of Spencer and Gillen's interpretative data is taken up by
Durkheim. They provide quite a detailed account of the social organization of the ritual and its avowed purpose. The ceremony enacts the relationship between the two moieties and provides the context for dispute
settlement through public displays of aggression (see Peterson 1970). The
man charging with the fiery bayonet engages with a man with whom
he had had a serious quarrel the year before. Durkheim does not refer
to these interpretations but instead focuses on the experiential dimension
of the ritual:

Feeling himself dominated and carried away by some sort of external
power which makes him think and act differently from normal times
... all his companions feel themselves transformed in the same
way ... everything is just as though he were really transported into
a special world, entirely different from the one in which he ordinarily lives, and into an environment filled with exceptionally intense
forces that invade him and metamorphose him.

(312/218)

And this passage too echoes words in *The Northern Tribes*:

The whole ceremony is a curious mixture of license and restraint [men and women] very often, in fact, doing just the opposite of what they would do in other circumstances ... In many respects it could only be described as a primitive form of saturnalia, free from all traces of sexual license, during which the ordinary rules that strictly govern everyday life were, for the time being, laid to one side.

(Spencer and Gillen 1904:378)

The passage could be used to develop a more relative and relational perspective on the sacred–profane distinction. Durkheim, however, chooses to reinforce the contrast between the sacred and the profane worlds and emphasize their separation:

How could such experiences as these ... fail to leave him with the conviction that there really exist two heterogeneous and mutually incomparable worlds? One where life drags wearily along; but he cannot enter into the other without at once entering into relations with extraordinary powers that excite him to the point of frenzy. The first is the profane world, the second, that of sacred things.

(312–3/218)

In this oscillation between a life of routine and a phase of frenzied excitement Durkheim finds the origin of the sacred.

Although it is possible to find a direct relationship between interpretative passages in Spencer and Gillen's writings and sections of *The Elementary Forms*, the most important influence may have been the subjective and qualitative impact of their descriptive writings on Durkheim as a reader. When he first introduces the concept of effervescence Durkheim (312/218) refers to no less than seven examples from Spencer and Gillen. Spencer and Gillen themselves found the experience of witnessing and participating in Aboriginal rituals overwhelming and they sought to convey their feelings through their ethnographies. The extensive use of photographic illustration to convey the atmosphere and experience of the rituals they witnessed also appears to have had the effect they desired on their readers. Durkheim, discussing the emotions felt at death as an expression of social solidarity, writes: 'It seems as though individuals feel a need to come together and communicate more closely; they are pressed tightly against each other and are intertwined, so much as to make a single mass, from which loud groans escape' (560/392). In a footnote he adds, 'A very expressive illustration of this rite will be found in *The Northern Tribes of Central Australia*' (560 n.2/392 n.1). The citation reads: 'women embracing and wailing after cutting their heads in mourning' (Spencer and Gillen 1904:525). Spencer and Gillen's attempts to convey ritual as aesthetic experience also made their mark on Durkheim (see 544ff./381ff.), or at least were in harmony with his own understanding of the relationship between the two.

The interpretations diverge

The areas where Durkheim diverges from Spencer and Gillen reflect differences in their research methods. Spencer and Gillen's ethnography developed partly through testing against the data they recorded, the hypotheses generated by others, and partly by inductive research. In relation to the evolutionary hypotheses of Tylor and Frazer they were often cold-water theorists: their ethnography demonstrated a lack of relationship or failed to demonstrate conclusively a relationship where theory predicted that there would be one. They failed to find group marriage, they failed to demonstrate a strong relationship between totemism and exogamy. Their inductive approach results in much more phenomenological accounts than their predecessors achieved, in that they represent the world as they understood it to be conceived of by the Aborigines. Thus they discovered the locality-based nature of Australian totemism and the network of ancestral tracks that became the Dreaming. Their descriptions became a potential source for other people's theorizing, and their refutations necessitated the development of new theories. Frazer's theories of totemism for example can be seen to have developed dialectically in correspondence with Spencer (see Marett and Penniman 1932).

In certain key areas Spencer and Gillen's data contradicted aspects of Durkheim's theoretical constructions of it. For example Durkheim coupled totemism with social organization: 'totemism is tightly bound up with the most primitive social system that we know, and in all probability, of which we can conceive' (267/187). The Aranda clan was theoretically reconstructed by Durkheim as solid entity, an exogamous quasi-kin group, which was necessary for the reproduction of society and of which the totem, as name and emblem, was an integral part (280/196). Durkheim implied that a single main animal was associated with each clan and that all members of the clan had quasi-kinship connections with it. Spencer and Gillen on the other hand gave a relatively messy account of Aranda social organization and allowed for a highly complex relationship between groups, individuals and totemism, as Mauss (1900a) recognized in his review. Individuals could become members of totemic cult groups in several ways, including through inheritance and by conception. Totems cross-cut territorial organization and in some exceptional cases moieties. Durkheim recognized the inconsistencies between his model and the Aranda reality and devised all sorts of arguments for explaining the fuzziness and the contradictions – the Aranda were too primitive through degeneration or too disturbed by contact (156–7/111–12). In retrospect we can see that Spencer and Gillen's ethnography pointed to the problematic status of the clan in Australia, whereas Durkheim's theoretical stance led him to reify the clan and regard significant complexities as peripheral 'noise'.

Durkheim's theory required that spiritual power or force should spread from the totem to the world outside. The totem as the representation of the clan was the objectification of the spiritual force of effervescence which had as its origins the clan. The clan itself, as a real constituent of society, could enforce adherence to the ideological rationalizations of praxis and cause people to congregate together on a regular basis, thus generating effervescence and demarcating the sacred from the profane. 'Since religious force is nothing other than the collective and anonymous force of the clan, and since this can be represented in the mind only in the form of the totem, the totemic emblem is like the visible body of the god' (316/221). Religious sentiments

> result from causes wholly foreign to the nature of the object upon which they fix themselves. What constitutes them are the impression of comfort and dependence which the actions of society provokes in the mind. Of themselves these emotions are not attached to the idea of any particular object, but as these emotions exist and are especially intense they are also eminently contagious.
>
> (462–3/323–4)

A logical consequence of Durkheim's position was that no source of spiritual power could be prior to or independent of the clan and that no objectification of power could be independent of the totem. Hence he had to defend the priority of totemism and religion over magic (517/362); emotion felt at the loss of a relative had to originate in the clan and the soul must have been a later creation than the totem (573/401); the land-based nature of ancestral beings had to be a secondary phenomenon; and mythology had to be a retrospective construction on the totems since the individual clan totem had to exist before it could interact with others (147/105, 533/373 ff.). All of the elements of Aboriginal religion that were central to Spencer and Gillen's descriptive ethnography, except the excitement generated in collective rituals, became secondary phenomena.

What Durkheim refers to as the 'totemic principle' has the role of a universal interpretant which of necessity gives a determined position to all other phenomena of Aboriginal religion. Yet the totemic principle is not abstracted from Aranda exegesis but is an a priori creation arising from Durkheim's theoretical thinking. Its dominant position is given by its necessity to the clan, an institution which is in turn ethnographically problematic. Necessity eliminates fuzziness and regulates individual interpretation and experience. Writing of the seasonal patterning of ritual, Durkheim argues:

> since a social interest of the greatest importance is at stake, society cannot allow things to follow their own course at the whim of circumstance, it intervenes actively in such a way as to regulate their course in conformity with its needs. So it demands that this ceremony, which it cannot do without, be repeated every time it is necessary.
>
> (525/367)

The result is the creation of the social as a separate level of determination to which all other forms of explanation become subordinated.

We can see why Stanner, who was looking for an ethnographically derived indigenous interpretant to make sense of Aboriginal religion, appeared to be well nigh offended by Durkheim's analysis. The ontology and ontogeny of Aboriginal religion, which in Spencer and Gillen's accounts were founded on the journeys of the Ancestral Beings in the Alcheringa and the transference of spiritual power through the *churinga* to the present generation of humans (see e.g. Spencer and Gillen 1904:Ch.8), is entirely unexplored by Durkheim.

Conclusion

Spencer and Gillen opened up areas of interpretation which Durkheim then closed off in the short term. His sociologically-grounded theory left little room for a more phenomenologically-based analysis of the content of Aboriginal ritual: the myths, songs, dances, and art forms which form its substance. His almost total neglect of the rich body of mythology published by Spencer and Gillen is an example. Ironically, he provided little alternative to the speculations of the intellectualists. Indeed Durkheim accepts many of the symbolic mechanisms of the intellectualists, such as contagion and mimesis, but reduces their effectiveness in each case to the same process: the spread of socially generated power. Hence the issues that concern the intellectualists are deemed irrelevant, and the differences between the symbolic mechanisms are stated but not explored. Durkheim even in effect accepts some of Frazer's arguments about the operation of processes such as sympathetic magic. He argues that society demands a certain state of mind that 'is above all doubt that like produces like', rather than that such imitative processes are intellectually plausible. Society cannot afford its continued existence to depend on the individual: 'Opinion cannot allow men to deny this principle in theory without also allowing them to violate it in their conduct.' The logical implication of Durkheim's position is that society imposes intellectual consensus. This is the Emperor's New Clothes theory of symbolic action, with the Emperor being replaced by society. The fact that something takes the form of imitative magic is deemed irrelevant to explaining its persistence and hence details of the form of ritual action do not have to be analysed. Durkheim opened the way for a series of studies of symbolism and meaning in which indigenous exegesis was largely irrelevant to the explanation of the phenomena, and this resulted in a separation of the study of social life from the study of cultural forms.

Notes

1   The research for this chapter has been supported by a British Academy grant to produce an edited edition of the letters of F. J. Gillen to Baldwin Spencer. I thank Alison Petch for producing a detailed comparison of *The Elementary Forms of Religious Life* with passages in the published and unpublished works of Spencer and Gillen, only a fraction of which I have been able to use. Frances Morphy has exercised her editorial pen to attempt to improve the text. I thank the organisers of the conference, in particular Bill Pickering, for creating a stimulating environment for presenting ideas.

2   Spencer and Gillen used the spelling Arunta. Until recently Aranda has been more common. Today the more phonologically correct spelling Arrernte is increasingly found.

3   Stocking (1995:14) brilliantly charts his way through this period of transformation while recognizing that 'The intellectual history of British anthropology between its two classical moments (social evolutionism and structural functionalism) still tends to be a rather shadowy, if not actually dark, age.' The fact that Spencer and Gillen's work occupied this time of paradigm change has made their work open to multiple interpretations.

4   Gillen's letters are published in Morphy, Mulvaney and Petch 1997.

2

DID LUCIEN LEVY-BRUHL ANSWER THE OBJECTIONS MADE IN *LES FORMES ELEMENTAIRES?*

Dominique Merllié[1]

On 29 May 1931 Lucien Lévy-Bruhl was the guest of Oxford University where he delivered the Herbert Spencer Lecture. In this text, interestingly one of its author's most comprehensive statements on 'primitive mentality', he begins by expressing his pleasure in accepting the invitation, acknowledging a debt not only to Herbert Spencer in particular, who had influenced his philosophic education in Paris at the end of the 1870s, but also to E. B. Tylor and Sir James Frazer, as well as to 'so many other British anthropological scholars':

> Even if I had at times to diverge from them, I could only do so on the basis of the results of their work and by utilising the mass of facts that they have made accessible.
>
> (Lévy-Bruhl 1931b:6)

This was much more than a polite tribute. In the same vein, and remaining within the Oxford context, there is the long article on Lévy-Bruhl by E. Evans-Pritchard (1934) and the detailed letter in which Lévy-Bruhl expressed his pleasure at the interest shown in him by the British field anthropologist and gave precise answers to the criticisms made of him. The fact that Evans-Pritchard was English meant much to Lévy-Bruhl, who patently wanted to be understood in Britain:

> Your article renders my theory the most valuable of services and only a scholar like you, who is English himself, could explain to English academics why they are wrong to scorn works ... which can be of use to them and which really have been 'misrepresented'.
>
> (Letter, 14 November, 1934:406)

And this letter provides him with the opportunity to repeat what he owes to Tylor and Frazer in enthusiastic terms:

I admire the *Golden Bough*; I always remember the extraordinary impression it made on me; for me, it was like a revelation. A new world appeared before my eyes.

(ibid.:413)

It seems to me that Lévy-Bruhl's interest in and sympathy for British authors was, relatively speaking, reciprocated. If his anthropological ideas are very generally presented in a negative and unfavourable light, this is even truer in France than in Britain. To give only one recent example of the negative reception accorded Lévy-Bruhl in France, one needs only to recall the last three books by Raymond Boudon which make Lévy-Bruhl a positive whipping boy in a recurring comparison between the theories of magic attributed to Lévy-Bruhl and Durkheim respectively. According to Boudon, the first seeks 'causes' external to the subjects to explain their beliefs and thus produces 'sociocentric' explanations, *ad hoc*, tautological and sterile. The latter, by contrast, is able to acknowledge their 'reasons' and 'good reasons', for his explanations rest on '"psychological" propositions' which show that 'there is nothing strange about magical beliefs', and which possess genuine explanatory power (Boudon 1990:35–45; 1992:508–15; 1995).

In short, Lévy-Bruhl's 'explanation of magical practices is purely verbal', whereas that of Durkheim, as of Weber, makes it possible to understand 'that magic provides an interpretation of the world which has nothing irrational about it in societies or social environments where scientific thought is unknown' (Boudon 1992:43). Because of this, 'on the question of the continuity or discontinuity between scientific thought and pre-scientific thought', Lévy-Bruhl 'was a fierce supporter of discontinuity', interpreting 'the discontinuities described by Comte in a radical way', whereas 'Durkheim supports the thesis of a deep-seated continuity between traditional religious thought and magic, on the one hand, and modern and scientific thought, on the other' (ibid.:495).

In the face of such analyses, which patently distort the spirit and letter of Lévy-Bruhl's writings but belong to a long tradition, it is easier in Britain than in France to find authors in the tradition of Evans-Pritchard, who have presented Lévy-Bruhl's theses or themes in a positive light. A case in point is another Oxford anthropologist, Rodney Needham in *Belief, Language and Experience* (1972), dedicated to the memory of Lévy-Bruhl and Wittgenstein. Emphasizing how crucial for the humanities is 'the question of the logical unity of mankind', Needham pays an emphatic tribute to Lévy-Bruhl:

We therefore have cause to be grateful indeed that it was taken up by a man of such intelligence, erudition, and liberality of mind as Lucien Lévy-Bruhl. It is all the more dejecting, however, that for the most part he vainly saw his views traduced and the problems he discerned largely ignored by the ethnographers and others, mostly British, who were in a position to profit from them in their observations.

(ibid.:160)

Although he cites and comments at some length on Lévy-Bruhl, Needham hardly contrasts him with Durkheim (preferring to stress the continuity between the two authors, even if they do not place the emphasis on the same things).

However, a year after the publication of his book, a collective work appeared, dedicated to Sir Edward Evans-Pritchard, entitled *Modes of Thought* and consisting of 'essays on thinking in western and non-western societies' (Horton and Finnegan 1973). It contains a long article by Robin Horton, 'Lévy-Bruhl, Durkheim and the scientific revolution', in which the attitudes of the two 'great French philosopher-sociologists' are sharply contrasted (ibid.:249). Lévy-Bruhl appears as the prototype of the theory of contrast, Durkheim of continuity:

> To put it in a nutshell, Lévy-Bruhl sees the relation between 'prim-itive' and 'modern' in terms of contrast, and the transition between them as a process of inversion, whilst Durkheim sees the relation in terms of continuity, and the transition as a process of evolution. For purposes of shorthand, I shall talk in what follows of a contrast/inversion schema as opposed to a continuity/evolution schema.
>
> (ibid.:270)

By so doing, Horton considers that he is presenting a version of Durkheim's principal thesis which is contrary to the one he thinks prevails, but is better founded on the text of *Les Formes élémentaires* (ibid.:267). However, the idea of a contrast between Lévy-Bruhl and Durkheim in this respect, which seems novel to him, is not new. It can be found in France as early as the first reviews of *Les Formes élémentaires*, and particularly in the long article that Gustave Belot devoted to a critique of the book in *La Revue philosophique* (Belot 1913).

For Belot this was 'a fairly instructive small inter-school quarrel', in which each betrayed Auguste Comte, Lévy-Bruhl by exaggerating the break, Durkheim by seeing 'in human history nothing but continual derivation, an unfolding with no real change' (ibid.:361–2). For Belot it is Comte who is right: 'he held the whole thing together and explained it, both the conti-nuity of the nature of the human faculties and the heterogeneous multiplicity of their manifestations' (ibid.).

This contrast is just as clearly expressed by the somewhat marginal Durkheimian, Célestin Bouglé who, in discussing religion and science, envis-aged scientific reason also as having been 'raised on the lap of the gods', and presented this idea as supporting Auguste Comte's thesis (Bouglé 1922:180).

> An audacious thesis which is set at exactly the opposite pole from the one formulated at the same time by another of Auguste Comte's disciples. When M. Lévy-Bruhl, in order to make us understand the specific nature of the mental processes in inferior societies, emphasizes the pre-logical character that they present – everything

participating in everything, and the confusion of modes, like incoherence of reasoning, being the general rule – he is wantonly digging
a trench between religion and science. To such an extent and so
well that the ultimate appearance of reason risks giving the impression of a miracle: how has the faculty of sound reasoning, by taking
into consideration the attributes of things, ever been able to rise up
in this cloudy world? It is precisely this impression of miracle that
M. Durkheim wants to dissipate. And that is why he builds bridges,
whereas M. Lévy-Bruhl digs trenches.

(ibid.:181)

Horton deduces this contrast between the positions of Durkheim and Lévy-
Bruhl from the text of *Les Formes élémentaires* itself, but he finds 'the strongest
possible evidence' for it in the review in the *Année sociologique*, where Durkheim
'compares and contrasts Lévy-Bruhl's *Fonctions mentales* with his own *Formes
élémentaires*' (Horton 1973:267). In fact, Durkheim's work was the object of
two comparative reviews in volume XII (dated 1909–12, published in 1913)
of the *Année sociologique*: the first, signed by Durkheim, concerns *Les Fonctions
mentales dans les sociétés inférieures* (1910) and *Les Formes élémentaires* (1913a(ii)(6)
and (7)), the second, signed by both Mauss and Durkheim, of Frazer's
Totemism and Exogamy and *Les Formes élémentaires* (1913a(ii)(11) and (12)).
(Frazer's book is also the subject of another review which concentrates on
his theory of exogamy (1913a(ii)(31)).

In fact, Durkheim had already indicated disagreement with Lévy-Bruhl
several times in *Les Formes élémentaires*, particularly concerning the meaning
of 'participation' which, according to Lévy-Bruhl, was typical of 'primitive'
thought, but was just as typical, according to Durkheim, of modern science.
He writes:

> Today, as formerly, to explain is to show how one thing partici-
> pates in one or several others. It has been said that the participations
> of this sort implied by the mythologies violate the principle of contra-
> diction and that they are by that opposed to those implied by
> scientific explanations. Is not the statement that a man is a kangaroo
> or the sun a bird, equal to identifying the two with each other? But
> our manner of thought is not different when we say of heat that it
> is a movement, or of light that it is a vibration of the ether, etc.
> Every time that we unite heterogeneous terms by an internal bond,
> we inevitably identify opposites.
>
> (341/238)

But the disagreement is confirmed in even clearer terms in the review in
the *Année sociologique* where Durkheim draws a marked contrast between 'the
form of a genuine antithesis' in Lévy-Bruhl, and his own evolutionist thesis:

> On the contrary we consider that these two forms of human
> mentality, however different they may seem, are mistakenly thought

to have originated from different sources: they grew out of each other and represent two stages in the same process of evolution . . . There is no gap between these two stages of the intellectual life of mankind . . . If then human mentality has varied over the centuries and with societies – if it has evolved – the different types of mentality it has successfully produced have each given rise to the other.

(Durkheim 1913a(ii)(6) and (7))

Did Lévy-Bruhl answer this criticism, and if not, why not? It was Horton who asked this question, which is why I have already quoted him at such length:

One of the enigmas of [Lévy-Bruhl's] later work, indeed, is that for all his positive response to the criticisms of Malinowski and Evans-Pritchard, he seems to have made no response at all to the lone but powerful voice which directed its criticism against these more enduring presuppositions of his thought. The voice in question was that of his colleague Emile Durkheim.

(Horton 1973:258)

To sharpen the question, it is to be noted that the two men were at least on friendly terms and Lévy-Bruhl always showed great respect for Durkheim's work. All his books on 'primitive mentality', not only the 1910 book that Durkheim was able to criticize, but the whole series of five others which followed it between 1922 and 1938, appeared in La Collection de l'Année sociologique. It is also true to say that Lévy-Bruhl always paid close attention to comments by field anthropologists, as has been seen from the terms, almost the enthusiasm, of his reply, quoted above, to the article by Evans-Pritchard.

A first possible answer to this question is to refer to a trait of character.[2] Nothing in Lévy-Bruhl's gentleness, even shyness, and also sense of humour brings him close to the prophetic temperament of Durkheim, the founder of a school. Lévy-Bruhl was not a man to engage in controversy. And in fact we possess the evidence of a former student which shows that he was wounded by the manner in which Durkheim's criticisms were expressed:

Lévy-Bruhl, grieved and disturbed by the attacks whose violence and injustice took him unawares, did not, as it were, defend himself. He suffered in silence, but I am sure that his views, much more nuanced and subtle than those of orthodox Durkheimians, did not give ground.

(Rivaud 1950)

The fact that Durkheim was dead in 1917 would then provide an additional explanation of why Lévy-Bruhl did not reply to him explicitly. And it can at least be noted that references to Durkheim, quite prominent in Les Fonctions mentales – but already fewer than in La morale et la science des moeurs (Lévy-Bruhl 1903) – become considerably rarer in Lévy-Bruhl's later works.

However, to pursue the trail of explicit references, a later passage can be found which makes it possible to say that Lévy-Bruhl did nonetheless sketch out an 'answer'. *La mythologie primitive*, published in 1935, is the work in which Lévy-Bruhl most directly confronts the cultures studied in *Les Formes élémentaires*. In it, he accepts a recurrent criticism made by Marcel Mauss and, by limiting his field of investigation, concedes that 'the term "primitives" should have been reserved for the Australians' (Lévy-Bruhl 1935:215). In any case, the book's sub-title is 'The mythical world of the Australians and Papuans'. When it is recalled that Lévy-Bruhl's early works did not carry sub-titles, this could almost sound like an echo of the sub-title of *Les Formes élémentaires*: *Le système totémique en Australie*.

The relevant passage appears in the chapter entitled 'The Persistence of the Mythical World'. Lévy-Bruhl first asks if the 'representation of the mythic world' which he has just studied 'is to be found . . . elsewhere, in societies which do not seem . . . ever to have been in contact with them' (ibid.:200–201). Examples borrowed from Radcliffe-Brown, Boas and other anthropologists who have worked in varied regions allow him to conclude that:

> In a large number of more or less 'primitive' societies in both hemi-
> spheres, one finds, if not the totality of the essential elements [of
> the mythical world of the Australian tribes], at least the most impor-
> tant among them.
>
> (ibid.:214)

But Lévy-Bruhl then debars himself from the generalization of this statement which would consist of saying that: 'This representation of the mythical world . . . is always found in approximately similar form in primitive societies.' In fact 'Even where the analogies are indubitable and striking, differences compel attention' (ibid.:215). Among these differences, he mentions the creation of 'divinities', of 'a veritable cult, which involves sacerdotal functions', the emergence of 'sacrifices, unknown in Australian and Papuan tribes' (ibid.:216).

It can be noted that the word religion does not appear in this context. And it is at this point that the reference to, and the aloofness from, Durkheim occurs:

> I will therefore not say, as did Durkheim in his famous book, that
> Australian societies offer us the 'elementary forms of religious life',
> but rather that the collection of beliefs and practices which has taken
> shape in their myths and their ceremonies constitutes a 'pre-religion'.
> The meaning of this neologism, for which I apologise, is sufficiently
> defined by what has been set out in preceding chapters . . . It has at
> least the advantage of bringing out the point where I diverge from
> the dominant views of the founder of the *Année sociologique*. In his
> thought, however varied the forms that religion may assume, whether
> it be captured in the Australian tribes, or in our western societies, or
> in the Far East or elsewhere, it always remains similar, not to say

identical, in essence. A study of the facts has led me to a somewhat different conception. It seems to me to be preferable not to apply such a strictly defined concept to every case. I will not give the name of religion to the collection of beliefs and ceremonies expressed by the myths, which has been described and analysed above. It is only when certain elements of this complex grow weaker and disappear, when new elements take their place in it and develop, that a religion properly speaking is formed and established.

(ibid.:217)

Hardly has he said this than Lévy-Bruhl seems to want to minimize its import:

In no way does making such a distinction between 'pre-religion' and 'religion' tend to contrast them. How could one possibly fail to recognize all that they have in common, which Durkheim has brought out so well? . . . Even the term *pre*-religion, without involving a necessary evolution, indicates that this is one stage to be succeeded later by a religion in the full sense of the word.

(ibid.)

But having made this concession, in the end Lévy-Bruhl again emphasizes the importance he attaches to the distinction:

But it has seemed useful to stress the differences between pre-religion and religion, instead of emphasising the resemblances, as has hitherto been the case. In this way one guards against serious possibilities of error. There is less risk of projecting characteristics which only appear in more advanced societies on to the quasi-religious facts which are observed in these societies, the most primitive that it is given to us to know at the present time.

(ibid.:217–18)

What, then, is interesting about this terminological quarrel, modest but yet persistently expressed? A sort of reversal of position is evident. Durkheim, in a book whose dominant theme was religion, criticized Lévy-Bruhl's excessively discontinuist thesis but on the grounds of modes of thought. More than twenty years later, after a long silence, in a book on *représentations*, the expert on 'primitive mentality' criticized Durkheim's thesis in regard to religion because it failed to make certain indispensable distinctions. Talking about pre-religion would be an indirect way of answering the criticism of the term 'prelogical': it would be as inordinate to rank the most purely primitive modes of thought and modern or scientific modes of thought in the same class (that of 'human mentality', an expression Durkheim used in the passages quoted above) as it would be to assimilate empirical realities as different as the myths and ceremonies of Australian aborigines with religions, properly so called.

However, it is possible to go a little further by recalling that Durkheim connected the origin of religion with the origin of science and for that very reason criticized Lévy-Bruhl for connecting religion with primitive mentality. Nothing of the kind, replies Lévy-Bruhl, because it is not religion but a form of pre-religion that corresponds to primitive mentality proper. Religion, if strictly defined, has even here to do with modern modes of thought. Moreover, this interpretation is in accordance with the Durkheimian definition of religion by the rift between the sacred and the profane, which implies the distinction made between two realms or spheres of activity. For Lévy-Bruhl, in fact, primitive mentality proper can only be understood if one sees that it remains alien to this dissociation – a theme developed particularly in *Le Surnaturel et la nature dans la mentalité primitive* (Lévy-Bruhl 1931a). However, this response would not only have been belated, but also somewhat indirect. Nevertheless, it is possible to find – especially in the same book – answers which are just as discreet but which bear more directly on the theme of modes of thought.

In the introduction to the same book, where Durkheim is neither quoted nor mentioned, if one bears Durkheim's criticisms of Lévy-Bruhl in mind, arguments are indeed found which really appear to be quite explicit answers to these criticisms. After recognizing that 'the fundamental structure of the human spirit is probably the same everywhere', he refers to the 'non-conceptual tendencies' of the 'primitives' attitude' in respect of the 'contradiction', to say:

> He (the primitive) indeed forms concepts: how could he completely avoid it? But these concepts are fewer in number than ours and are not systematised like them. Consequently, their language does not enable them to pass effortlessly from one given concept to other, less general, ones which are comprised in it, or to more general ones which comprise it.
>
> (Lévy-Bruhl 1935:xii)

How can this not be viewed as a response to the passage in *Les Formes élémentaires* which states, as a criticism of *Les Fonctions mentales*, the universality of conceptual thought:

> Saying that concepts express the manner in which society represents things is also saying that conceptual thought is coeval with humanity itself. We therefore, refuse to see in it the product of a more or less relatively late culture. A man who did not think with concepts would not be a man, for he would not be a social being. Reduced to having only individual perceptions, he would be indistinguishable from the beasts. If it has been possible to argue a contrary thesis, it is because concepts have been defined by characteristics which are not essential to them. They have been identified with general ideas [a footnote refers to *Les Fonctions mentales*] ... Thinking conceptually is not simply isolating and grouping together

the common characteristics of a certain number of objects; it is subsuming the variable in the permanent, the individual in the social. And since logical thought commences with the concept, it follows that it has always existed.

(626–7/438–9)

Likewise, Lévy-Bruhl is answering the same criticism once again when he recalls in the same introduction that, for him, '*représentations* which have not taken the form of regular concepts are not necessarily devoid of generality' (which led him to speak of an 'affective category of the supernatural' (Lévy-Bruhl 1935:xv).

It is therefore possible to say that Lévy-Bruhl did indeed reply to Durkheim's criticisms. Nevertheless the belated and quasi-cryptic nature of this response can still call for analysis.

Another possible form of response to the queries raised by Horton is therefore that perhaps Lévy-Bruhl was not really interested in the question, posed in that way. Reading the two authors can in fact lead one to think that, beyond the contrast pointed out by Horton, the true difference between them lies in the nature of their project. It would then be somewhat misleading to read them as contrary answers to the same question, in so far as they would not be asking the same question. And in fact Lévy-Bruhl's basic inquiry is not of a directly theoretical nature, but of an empirical nature. He never denied the unity of human nature (and the passage on this subject quoted above from the introduction to the 1935 book already appeared by way of hypothesis in *La Morale et la science des moeurs* (Lévy-Bruhl 1903:82). But he strove to make intelligible to westerners alien thoughts which lent themselves to every type of misconstruction. This leads him to say that they do in effect lead to misconstructions, and then to try to explain them. The stress placed on otherness is not based on an ethnocentric attitude but on the denunciation of ethnocentrism. In this sense it can be said that his objective is first and foremost descriptive, almost more ethnographic than anthropological.

A French anthropologist, whose work is not without an echo of Lévy-Bruhl's, seems to me to express quite well the fundamental difference between Durkheim's and Lévy-Bruhl's type of inquiry. I have in mind Roger Bastide. His work of 1965 is devoted to a 'confrontation between Leenhardt and Lévi-Strauss'. 'The problem' with this confrontation, Bastide begins, 'is of the same nature as of the comparison between Durkheim and Lévy-Bruhl', because of a certain relationship between Claude Lévi-Strauss and Durkheim and between Maurice Leenhardt and Lévy-Bruhl:

> Durkheim only wants to see the unity of reason, because reason is of social origin and all men belong to society – whereas Lévy-Bruhl wants to see only the multiplicity of reasons, because human intelligence is always fashioned by the culture of the surrounding environment, and there is a multiplicity of cultures.
>
> (Bastide 1965:123)

It is clearly the contrast brought out by Horton which attracts Bastide's attention. But he then suggests the following explanation, or rather interpretation:

> Durkheim wants to explain; his work takes its place in the great current of positivism. Lévy-Bruhl wants to understand (or more accurately draw our attention to the danger of understanding) the 'primitives' via another mentality, our own, which has been fashioned by centuries of western culture; he opens the path to a new sociology which will subsequently be called the 'sociology of understanding' [akin to *Verstehen*].
>
> (ibid.)

Explanation on one side; understanding or even attention to the dangers of incomprehension on the other. Those terms which place the emphasis on the phenomenological or hermeneutical side of the Lévy-Bruhlian enterprise seem sound to me.[3] Far from denouncing irrational thinking or thinking without reason, Lévy-Bruhl set himself the task, as do our modern 'ethnomethodologists', of accounting for the specific 'logic' at work in nonwestern societies.

Notes

1 Translated from the French by Miriam Kochan.
2 I have dealt more comprehensively with the relationship between the two men in an earlier article (Merllié 1989).
3 In a very short article on 'Lévy-Bruhl's originality', Emile Bréhier similarly emphasizes that Lévy-Bruhl's efforts consisted of a 'search for the structure replacing a search for genesis' which put him at odds with Durkheim's enterprise: he was seeking 'not the steps in a genesis, but a different structure' (Bréhier 1949:385–6). On these grounds, Bréhier compares his enterprise 'with the whole current of ideas which are manifested in very diverse domains, for example in Gestalt psychology and also in phenomenological analysis (ibid.:388).

3

RELIGION AND SCIENCE IN *THE ELEMENTARY FORMS*

Robert Alun Jones

Introduction

'The believer who has communicated with his god is not merely a man who sees new truths of which the unbeliever is ignorant; he is a man who is stronger' (595/416). Durkheim's emphasis on religion as a form of action as well as thought thus has two important ideas, each 'irrationalist' in disposition and Calvinist in origin. The first was 'the ritual theory of myth', inspired by Robertson Smith and later applied to the study of classical antiquity by the Cambridge Ritualists (see Smith 1889/1972:18–20; Ackerman 1975, 1987; Jones and Vogt 1984). The second, which Durkheim owed to William James, was that religious beliefs are not illusory, but rather rest upon concrete experiences like those of the sciences (596/417; James 1902). Like the ritualist, Durkheim believed that primitive religion was more a matter of things done than of things believed; and like the pragmatist, Durkheim believed that 'a tree is known by its fruits', fertility being the best proof of what the roots are worth. For Durkheim, of course, 'the concrete experience' in question was the periodic gathering of the clan, which raised individuals above themselves, and thus produced the 'experimental proof' of their beliefs (596/417).

But Durkheim then encountered an objection. If religion is the effect of real, social causes, does it reflect these causes in such an idealized form? An ideal effect seems to presume an ideal cause; but an ideal society would presuppose religion, not explain it (601/420; Boutroux 1909a:201–2). Durkheim took this objection seriously, and his answer was decisive for his sociology of religion. Briefly, when the cult gathers, it arouses a state of 'collective effervescence' that alters the conditions of psychic life, arousing stronger sensations and more active passions. It is to account for these passions and sensations that members of the cult attribute extraordinary powers and virtues to otherwise ordinary, profane objects. Above the real world, therefore, the cult creates another which exists only in thought, but to which it attributes a higher dignity, that is, the idealized world of 'sacred' objects. Religion was thus the natural product, not just of social life, but of society become conscious of itself. For Durkheim, therefore, everything passes into the world of the ideal. Durkheim's answer to this objection has thus, quite appropriately, been construed as an attempt to distinguish his own theory of religion from that of historical materialists; but as I shall suggest below, the objection had come from Emile Boutroux.

Boutroux's objection answered, Durkheim quickly formulated three propositions on the relation between religion and science. First, all societies need to affirm and reaffirm their collective sentiments and ideas at periodic intervals; there is thus 'something eternal' in religion 'destined to survive all the particular symbols in which religious thought has successfully enveloped itself' (609/427). Religion as *practice* is thus the expression of a concrete reality, and no science makes the reality to which it is applied disappear. Second, religion also comprises a system of speculative *ideas*, and 'in all that which concerns the cognitive and intellectual functions' (614/430), Durkheim embraced the more Frazerian view that religion would be gradually replaced by science. This, he insisted, is what the conflict between religion and science 'really amounts to' (ibid.). Third, Durkheim articulated a Jamesian, pragmatic view of the relation between thought and action. We cannot celebrate ceremonies for which we see no reason. Religious faith must be *justified*, and while faith must take science into account, science alone will always remain insufficient; faith is an impetus to action, while science is always fragmentary, advances slowly, and is always incomplete. Life, in short, cannot wait for science (616/431).

The Development of Durkheim's views on religion and science

This was Durkheim's most detailed and nuanced treatment of the relations between religion and science, and it seems to have emerged relatively late in the development of his thought. Indeed, Steven Lukes referred long ago to the thinness and inconclusiveness of Durkheim's early writings on religion (Lukes 1973:44). In 1886, for example, Durkheim admitted that he felt 'unqualified to speak' on the history of religion, appeared ignorant of totemism, and was inclined to accept the naturistic hypothesis of Albert Réville. He also emphasized the regulatory function of religion which, like that of law and morality, was 'to maintain the equilibrium of society and to adapt it to environmental conditions' (1886a/t.1975a:18, 20). In 1887, Durkheim again pointed to the 'confused synthesis, of early moral, legal, and religious customs, and criticized Jean-Marie Guyau for ignoring 'the obligatory nature of religious prescriptions' (1887b/t.1975a:34). In 1893, Durkheim could still complain that 'we do not actually possess any scientific notion of what religion is', though he linked it to the *conscience collective* and granted it a declining role in social life with the evolution of organic solidarity (1893b/t.1933b:168–9).

Durkheim's lecture-course on religion at Bordeaux in 1894–5, clearly marked a great watershed in the development of his thought. But even in 1899, his discussion of religion and science was still limited to the observation that beliefs and practices of the religion are 'obligatory', while those of science are not (1899a(ii)/t.1975a:91). The more detailed and imaginative essay on totemism in 1902 at last revealed the powerful influence of Frazer and Smith; but here there was no discussion of the relation of religion and science whatsoever (1902a(i)). Even in Paul Fontana's summary of Durkheim's lecture-course on 'La Religion: les origines' (1906–7), the view seems to have been simply that religion is a primitive form of both science and morality (1907f:110). It is only with the appearance of *Les Formes élémentaires*, therefore, that Durkheim mounted a substantial effort to explain how the idealized world of sacred objects might be explained as the product of real social forces, and how individuals are thus 'raised above themselves'. Indeed, in his defence of *Les Formes élémentaires* before the Société Française de Philosophie in 1913, Durkheim emphasized this 'dynamogenic' quality of religion, that is, its capacity to give rise to actions as well as thoughts, to enable the believer to transcend his merely individual powers, to become capable of greater things' as one of the two central ideas of his book (see 1913b/t.1984b:3–11; Jones and Vogt 1984:47–8).

Any attempt to reconstruct the historical development of Durkheim's view of the relationship between religion and science, therefore, must grant special emphasis to the period between 1907 and 1912.[1] As we shall see, this quite naturally draws our attention to the publication of Emile Boutroux's *Science et religion dans la philosophie contemporaine* (1908), as well as Boutroux's discussion and defence of this book before the Société Française de Philosophie in 1909. Born at Montrouge, near Paris, in 1845, he attended the Ecole Normale Supérieure from 1865 to 1868, where he came under the influence of the neo-spiritualist philosopher Jules Lachelier (1832–1918). Dissatisfied with the reigning mechanistic and deterministic perspective of French philosophy, Lachelier urged his pupil to study Kant, and Boutroux's student papers suggest that he soon embraced the anti-determinist position (Smith 1967a:355). Successful in the *agrégation* in 1868, Boutroux spent the following year studying in Heidelberg, returning in 1871 as an instructor at the lycée of Caen. Boutroux's first major work was *De la Contingence des lois de la nature*, a study of determinism in its relation to the physical and moral sciences, for which he received his doctorate in 1874 and which ultimately proved to be his *magnum opus*. After teaching at Montpelier and Nancy, in 1877 Boutroux received an appointment in philosophy at the Ecole Normale Supérieure, where he remained for the next nine years, including the period from 1879 to 1882, when Durkheim was his student. From 1886 to 1902, Boutroux occupied a chair in philosophy at the Sorbonne. *De l'Idée de loi naturelle dans la science et la philosophie contemporaines* (1895) extended further the ideas that had first been expressed in his doctoral thesis and later taught in his lecture course (1892–3) at the Sorbonne.

In his preface to the English translation of *De la Contingence des lois de la nature*, Boutroux recalled the problem that led him to write the book: 'If [the laws of nature] were actually necessary', he reasoned, '[they] would signify the immutability and rigidity of death. If they are contingent, they dignify life and constitute points of support or bases which enable us constantly to rise towards a higher life' (Boutroux 1916:vii). Boutroux's goal was thus to show that the laws of nature are contingent rather than necessary, and that they indeed make a 'higher life' possible.

Boutroux did not deny that the principle of causality could be stated in such a form that it would be necessarily true. But he did insist that this is not the sense in which the principle is actually used in the natural sciences. On the contrary, for the purposes of scientific practice, the more Humean, empiricist notion of 'relatively invariable relations' between the phenomena is all that is required for the formulation of scientific laws. The idea of necessity is not required. The principle of causality is derived from experience, as 'a very general and abstract expression of observed relations' (Copleston 1977:189; Boutroux 1916:23–5). So the development of the sciences themselves suggests that the laws of nature do not express objectively necessary relations. Scientific laws are useful, but they are not definitive. 'There is no equivalence,' Boutroux thus insisted, 'no relation of causality, pure and simple, between a man and the elements that gave him birth, between the developed being and the being in process of formation' (Boutroux 1916:32).

In opposition to the rationalist conception of a single world comprised of logically-deducible necessary relations, therefore, Boutroux insisted 'on several worlds, forming, as it were, stages superposed on one another' (ibid.:151–2). These include the world of pure necessity (i.e., of quantity without quality), the world of causes, the world of notions, the mathematical world, the physical world, the living world and, at last, the thinking world. At first, Boutroux acknowledged, each of these worlds seems to depend on those beneath it, and to receive from them its existence and its laws; but again, the examination and comparison of these forms of being, as well as the sciences that study them, shows that it is impossible to connect the higher to the lower forms by any link of necessity. This means, in turn, that the universe is not made up of equal elements capable of being transformed into one another like algebraic quantities; on the contrary, each world contains something new, something more than the worlds below, so that within each world the amount of being and the degree of perfection are indeterminate (ibid.:158–9). Each world, in short, is indeterminate and contingent, which means it might not have existed, or might have existed in some other form, rather than logically or causally necessary. As a devout Roman Catholic, Boutroux considered God the creator of both the existence and the essence of all beings. From the religious standpoint, therefore, the doctrine of contingency was quite literally a theory of divine providence (ibid.:180).

An obvious corollary of this contingency and indeterminacy is freedom of individual thought and action. The individual, Boutroux thus insisted, 'is not only the creator of his character, he can also intervene in the events of his life and change their course; every moment he can strengthen his acquired tendencies or endeavour to modify them' (ibid.:172). Forty years after *De la Contingence*, Boutroux could thus write: 'I have restored to man, *qua* man, his thoughts and feelings, his will and action, that reality and effective influence over the course of things which common sense attributes to them' (ibid.:vi–vii).

The significance of Boutroux's doctoral thesis to the development of Durkheim's sociology is well-known. In 1907, responding to Simon Deploige's claim that the distinction he had drawn between psychology and sociology had been borrowed from Wundt, Durkheim insisted that he had acquired the idea elsewhere:

> I owe it first to my master, Boutroux, who, at the Ecole Normale Supérieure, repeated frequently to us that each science must, as Aristotle says, explain [its own phenomena] by 'its own principles' – e.g. psychology by psychological principles, biology by biological principles. Most impressed by this idea, I applied it to sociology.
>
> (1907b:612–13)

But in fact, Durkheim's ambitious claims for sociology went far beyond anything that Boutroux might have condoned. In his inaugural lecture at Bordeaux (1888), Durkheim made it clear that the search for necessary laws was the task of all positive science, including the social sciences (Durkheim 1888a/t.1978a:47; see Lukes 1973:58). Confronted with the objection that such laws, applied to the study of human behaviour, would contradict free will, Durkheim responded that the question of man's freedom 'belongs to metaphysics, and the positive sciences can and must ignore it'. In short, one must choose: 'Either one recognizes that social phenomena are accessible to scientific investigation,' Durkheim insisted, 'or else one admits, for no reason and contrary to all the inductions of science, that there are two worlds within the world: one in which reigns the law of causality, the other in which reign arbitrariness and contingency' (Durkheim 1888a/t.1978a:48; see Lukes 1973:57–8).

Boutroux, of course, would have resisted such a conclusion, however provisional and abstract. But *De la Contingence des lois de la nature* contains no explicit discussion of 'laws of social behaviour', for Boutroux's theory of qualitatively different, irreducible levels of being culminates with the 'thinking world' of human self-consciousness, not human societies. In 1892–3, however, Boutroux gave a series of lectures at the Sorbonne, subsequently published under the title *De l'Idée de loi naturelle dans la science et la philosophie contemporaines*, which were published in 1895, in which the status of sociological laws was treated in much greater detail (see Boutroux 1914). Predictably, Boutroux objected strongly to sociological laws based on the models of either mathematics or the natural sciences. History provided a more attractive alternative; but Boutroux, like his colleague Fustel de Coulanges, questioned whether historians discover 'laws' at all.

Boutroux thus turned to a second alternative, namely, that we connect social facts, not with their equally social antecedents, but with external conditions capable of being observed and measured (e.g., geographical features, density of population, amount of sustenance, etc.). But Boutroux also had objections to this alternative, including one he illustrated with an example familiar to us all.

Suppose, for instance, we explain the development of the division of labour by the progress of social density, the interdependence of the members of a society. The saying of Darwin is recalled, that different beings live side by side more easily than similar beings: they inconvenience one another in a less degree and the struggle for life amongst them is not so keen. Man obtains this salutary diversity by developing division of labour, and so this division of labour shows itself as the necessary result of the struggle for life. Vital competition: a physical cause, thus explains division of labour: a social fact.

(ibid.:198)

It is hard to imagine a more succinct description of Book II of *De la Division du travail social* (1893b), which was Durkheim's doctoral thesis, defended just months before Boutroux's lectures were delivered (see Durkheim 1893b/t.1933b:256–82). In fact, Durkheim's thesis was dedicated to Boutroux. But according to Bouglé (see Lukes 1973:296), Boutroux accepted the dedication with a grimace, and in the doyen's report of the defence, Boutroux's discontent was particularly addressed to Durkheim's mechanical, necessitarian mode of explanation.[2] Concerning the 'law' that the increase in the division of labour is a direct result of the increasing density and volume of population, for example, Boutroux argued that the increasing division of labour was not the only possible solution. 'I did not wish to show that my law was the only possible consequence,' Durkheim replied during his defence, 'but rather that it was a necessary consequence. There are others, but they are secondary and weak (ibid.:298).

Boutroux was apparently unhappy with this reply; and he was no happier two years later when his lectures were published. The division of labour, Boutroux insisted, is not a necessary, invariable consequence of the Darwinian struggle for existence; and even if it were, this would still not constitute 'a relation of necessity' in the Newtonian sense. For in Durkheim's theory, the division of labour is a condition essential to the realization of a particular end, that is, the cessation of the struggle for life, which is by no means a mechanical and inevitable necessity. On the contrary, the struggle for life 'admits of other solutions, the simplest of which is the eating of one another. That is really the law of nature, and division of labour is instituted for the very purpose of impeding the fulfilment of this law' (Boutroux 1914:199). The division of labour is necessary, Boutroux thus concluded, only in the sense of being preferable and 'more in conformity with the idea of humanity which responds more completely to that sympathy with the weak which we assume to exist in man'. What can this mean, Boutroux asked, except that 'what we took to be a crude law of causality involves a relation of finality, and that we are assuming the intervention of the human intellect and will where we think we are bringing into action none but external and material conditions?' (ibid.:199–200).

Like his notion of the irreducible levels of being, Boutroux's insistence on the contingency of natural laws, including sociological laws, was more than an abstract exercise in the philosophy of science. On the contrary, as a devout Roman Catholic, Boutroux was attempting to describe the limitations of science itself (Copleston 1977:192).[3] Like the other Catholic Modernists (e.g., Alfred Loisy, Lucien Laberthonnière, Maurice Blondel, Edouard Le Roy, and others), Boutroux felt that the Church had closed its mind to a variety of intellectual difficulties, such as the conflict between Scholastic philosophy and evolutionary biology, the challenge of scientific historical criticism of Scripture, the emergence of neo-Kantian and neo-Spiritualist philosophies; and he particularly sought to reconcile the claims of modern science with those of Christianity. Initially tolerated by Pope Leo XIII, the Modernists came under increasing suppression after the accession of Pius X in 1903. By 1907, the Church had published a catalogue of errors, modelled on the *Syllabus Errorum*, entitled *Lamentabili sane exitu*. The catalogue condemned sixty-five Modernist 'errors' concerning Scripture and Church doctrine, most extracted from the writings of Loisy, in effect calling 'a halt to a genuinely historical study of the Scriptures and tradition' (Livingston 1971:291). In the same year, the Pope published the encyclical *Pascendi dominici gregis*, which re-affirmed the teachings of the Church in opposition to the Modernist position, and enumerated the steps to be taken 'to fight the growing contagion' (ibid.:292). Loisy was excommunicated just one year later, and in 1910, the Church imposed the *Motu Proprio Sacrarum antistitum* – the detailed anti-Modernist oath which is still required of all candidates for the priesthood before ordination. It was at the height of this Modernist crisis that Boutroux published his *La science et la religion dans la philosophie contemporaine* (1908). It was the work to which Durkheim's theory of the relation of religion and science was in some sense a response.

Boutroux on science and religion

Boutroux's doctrine of contingency made history singularly important, and his treatment of the relationship between religion and science dealt with the mathematical and natural sciences from antiquity to the early twentieth century (see Boutroux 1916:166–7). But Boutroux particularly emphasized the changes brought about by psychology and sociology, which had introduced two new elements into the relationship of religion and science. First, these sciences no longer asked whether their conclusions were consistent with religious doctrine, but brought religion itself – religious experience, beliefs, and institutions – under the scrutiny of science. Second, in doing so, this 'science of religions' had 'this remarkable property of destroying its object in the act of describing it, and of substituting itself for the facts in proportion as it analyses them' (Boutroux 1909a:196–7). In sum, the scientific study of religion, if successful, would destroy religion itself.

To whom was Boutroux referring here? There can be little doubt. In 1906–7, Durkheim had offered a lecture course, 'La religion: les origines', at the Sorbonne. Paul Fontana's detailed account of those lectures appeared almost immediately in the *Revue de philosophie*; and they are, in effect, a preliminary outline of *Les Formes élémentaires* (Durkheim 1907f). As we shall see,

Durkheim denied that his science could have the effect of 'destroying its object in the act of describing it'. But the equation between God and society was already sharply drawn in the Sorbonne lectures, and Boutroux thus set himself the task of attacking Durkheimian sociology *tout court*.

Boutroux acknowledged that sociology begins with 'conspicuous and objectively cognisable' things rather than the subjective sentiments studied by the psychologist (see Boutroux 1909a:187–90). But as he had in *De l'Idée de loi naturelle*, Boutroux denied that sociology is concerned with facts and laws in the same sense as physics. The physicist who has found the means of expressing the scale of heat sensations by changes in the elevation of a liquid column no longer needs to consult his subjective appreciation of heat; but the sociology uses 'objective documents' only by considering them as mere symbols of the subjective realities supplied by consciousness. So in reality, the distinction between sociology and psychology is delusive, for beneath every sociological explanation, an irreducible psychological element is concealed.

Boutroux thus attacked Durkheim's social realism, namely, the notion that society was an objective reality rather than a subjective fact. 'That which is [in society] real and living – which is the motive and the characteristic adapted for explaining the phenomena in so far as they are explicable – is found, in the last analysis, to be the wants, the beliefs, the passions, the aspirations, the illusions of the human consciousness' (ibid.:201).[4] Moreover, society is not only a subject but, unlike the individual consciousness (a 'given' subject), the collective consciousness is an *ideal* subject. 'If the community itself' Boutroux explained, 'gives instinctively and spontaneously to its institutions a religious character in order that they may have more prestige and more power, we may infer that the community pursues an ideal not easily realisable by the individual consciousness. May not, then, the conception, the pursuit of this ideal be, itself, the effect of a religious inspiration?' (1909a:201). This argument, that the ideal society presupposes religion rather than the reverse, was the one to which Durkheim responded in the conclusion of *Les Formes élémentaires*, defending an essentially idealist theory of society (see above and 600/420).

When Durkheim acknowledged that 'all passes in the world of the ideal' (603/422), therefore, he was responding to Boutroux as well as attacking Marx and historical materialism; and as a consequence, of course, Durkheim's sociology of religion became more nuanced and complex, embracing a vocabulary of 'idealization' and 'transcendence' as well as 'obligation' and 'constraint'. But this *ideal* community, Boutroux insisted, 'is no longer something definite and given which can be compared with a physical fact; to explain religion by the exigencies of this community, is no longer to resolve it into political or collective phenomena that can be observed empirically' (Boutroux 1909a:212). On the contrary, the ideal community inclines us 'to put the claims of God in opposition to those of Caesar – personal dignity in opposition to public constraint' (ibid.:211–12). In this sense, Boutroux argued, 'the science of religions' is quite literally a contradiction in terms.

What, then, of the larger conflict between religion and science? This conflict, Boutroux observed, is not between the doctrines of religion and the conclusions of science, but rather between two different mental dispositions, of the scientific spirit and its religious counterpart. As in his Gifford Lectures, Boutroux described the modern scientific spirit as 'a system of symbols' that provides 'a convenient and usable *représentation*' of realities that cannot be directly known. Acutely aware of the principles of evolutionary biology, *pace* Descartes, the scientific spirit no longer views anything as stable or definitive: 'Not only is a purely experimental science, by definition, always approximative, provisional, and modifiable,' Boutroux observed, but 'according to the results of science herself, there is nothing to guarantee the absolute stability of even the most general laws that man has been able to discover. Nature evolves, perhaps even fundamentally' (ibid.:357). But if the scientific spirit is thus no longer dogmatic in the metaphysical sense, it still regards itself as the supreme example of judgment and reason, and 're-establishes for its own use a kind of relative dogmatism actually based on experience. It believes in its power of unlimited expansion, and in its indefinitely increasing value' (ibid.:358).

What, then, is the *religious* spirit? In the face of the 'unbounded confidence' of its scientific counterpart, can room be found for it in human consciousness? One answer to this question, of which Boutroux was well aware, was to equate science with reason itself, so that everything outside of science – religion included – would be outside of reason, 'relegated among those raw materials of experience which it is the special aim of science to transform into objective symbols capable of furnishing truth' (ibid.:360). At least since A. D. White's *History of the Warfare of Science with Theology in Christendom* (1896), writers have employed this 'non-cognitivist' strategy to separate religion from theology, and thus to render the former immune to scientific (indeed, to any intellectual) criticism whatsoever. Though hardly motivated by the desire to immunize religious orthodoxy, Durkheim's distinction between the speculative and practical aspects of religion belongs in part to this tradition.

But, as Boutroux was aware, this strategy is open to serious objections. Most Christians, for example, are committed to a creed that contains factual assertions, for example, that Christ rose from the dead, that there is a life after death, and so on; and if religion is not a matter of fact, there is the problem of deciding rationally between one's own religion and other religions (Smart 1967:159). In sharp contrast to the 'noncognitivist' apologetic, therefore, Boutroux insisted that science itself acknowledge the claims of 'a more general reason' – a conception of reason of which science is undoubtedly the most definite form, but which science does not itself exhaust. 'The *scientific* reason,' Boutroux explained, 'is reason in so far as it is formed and determined by scientific culture. Reason, taken in its *fullest* sense, is that outlook upon things which determines, in the human soul, the whole of its relations with them' (Boutroux 1909a:360. Emphasis added.). In short, Boutroux insists, a man 'ought to be allowed to consider the conditions, not only of scientific knowledge, but of his own life' (ibid.:366).

Boutroux's position here, that *science* does not exhaust the possibilities of *reason*, recalls Durkheim's own acknowledgment, in the conclusion of *Les Formes élémentaires*, of the limitations implicit within science. We cannot practise ceremonies for which we see no reason, Durkheim there observed, nor embrace an incomprehensible faith. So a type of reason – one which takes science into account, but is not itself 'scientific' – must be a part of religion, justifying our faith. Faith, in turn, becomes an impetus for action, which is necessary for life – an impetus that science cannot provide (616/431). In any case, just weeks after Boutroux's book appeared, we have concrete evidence of Durkheim's interest in this argument.

Durkheim, Boutroux, and the Société Française de Philosophie

'I have just read Boutroux's book' Durkheim wrote to Xavier Léon on 8 May 1908.

> It would be really interesting if on Tuesday you could raise at the Société de Philosophie the question of the relations between philosophy and religion. There is a question which hovers over all the recent discussions which I have attended and which this book raises once again, namely, whether there are two types of reason, the one relating to science, the other to philosophy and religion.
>
> (Cited in Lukes 1973:406)

Six months later, on 19 November 1908, the Société Française de Philosophie devoted an entire evening to the discussion of Boutroux's book, providing Durkheim with an opportunity to respond to its author's conception of the relation of religion and science.

Why, Durkheim asked, do we continue to place religion outside science? In effect, Durkheim's answer contained three elements. The first concerned Durkheim's conception of religion, which differed substantially from Boutroux's. Religion, Boutroux had insisted, was the realm of life, action, and ideals, while science was concerned only with fixed, given, fully-realized facts. But this distinction, Durkheim insisted, refers only to the religion of prophets, namely, that 'dynamic' religion that is still being made. Such 'dynamic' religion, Durkheim continued, always passes to a more 'static' condition, where these ideals become crystallized in dogmas and rites. 'It is then a reality, a system of acquired and given facts, comparable at every point to those studied by the sciences, and not just an ideal in the process of becoming. So why, under this form' Durkheim asked 'would religion not be the object of science?' Fortified by an assumed acceptance of this first argument, Durkheim returned to 'dynamic' religion: 'If religion, once constituted and organized, is the object of science,' he asked, 'why would the evolution from which it results escape scientific explanation? If the static condition is scientifically intelligible, how would the dynamic condition, of which the former is only the consequence and prolongation, be refractory to this same intelligibility?' (1909a(1):56–7).

The second element concerned Durkheim's fundamental disagreement with Boutroux over the nature of science. To refuse to religion the object pursued by science, Durkheim insisted, is 'to admit that science does not explain, that it is limited to summarizing experience, to ascertaining the order of facts once the facts have been given.' This, Durkheim observed, is the empirical conception of science, which has value only if one is an empiricist. If, by contrast, one acknowledges that 'science has explanatory value' the 'immanent intelligibility in the facts which it explains should be found again, in the same manner, in the development of which these facts are the end result' (ibid.:57). In short, while Durkheim could occasionally utter searing criticisms of Descartes, and frequent encomiums for the results of German empiricism, he was, in the last analysis, a rationalist who believed that the facts contain their own 'immanent intelligibility'.

The third element concerned Boutroux's fear that the submission of religion to reason is equivalent to the 'negation of religion in the name of reason'. But a science, Durkheim insisted, advancing an argument he would repeat in the conclusion of *Les Formes élémentaires*, 'cannot make the reality to which it is applied disappear . . . Why would religion be an exception? Religion is a fact. Over the centuries, it has undergone the test of history. One can thus be assured in advance that it is not a pure fantasmagoria, but corresponds to something real' (ibid.). Again as in *Les Formes élémentaires*, Durkheim added the crucial stipulation that, while this reality clearly exists, the conception of it held by believers is represented in a 'vulgar way', as 'something irrational and mysterious that eludes science'. The determination of the true nature of the reality that religion expresses, therefore, is a problem – indeed, the only problem – that the science of religion can solve. The character with which sacred objects are marked, which makes them truly 'religious' beliefs, is thus 'the result of a physical process which seems perfectly natural, and from which science, consequently, should be made. And, far from having as its object the reduction of the religious fact to a *flatus vocis*, this science of religion should express it while preserving all its specificity. Science must explain the distinct characteristics of religion,' Durkheim argued, 'not deny them' (ibid.).

What is not clear from *Les Formes élémentaires*, however, is the extent to which Durkheim felt that this third argument would secure the support of religious believers – at least those who, like the Catholic Modernists, were open to science and of dubious orthodoxy. Aside from those committed to a 'determined confessional formula' Durkheim observed 'I do not see why a believer would refuse to see the problem in these terms' (ibid.:58). And here Durkheim introduced the second argument concerning science and religion that would appear in *Les Formes élémentaires*. Historically, Durkheim observed, religion has performed two, very different functions. One function has been 'vital, of a practical order – i.e., religion has helped people to live, to adapt themselves to their conditions of existence'. Another, quite different function has been 'speculative thought, a system of *représentations* uniquely destined to express the world, a science before science, and a science concurrent with science as the latter became established' (ibid.). The second function declines with the advance of science, but the first function – the vital, practical role – remains whole. 'All that science can and should do,' Durkheim insisted, 'is to explain [this function], to illuminate in what it consists and to what it responds. Here, science will be able to substitute itself for religion in no way whatsoever'. In particular, Durkheim suggested that Boutroux should accept this conclusion, for he 'seems to admit that religion is essentially a matter of order, action, and life' (ibid.). But instead, Durkheim complained, Boutroux had placed religion outside of science.

Boutroux's initial response concerned the second element – i.e., Durkheim's philosophy of science. '[T]here is one way of understanding science,' Boutroux acknowledged, 'that does not prejudice the nature of the reality to which it is applied'. This is the way that Durkheim called 'empirical', that Boutroux preferred to call 'experimental or modern', and that I, for want of a better term, shall call *empiricism*: 'Science ascertains what is, and tries its best to organize and systematize it, without knowing in advance the extent to which reality will go along with this systematization' (Boutroux 1909b:60). In fact, Boutroux was acutely aware that the scientific rationalism of the seventeenth and eighteenth centuries had largely been replaced, in the nineteenth century, by more empiricist, experimental methods; and in his more anti-Cartesian, Germanic moods, Durkheim – who learned history of philosophy from Boutroux – knew it as well. But at this *séance* on science and religion Boutroux observed 'it is not this science of which Durkheim speaks. Science, for him, explains things rationally', namely, 'derives the facts, following a logical necessity, from a postulated principle'.

What were the consequences of Durkheim's rationalism, Boutroux asked, for his sociology of religion? First, for Durkheim to say that 'everything is a matter for science, is to impose on being, a priori, the form of identity'. This means that the scholar must 'abstract from the idea that religion has of itself, to consider religious phenomena only from an exclusively objective point of view' (ibid.:61). Such a thesis, Boutroux observed, would surprise the religious man; and to make this clear to Durkheim, Boutroux brilliantly reversed the case. 'What would [Durkheim] say if, in order to show him the degree to which we accept the reality of science, we told him that we will abstract from the meaning that he attaches to his demonstrations, in order to consider them only as the necessary products of his cerebral or psychic activities?' The religious man, Boutroux insisted, 'finds himself no less mystified when [Durkheim] attempts to reassure him while revealing, in his dogmas and his feelings, the necessary results of social conditions, or of other given circumstances' (ibid.).

Durkheim's response to this, of course, was that he had 'justified' the believer's activity by showing that it corresponds to some concrete reality. But Boutroux argued that, of the 'activity' of the believer, Durkheim had preserved only the name, for in the eye of the conscience, he had elim-inated everything that characterizes it as *activity*. What, Boutroux thus asked, does it mean *to act*? 'When I ask if I am truly acting, or if I am only a thing', Boutroux explained, 'I ask what value I have the right to attribute to the idea that, in my mind, I make of my personal determinations. It is my subjective interpretation of my acts, and this subjective interpretation alone, which is at stake here.' In its proper sense, therefore, the word 'action' belongs to the vocabulary of subjective consciousness. For those who, like Durkheim, submit everything to the logical conditions of purely objective science, there is no longer any place for action or for religion 'in that which characterizes them from their own point of view, which is to say, in that which characterizes them' (ibid.). As Durkheim uses the terms 'action' and 'religion', therefore, they are simply metaphors presumably for those social 'realities' that they 'express'.

Not surprisingly, therefore, Boutroux agreed with an earlier objection of Le Roy, that it 'is not at all clear that science can never make the object of its research disappear'. Indeed, as Comte recognized, there is a sense in which science 'dissolves and makes disappear' everything that it touches: 'Everywhere that man puts will, intention, or strength', Boutroux observed, 'science dissipates these phantoms, replacing them with facts and laws' (ibid.:62). If we believe Durkheim, religious facts are social facts; but facts that are simply social are deprived of everything that makes the specificity of religious facts. 'It is inconceivable,' Boutroux concluded, 'that everything specific to a religion would not disappear sooner or later, assuming that the religion is truly explicable, in its entirety, following the principles of a dogmatically rationalist, determinist, and objective science' (ibid.).

Conclusion

What can we learn from this brief account of Durkheim's relationship with Boutroux? First, it is arguable that some of the most familiar and characteristic aspects of Durkheim's treatment of the relationship between religion and science were formed in response to Boutroux's *La science et la religion dans la philosophie contemporaine*. As we have seen, Durkheim's insistence that 'all passes in the world of the ideal' was a response to Boutroux's argument that society presupposes religion rather than the reverse, and also that this insistence marks a significant step in the development of Durkheim's sociology of religion. Similarly, Durkheim's acceptance of the limitations implicit within science, and of a type of reason which takes science into account but is not itself 'scientific', owes much to Boutroux.

More generally, the conflict between Durkheim and Boutroux over science and religion, culminating at the November *séance*, invites us to think seriously about the criteria we use to evaluate past ideas. Durkheim provided a scientific explanation of religious belief as the consequence of a natural, externally observable, social process. Because religious belief thus expresses and corresponds to something real, Durkheim could not understand why believers would disagree. No science, Durkheim insisted, makes the phenomena it explains disappear; and it was in this sense, of course, that he argued that the vital, practical function of religion is eternal. At hearing this argument, Boutroux, Le Roy, and Lachelier were almost incredulous; and their chief objection was stated most clearly by Le Roy four years later, when *Les Formes élémentaires* itself became the subject of a *séance* of the Société (see Le Roy 1913:45–7). Explaining religion, Le Roy paraphrased Boutroux, is not the same as explaining the effects of gravitation or physio-chemical processes. For one of the constitutive elements of religious belief – indeed, the element that renders such a belief 'religious' by contrast with our other beliefs – is the conviction that it *cannot* be explained as the consequence of natural causes. Whatever takes place in other sciences, therefore, the sociological explanation of religious belief rather clearly *does* seem to destroy the phenomenon it attempts to explain.

If the criterion we use to evaluate past ideas is their truth or falsity, most of us will have little difficulty deciding on Durkheim's behalf; and Boutroux himself would have argued that the practice of the science of religions entails just such a decision. But the practice of intellectual history is less concerned with the *truth* of past beliefs than with their *rationality*. What, then, does it mean to hold *rational* beliefs? Very briefly, it means only that the beliefs in question should be suitable beliefs for people to hold under the circumstances in which they find themselves. Beliefs that are 'rational' would thus be those beliefs that people have achieved through some socially accredited process of reasoning. This process, in turn, would be one that, according to the prevailing norms of epistemic rationality, might be said to give people good reasons for assuming – by contrast with merely desiring or hoping – that the beliefs in question are true (see Putnam 1981:150–200; Skinner 1988:239–40).

This illuminates what was really at stake in the dispute between Durkheim and Boutroux. For it seems obvious that the beliefs of both were rationally held, their disagreement coming rather from the fact that, in their respective vocabularies, words like 'reason', 'religion', 'science', and so on, were used in different ways and thus meant different things. Disagreement over *beliefs* presumes that adversaries understand one another and agree on the application of crucial concepts like 'reason', 'religion', and 'science'. By contrast, Durkheim and Boutroux used these concepts in *different ways*, so that one 'understood' Christianity only in a sense that the other did not, and vice versa. So what at first appeared to be a disagreement over beliefs turns out, in the end, to be a misunderstanding over *criteria of intelligibility* – quite literally, over what it means 'to believe'.[5]

Notes

1   On the distinction between rational and historical reconstructions of past ideas, see Rorty 1984.
2   *Revue universaitaire* 1893, I:440–43, cited in Lukes 1973:297–8.
3   See also Boutroux's Gifford Lectures (1903 and 1905), published posthumously as *La Nature et l'esprit* in 1926.
4   Here again, the similiarity to the views of his student, Bergson, is evident.
5   This point, and my entire conclusion, owes a debt to MacIntyre 1970.

4

THE CONCEPT OF BELIEF IN *THE ELEMENTARY FORMS*

Sue Stedman Jones

'A religion is a unified system of beliefs and practices relative to sacred things' (65/47). This final definition of religion by Durkheim postulates a relation between belief and action or ritual that has been debated ever since. Which is primary? Of three possibilities, that ritual precedes belief, that they have equal parity, and that belief has primacy over ritual, Pickering argues that, although Durkheim wanted to maintain the second position, he finally decided on the third. That is, 'he secretly awards first prize to belief' (1984:379). Of course, Durkheim stressed the active aspect of religion (under-lined by Parsons) and its expressive function, which is seen in moments of 'effervescence'. Nevertheless in his 1886 review of Spencer he argued, 'In short religion starts with faith, that is to say, with any belief accepted or experienced without argument' (quoted in Pickering 1984:369). Davy argues that the reality of totemism for the Arunta is located in their beliefs. Thus 'all turns on belief'. For Pickering this is an indication, in the most devel-oped stage of his thought, of the 'primacy of *représentations* over action and ritual' (ibid.:372). Indeed it could be added that, *au fond*, what else is ritual reinforcing if not the beliefs? 'The true justification of religious practices does not lie in the apparent ends which they pursue, but rather in the invis-ible action which they exercise over *consciences* and in the way they affect the level of our mental state' (514/360).[1] The stress on belief, more than ritual, allows his comparison of individualism to religion. This system of beliefs does not involve 'rites properly speaking' (1898c/1970a:270). The cult of man 'has its first dogma in "the autonomy of reason" and first rite in free thought' (ibid.:268).

Religion for Durkheim is an institution, indeed the primary social insti-tution. In this he opposes classical philosophical and theological viewpoints. He stresses its communal, expressive function, particularly in the reinforce-ment of group identity and in the direction of action. Revolutionary moments and modern individualism share in the expressive power of religion: they are beliefs which focus on symbols and ideals, which generate passion and action. A necessary part of the argument for the social significance of reli-gious beliefs is a logical argument about belief and its objects. The concern of this article is precisely here.

There is a difference between beliefs and belief. The corpus of beliefs is what is believed in socially and historically: this could be Protestantism, Buddhism, individualism. Underlying this is an argument about belief and its objects. That there is a belief and a reality relative to belief is a necessary part of social beliefs. The believing function is a central feature of human *conscience*: indeed it plays a role in the constitution of the reality believed in. The unravelling of the psychic mechanisms that are essential to believing is part of sociological explanation for Durkheim. 'Social action follows ways that are too circuitous and obscure, and employs psychic mechanisms that are too complex to allow the ordinary observer to see whence it comes' (299/209). The hook by which social and historical beliefs are caught is the believing function of consciousness – that is belief.

Beliefs thus require belief – the constituting, symbolizing functions of *conscience*. That is, the ideals, the symbols that are believed in socially, have no logical existence outside of the *consciences* which believe them, even though expressed in action and ritual. To recognize Durkheim's argument for the constituting power of *conscience* in belief is not only to deny that he is a behaviourist, but is also to deny that he is either a philosophical realist or a positivist in his theory of religion, for both in different ways deny the constitutive functions of *conscience* in the formation of reality.

Further, this is central to the sociological argument that religion stems from the collectivity. The collectivity's beliefs are symbolized in sacred things or ideals and are reinforced in action or ritual. This boomerangs back on the collectivity and reinforces it, emotionally, expressively and in terms of solidarity. There is a circularity of expressive communication here; but the subject and object of this is the community itself. That there is a reality relative to belief is a logical condition of this sociological argument. Philosophical history is present, which elucidates this necessary feature of religion and is to be found in Kant and Renouvier. I will compare and contrast Durkheim's account with two other theories of belief, those of Bertrand Russell and William James.

The Elementary Forms and the concept of belief

The importance of belief is not immediately obvious in the argument of *The Elementary Forms*. 'Religious phenomena are naturally arranged into two fundamental categories: beliefs and rites' (50/36). Durkheim argues, however, that rites cannot be defined until belief has been defined: all religious beliefs presuppose the classification of things into the sacred and the profane. And it is these sacred things which then become a centre of organization around which revolve beliefs and rites.[2] In Book I, beliefs are defined in relation to sacred things: these constitute a centre of organization around which beliefs and rites gravitate. However, it is clear that these sacred things and rites are themselves the expression of beliefs: beliefs are made manifest in the rituals and cults. 'Also, this community of beliefs is sometimes shown in the cult' (221/155). The point of ritual is to reinforce beliefs. 'The rite does not limit itself to expressing this kinship [of clansmen and totem]; it makes or remakes it. For the kinship exists only in so far as it is believed in, and the effect of all these collective demonstrations is to support the beliefs on which it rests' (511/358). Totems as sacred things are symbolic expressions of totemic beliefs. In the logical relation between totem and the beliefs which they inspire, it is fundamentally the totems that rely on the beliefs. 'Among the beliefs upon which totemic religion rests, the most important are naturally those concerning the totem' (142/102). Indeed, it becomes clear that beliefs are the foundation of religion. 'Mythological constructions ... cover over a system of beliefs, at once simpler and more obscure ... which form the solid foundations upon which religious systems have been built' (289/202).

Durkheim has moved from defining belief by sacred things to defining sacred objects by the beliefs that underpin both sacred things and rites and cults. 'Of course the cult depends on the beliefs, but it also reacts on them' (424/296). Totems as physical objects, indeed any religious artefacts thus symbolize the belief; it is a material *représentation* of that which is believed.

It is belief that is a constituting feature of religion, for by definition sacred things represent that which is believed in. 'The sacred character which makes them objects of a cult is not given by their natural constitution; it is added to them by belief' (492/345). Gods are constituted by belief. 'The idea of the supreme god even depends so strictly on the ensemble of totemic beliefs that it still bears their mark' (418/291). Gods depend on the system of collective belief. 'Sacred beings exist only because they are represented as such in minds. When we cease to believe in them it is as though they did not exist' (492/345). Similarly for Durkheim, the notion of the soul is a result of belief. 'The notion of the soul is a particular application of beliefs relative to sacred beings' (375/262). Indeed more strongly, 'Our moral *conscience* is like a kernel around which is formed the idea of a soul' (401/280). So strongly connected are the concepts of religion and belief that Durkheim says to explain the one is to explain the other.

Objects of religious belief are constituted by those beliefs. In this sense, belief plays a pivotal, foundational role in establishing the nature of those beliefs and, further, in the constitution of the reality that is believed in. To explain totemism is 'to seek for how men have been led to construct that idea and out of what materials they have constructed it' (293/205). The concept of force, also important to the concept of the sacred, exemplifies this logic of argument. 'The force isolating the sacred being ... is not really in that being; it lives in the *conscience* of the believers' (522/365).

Religion and its panoply of gods, rituals and cults do not exist without belief. This logical relation between belief and its objects is the backbone of Durkheim's sociological explanation of religion. It has a philosophical ancestry and unexpected philosophical affiliations which it is important to unravel.

Kant and the concept of belief

The above arguments are in part a philosophical descendant of Kant's arguments about theism. Kant rejected the claims of theology, that God or the soul is an object of knowledge and argued that theoretical reason is essentially limited when it comes to determining transcendent existence. Kant rejected the Cartesian ontological argument for God's existence: we do not know about God because of what has been implanted in our mind through the divinity. He argued that we cannot infer God's existence from the idea we have of the infinite perfection of God: existence is not a predicate. The conclusion of his argument is that there is no theoretical or existential knowledge of God. He claimed that God is a morally necessary postulate of practical reason: God is the object of rational faith or belief.

In this Kant overcame the traditional division of faith versus reason by encompassing the concept of faith within philosophy, when it had been traditionally the concern of theology. The concept of faith for him was so important in morality and religion that he said in the preface to the *Critique of Pure Reason*, 'I have found it necessary to deny knowledge in order to make way for faith' (1963:29 Bxxx). He argued that faith is an aspect of practical reason. Belief is called 'faith of pure practical reason', 'practical belief' or even 'moral belief'. Faith and knowledge are contrasted. For Kant representations are the sphere of knowledge; belief and knowledge are split. He then faces the problem of how beliefs relate to the real, if by real we mean that which exists in space and time and is the object of knowledge, as determined by the categories.

L. W. Beck expressed Kant's position thus. Knowledge is assent on grounds that are objectively and subjectively sufficient, but faith is assent on grounds that are subjectively sufficient in spite of being objectively insufficient (Beck 1966:253). Faith in the objects of practical reason (faith-belief) is needed to orientate ourselves in 'the empty space of thought beyond experience which is 'the native home of illusion' (Kant 1963: A238, B295). God, freedom and immortality are the necessary objects of rational belief. They function also to aid action and to offer hope for morality.

The connection of God with practical reason – indeed the latter as foundation of the former – overturns the traditional theological relation between God and man. The concept of God as a necessary object of moral belief, implies a constitutive role for practical reason. This reverses the traditional dependence of man on God so characteristic of pre-Kantian theological thinking. More strongly, God as divine being is practically dependent on practical reason. This is central to the establishment of the politics of autonomy for Kant. (It is important to note that this does not entail for him the illusory or even the subjective nature of God.) Durkheim underlined 'that state of dependence in which the gods stand in relation to the thought of man' (493–4/345). He could rely on Kant's argument as a stage in his argument for the social origin of religion: gods are the objects of collective beliefs, the *croyances collectives*. It is not by the elucidation of God that we can understand mankind, it is only through the collective nature of mankind that we can understand God.

Durkheim's concepts of belief and reality

For Durkheim the gods and sacred beings are not only the objects of belief, they are constituted by those beliefs. As such they underlie the collective morality and action so essential to the existence of society. This argument is remarkably Kantian. Further, as for Kant, there is for Durkheim a non-visible world, which is not available to the senses. 'It is religious beliefs that have substituted for the world, as it is perceived by the senses, another different one' (338/236). One would expect that since Kant personally was a deist and Durkheim an atheist, that Kant would find God as object of belief objectively sufficient, and Durkheim would find God only subjectively sufficient. On the contrary, for Durkheim the idea of God is objectively sufficient in the sense that it is the object of collective belief and expresses a reality – society. The failure of animism is that it makes religious beliefs 'hallucinatory *représentations* without any objective foundation' (97/68). Religious beliefs have 'a foundation in the real' (ibid.). As objects of belief, God or gods and sacred beings are 'collective states that have been objectified (*objectivés*)' (590/412).

For Kant, religious beliefs do not refer to an objective reality, in the sense of that to which the categories apply. Durkheim, in holding that religious beliefs have an objective reference, is paradoxically making a claim similar to that made by Bertrand Russell in *The Analysis of Mind* (1921). There is no question of influence, nor indeed of philosophical similarity, for Russell was a logical empiricist and Durkheim rejected empiricism, both in *The Rules* and in *The Elementary Forms*. Durkheim, however, shares with Russell a view of the centrality of belief to all mental acts. For Russell 'Believing seems the most mental thing we do, the thing most remote from what is done by mere matter. The whole of intellectual life consists of belief' (Russell 1989:231). Durkheim also regards beliefs as part of our mental operation, even when 'the symbols employed are the most disconcerting for reason' (612/428).

The field of religion is the field of belief: belief is a *représentation* and these are mental and irreducible to matter for Durkheim. Further, for Russell as for Durkheim, there is an objective reference of belief: a belief is true in so far as it refers to a state of affairs. Of course for Russell this applies to empirical belief – a religious belief is quite different and lacks the possibility of empirical confirmation. For Durkheim also, there is no empirical co-efficient for religious belief for, as we have seen, religion establishes a world distinct from the senses. It is, however, not false for it points to a collective reality. It is a human institution that guarantees the truth of a belief. Beliefs are objectified into symbols or gods: thus society worships itself. Beliefs are central to the affirming and re-affirming of collective identity. Ritual action which expresses them supports collective action and morality, which are the cement of society.

There is, however, a reality affirmed for the believers. Durkheim, like William James, argues that religious beliefs are not illusory. 'Our entire study rests upon this postulate that the unanimous sentiment of the believers of all times cannot be purely illusory' (596/417). For James the constancy and the universality of religious beliefs point to some truth in them. For Durkheim they are not illusory, but the reality they have does not accord with the testimony of the believers. Because so many people believe in gods, it does not mean that therefore gods must exist: the universality of belief does not support deism. In this Durkheim is quite unlike Kant or James. For him, the central element of the reality of religious belief is its collective nature.

Can Durkheim really maintain this argument? How can it be that religious beliefs have no transcendent object nor empirical referent, but nevertheless have an objective reference in society, and thus that their truth lies in the human institution they underpin? That is, can Durkheim both maintain that religious beliefs are empirically 'empty', but are affectively and cognitively 'full' in terms of the collectivity? I suggest that his argument revolves around a particular view of belief and reality which is distinct from that of either Kant or Russell.

What does Durkheim mean by belief?

To begin to evaluate these claims we must examine what belief actually is for Durkheim. Durkheim claims that belief is the result of a 'psychic process ... This impulse towards believing, is just what constitutes faith; and it is faith which establishes the authority of the rites, for the believer, whoever he may be, Christian or Australian. The only superiority of the former is that he better realises the psychic process from which his faith results; he knows "it is faith which saves"' (515/360). There is a 'psychic mechanism' involved in both expiatory and piacular rites (584/408). 'Beliefs ... are states of opinion, they consist in *représentations*' (50/36). The sacred beings who are the object of belief are developed in the *consciences* of the believers. 'It is in human *consciences* that (religious life) is elaborated' (462/323). Further 'sacred beings ... can only live in human *consciences*' (495/347). Beliefs are thus the result of a psychic process, they are *représentations* and are located in *consciences*. Further, they are closely associated with symbolization and idealization, which are necessary to flesh out the creatures of the religious imagination as it peoples the region beyond sense with sacred beings. Only thus, if belief can represent, symbolize and idealize, can it be involved in the constitution of an ideal world that is superimposed on the real. 'What defines the sacred is that it is superimposed on the real; now the ideal conforms to the same definition: so we cannot explain the one without explaining the other' (602–3/422). For the Arunta Dreamtime beings are 'ideal beings' (602/421). Ideals, symbols and indeed *représentations* are part of the psychic activity which is central to social life. Only by understanding these can we make sense of Durkheim's argument for their pivotal historical role in the constitution of science and philosophy, and their association with other features of human reality.

Durkheim's concept of belief is similar to that of William James.[3] In his famous article *The Will to Believe*, written in 1896, James argues for the centrality of belief to action. Anything that is addressed to our belief is a hypothesis and this in turn can be live or dead, and whether it is live or dead can be measured in the willingness to act. 'The maximum of liveness in an hypothesis means willingness to act irrevocably. Practically that means belief: but there is some believing tendency wherever there is willingness to act at all' (James 1907:3). Further, for James belief always involves our passional and volitional nature; that is, our non-intellectual nature influences our beliefs. For Durkheim too there are feeling and, to some extent, volitional effects and influences on beliefs. He argues that religions are too complex to have originated from 'a well-reflected act of will' (245/172). There is 'an impulse (*élan*) to believe' involved in religion, such that it is 'faith which establishes the authority of the rites for the believer' (515/360). The conception of social authority in religion is tied to that of belief.

For Durkheim, as for James, belief leads to action, and these are expressed in rites: the connection with action is one of the most important aspects of religion for the believers. 'The real function of religion is not to make us think . . . but to make us act, to help us live' (595/416). Further it transforms feeling. 'A faith is above all warmth, life, enthusiasm, exaltation of all mental activity, a transport of the individual above himself' (607/425). This is particulary noticeable in periods of effervescence. 'A state of effervescence . . . implies the mobilisation of all our active forces' (582/407).

We must now consider how it is that Durkheim can make these claims for belief: how is it that belief is a *représentation*? 'Sacred beings exist only because they are represented as such in minds' (492/345). It is clear that these sacred objects must be representable to be believed in. 'Beliefs express [religious life] in terms of *représentations*' (592/414). Further, how is it that belief is connected with symbol, ideal and feeling? All of these are central to Durkheim's account of the nature and function of religious belief in society. These claims have a philosophical origin and history.

Renouvier, the critique of Kant and the development of the concept of belief

To understand these positions, I suggest we must look at the seminal influence of Renouvier on Durkheim, for in the above characterization of the nature of belief he is not like Kant. First, for Kant beliefs are quite separate from representations. Representations are the object of the *Critique of Pure Reason* and are associated with science and knowledge, not belief. There is an antinomial split between reason as expressed in the representations of science and theoretical understanding, and reason as expressed in morality, practical reason and the concerns of the *Critique of Practical Reason*. Further, just as there is for Kant a sharp separation of practical reason and feeling, there is no account of the idealization and symbolization functions of *conscience*. In particular we see how Renouvier approaches and criticizes Kant, for Kant is clearly a seminal influence in this whole conception of belief. In Durkheim's theory of belief and its foundation in *conscience*, its association with other functions of *conscience* and its constituting role in the affirming of a reality, we see something of the influence both of Kant and Renouvier.

For Renouvier, Kant had established a new method for theology. 'The former theological procedure is overturned. We start from ourselves, both from our passions and our moral law, and we put into the heart of the universe what must correspond to them, so that there is harmony' (Renouvier

1859:631). In all questions of divinity we must start with ourselves. With Kant he agrees that the objects of theology have their foundation in practical reason: in his terms, God is thus an affirmation of *conscience*. As such He responds to the functions of end (*fins*) and feeling (*passions*), and above all, belief (*croyance*). Practical reason in effect is what the laws of *conscience* demand (ibid.). He criticized Kant for the radical separation of reason and feeling, and for the concept of pure will. For him reason, will and feeling are the central functions of *conscience*, and are needed in the determination of all reality, but above all in that of religious reality. God is thus a determination of the three functions of *conscience*. He is discriminated as an object to be believed in, is willed as an object of belief and is wanted as an object of feeling. This argument opposes the conception of God as an absolute: pure reason as defined by Kant is an absolutist conception which must be rejected. 'Theism and the absolute reappear transformed in the ideal of moral perfection' (ibid.:626).

Certainly Renouvier praised Kant for his theory of belief. Indeed he insisted that belief is a better concept than faith, with its association with theology. He agreed with Kant's critique of Hume, for whom belief is a lively idea. He proposed to extend the concept of belief beyond its location in religion to a wider sphere of human beliefs: faith should be extended to the *croyances collectives* of history.

> Why should the faith of practical reason stop with those still very general objects of what they call natural religion? Why not extend it to the historical and theological mysteries, to familiar affirmations of such and such a sect or people, in other words to the super- stitions of which such a great number of human beings claim to experience the need.
>
> (ibid.:408)

However, Renouvier criticized Kant for leaving belief in a void, and without foundation. Kant's critical philosophy endorses a separation of theoretical and practical reason. Renouvier rejected Kant's claim in the second preface to *Critique of Pure Reason*, that he had to abolish science to make room for faith. Reason does not have to become antinomial. It is not necessary to put science on one side – in the *Critique of Pure Reason* – and faith on the other – in the *Critique of Practical Reason*. It implies that the human agent is divided in terms of knowledge and belief, which is disastrous both for knowledge and action. He aimed at unifying the separated reasons of Kant's account, to give a more coherent account of both knowledge and action. This line of argument is reflected in Durkheim's claim that there is no antinomy between science and morality, for both as aspects of human activity come from the same source (635/445).

As the human being cannot be so divided, philosophy must testify to the human reality of the integrated functions of consciousness, which co-operate in both knowledge and action. To make belief safe from theoretical reason and its determinism is to make belief irrational. This does not establish a good foundation for action and morality, for it separates knowledge and will. He argued that feeling is the essential intermediary between them. 'Between intelligence and the will, *passion* is a kind of centre for human phenomena ... it profoundly marks each full moment of our existence. Without passion, one could say that the elements of human nature would be disunited ... the understanding frozen, the will unfocused and machine-like' (Renouvier 1859:161).

Renouvier claimed that to introduce knowledge into belief is to purify belief of dogmatism, whilst to introduce belief into knowledge is to unify it into action. Kant had left belief in an epistemological void: what is required is a foundation for belief. 'Nowhere as far as I know, did he establish the nature and determine the elements of *conscience* of that faith, independent of the objects to which it applies' (ibid.:408). This entails the necessity of a concept which indicates the role of belief in knowledge, that is, which shows how it is integrated with other cognitive activities of consciousness. Renouvier argued that belief enters into all knowledge: in his terms belief (*croyance*) is not separate from *représentation*. The result is the theory of *conscience*, which shows how human consciousness operates in experience and in which belief plays a pivotal role.

I have just mentioned how the concept of God responds to the concept of end. Further, central to *conscience* are the affective, voluntary, symbolization and idealization functions. All of these contribute to the establishment of religious reality. Of course religion offers a world that transcends the senses, and thus is not limited to sensory experience. Durkheim said 'the gods ... are conceived not perceived' (617–18/432). In terms of Renouvier's theory of mind, religious experience can be made significant in a way that is impossible on the pure Kantian account. Renouvier offers us a theory of mind in which we can make sense of how belief has objects that are projected – it constitutes objects which are symbols and ideals which are made real by being believed in. Further, a central function is will – it is our will that makes us believe. Thus, integrated functions of *conscience* are essential to the activity of belief and the constitution of its objects, but will and feeling are primary. This gives the connection with action that is demonstrated in Durkheim's argument about action being the important consequence of religion. 'For them [mythic beings] to have the useful action on the soul which is their raison d'être, it is necessary that they are believed in. Now beliefs are only active when they are shared' (607/425). Renouvier showed how shared beliefs enter into society and history. Collective beliefs (*les croyances collectives*) are the coefficients of 'human determinations' (Renouvier 1864:2).

Most importantly, we have seen that it is the feeling quality of belief that makes it so important for Durkheim particularly in the periods of effervescence. Renouvier argued that it is only through the indissolubility of the functions of *conscience* that we can make sense of any world or indeed undertake any action: feeling is an essential function of *conscience*. Passions are 'the stimulants and the substance of life'. The great intellectual facts of history cannot be distinguished from the passions and morality (ibid.). With this theory of *conscience* and its central functions we can see why Durkheim says of religious life that 'it is in human *consciences* that it is elaborated' (462/323).

For Renouvier the concepts of feeling and end of action in turn lead to the concept of the ideal. 'The ideal . . . whose nature is not to be actually given, nor even actually to be thought, but is present to the mind by its elements' (Renouvier 1908:190). It relates to our intellectual, feeling and sensible functions. But it arises out of the gap between what is and what ought to be. It is an unrealized object which possesses qualities relating to beauty. 'The ought to be', which is a characteristic of the ideal, establishes an affinity between aesthetics and morality.

We have seen that Durkheim holds that beliefs are *représentations*. It is an important claim, for it is part and parcel of the claim that sociology can scientifically explain beliefs. If they are not *représentations* then they cannot be known or be the object of a science. How is this possible? They are not derived from the real, in terms of empirical existence; they transcend sense-data and are superimposed on the real. I suggest we can only understand this through Renouvier's claim that anything that is present to the mind is a *représentation*: the mind is essentially *conscience* for Renouvier. The mind in considering itself is aware that it believes: it thus holds belief in its own awareness. In this sense it can be known.

Renouvier thus completes the Kantian transformation of theism and paves the way for a sociological explanation of religion by showing that human *conscience* is central to the elaboration of the concept of a supreme being. He shows how all the central functions of *conscience* co-operate in this. He thus provided a conceptual foundation for belief in a way that Kant did not.

Collective beliefs and *représentations*

Thus far I have examined the development of the concept of belief and its association with other mental factors and the role this plays in a theory of religion. However, belief plays a fundamental role in one of Durkheim's boldest claims in *The Elementary Forms* – that it is from *les croyances collectives*, collective beliefs, that stem the first system of *représentations*. Because of this, Durkheim can claim that science and philosophy arise out of religion. This position implies that for Durkheim belief has primacy over cognition. Belief is thus given, not just a role alongside knowledge, but a foundational role *vis-à-vis* knowledge. Here we can clearly see the influence of Renouvier.

For Renouvier all forms of knowledge are actually forms of belief, in the sense that everything that is known is not apodictically known but is *held* to be true. This explains the diversity of systems of knowledge in history and society. Durkheim reflects this in his statement 'The concept, which is primitively held to be true because it is collective, tends not to become collective except on condition of being *held* to be true' (624/437). Renouvier argues that in all knowledge, even the most apparently necessary and universal, we are always *holding* it to be true. This holding something to be true is belief. He argues that in all cases where I claim to know or to see, what I should really say is that I believe that I know or that I believe that I see.

Renouvier argued that it is from belief that all knowledge stems: the principle of belief (*croyance*) is extended to all reality. How is belief connected with reality? Without intending to undermine science or the principle of knowledge, Renouvier argued that if we admit the role of belief in knowledge, then we have to recognize its crucial role in the central problem of certainty. It is in relation to this that we encounter the fundamental role of belief in relation to knowledge. We cannot talk of reality without approaching the problem of certainty. That is, we confront the question, how can we be sure of our knowledge? Neither Kant nor Descartes had recognized that pure reason alone cannot answer the problem of certainty. Against classic rationalism, Renouvier argues that belief, in collaboration with reason and feeling, answers the problem of certainty. As we have seen above, he argued that different functions of *conscience* co-operate to produce this state of mind called belief where we hold something to be true, that is, 'indubitable' for us. Given this logic it is understandable that Durkheim could argue that science and philosophy stem from collective beliefs, that is, that collective beliefs are more fundamental than collective *représentations*.

Durkheim, the logic of belief and the conception of reality

I have questioned whether Durkheim can maintain his argument that religious beliefs, although lacking empirical corroboration, still have an objective reference. I suggest that it relies on two positions. First, the conception of reality as affirmation. And second, the conception of the self-referentiality of belief. The first is Renouvierist whilst the second is more clearly Kantian.

First, the concept of reality as affirmation is found particularly in the account of the cultic action. In cultic or ritual action Durkheim says the group affirms itself, and strengthens itself through strong feeling. When the community comes together, he argues, 'The sharing of these feelings has, as always, the effect of intensifying them. In affirming themselves, these feelings are exalted and inflamed and reach a degree of violence' (582/407). What does affirmation mean in connection with social reality? I suggest it is implied by the cognitive acts of collective beliefs affirming a reality in collective *représentations*.

I have argued that for Durkheim the *croyances collectives* constitute a reality. Here it is implied that non-material objects of reference become real because they are believed in. Sacred things represent reality and thus symbolize beliefs. This is real for the *consciences* who have constructed a super-sensible world through the psychic processes of idealization and symbolization. Because this reality is believed in, it is affirmed by the believers. That is, if, following Renouvier, we accept that all questions of reality involve the problem of certainty, and that questions of certainty are solved by the practical, believing functions of *conscience*, then it follows that reality itself is dependent on the practical orientations of our consciousness. He thus means that at the deepest level, under all questions of evidence and necessity, underlying the most empirical sciences are cognitive acts of belief which affirm the reality in question. So Durkheim says in *Pragmatism and Sociology* that theoretical certainty is another form of practical certainty, and in this way 'we are in the Kantian tradition' (1955a:202). Now just as for Kant to deny that God is the object of theoretical knowledge is not to undermine, but to save deism, so for Renouvier, to deny that the real is the object of evidence and necessary theoretical determinations, does not undermine the concept of reality. Affirmation is the act of practical consciousness by which we relate to all reality.

This approach to reality is important for Durkheim: it indicates the human contribution to the concept of reality, and the practical constructive spirit in which it is made. Affirmation is central to his constructivism: it is central to the constitution of reality. It indicates the passage not just to the sociology of religion but to the sociology of knowledge. Renouvier thus establishes a connection between belief (*croyance*), affirmation and reality that Durkheim can use in his argument for the reality of religion relative to the *croyances collectives*. Here belief is central to the constitution of a reality, because we can see that belief leads to affirmations of the real which are central to the cognitive activities of *conscience*. Indeed any reality is founded on the practical necessity of affirmation.

Second, I have suggested that there is distinctive logic to this claim of Durkheim: these beliefs spring from community. Just as a concept as impersonal as *représentation* is common to all 'because it is the work of the community' (619/434), so beliefs in turn act back on the community from which they spring to reinforce action and the moral solidarity of society. 'It is this character of the ceremony which makes it instructive. It tends to act entirely on *consciences* and on them alone' (537/375). Beliefs which stem from the society are represented in sacred objects, are realized in rites and cults, and boomerang back with moral effect on the community from which they sprang. 'The rite thus serves, and can only serve to maintain the vitality of those beliefs ... to revive the most essential elements of the collective *conscience*' (536/375).

There is a self-referentiality of belief systems, which lies at the centre of the logic of social reality. Beliefs stem from *consciences*, are expressed in sacred objects, enacted in rites and cults, and flow back to and reinforce the social relations from which they came. (I suggest this is Kantian because the logic of the transcendental argument at the heart of Kant's first *Critique* is a form of self-referentiality.)

This logic allows Durkheim to argue for the collective origin of belief systems: this logic is thus at the heart of a sociological explanation of religion. It further allows him to argue for the functional necessity of religion as affirming the collectivity in a way no other human institution can quite match. Durkheim can maintain his argument that religious beliefs are true and have an objective reference because they refer to society, even though empirically they are false. The concept of affirmation and self-referentiality are essential to understanding the logic of this argument. I have argued that in believing, human beings affirm a reality. This is a symbolic *représentation*, in ideal and symbolic objects, of the beliefs themselves. The object of these are ideal beings, but their reference, that from which they spring and refer back to in reinforcing rituals, are the *consciences* which make up society. In so affirming themselves symbolically, they create a world of ideals and values; because this springs from society, it represents society.[4] So society can be compared to the gods; it also will die if they are no longer believed in.

> Were the idea of society to be extinguished in individual minds, were the beliefs, the traditions, the aspirations of the collectivity to cease to be felt, and shared by particular persons, society would die. One can then repeat for it what has been said above about divinity: it has reality only in the measure to which it has a place in human *consciences*, and it is we who make that place.
>
> (496/347)

Notes

1   *Conscience* (here and elsewhere untranslated) is a theoretically important term, central to Durkheim's rationalism, which cannot be adequately accommodated by the common-sense term 'consciousness'.
2   In this paper I concentrate on the logical aspects of Durkheim's thought in certain parts of *The Elementary Forms*. Further, I leave to one side the debate over the validity of his use of totemic material for a general definition of religion.
3   William James acknowledges a debt to Renouvier (1908:143). James' pragmatism was, however, distinct from Renouvier's rationalism.
4   My position here might help to elucidate an ambiguity in Durkheim's thought. When he argues that beliefs spring from the community, he is claiming that 'all that is religious is social', since religion reacts back on the community through its symbols and idealized beings. It also follows that 'all that is social is religious' (Pickering 1984:262–74). For an interesting discussion, see Ono (1996).

5

DURKHEIM, KANT, THE IMMORTAL SOUL AND GOD

W. Watts Miller

This essay explores some questions to do with the immortal soul and God. My interest in them has arisen through work on Durkheim's ethics, which meant relating it to Kant's, but also to the views of both on religion. Kant holds up to us the ideal, based on autonomy, of a kingdom of ends. Durkheim's project involves translation of this into a republic of persons. But Kant also announces in the second *Critique* – the *Critique of Practical Reason* – three necessary postulates of morality. They are freedom, the immortal soul and God. So it is not enough, to rework the kingdom of ends as a republic of persons, to rework Kantian as Durkheimian autonomy. Something must also be done about the immortal soul and God. How might a secular republic manage without them?

Religion via practical reason

Durkheim often says that religious beliefs are false as literal beliefs and yet are not mere illusions. They capture, symbolically, something that is true. But he never makes clear the basis of saying they are false as literal beliefs. Above all, what is the basis in the case of the immortal soul and God? Are they not inaccessible to scientific and, in Kantian terms, theoretical reason?

Far from rubbishing religious beliefs as all incoherence and contradiction, Durkheim criticizes secular rationalist philosophers who do. Yet in that he eschews their resort to pure logic, but wants to appeal to science, how is he entitled to deny – any more than others appealing to it are entitled to affirm – the existence of an immortal soul and God?

In an article on sociology and its scientific domain he argues that such things are beyond theoretical reason's remit and interest (1900c/1975b, 1:27). The message is the same in the lectures on moral education: 'Because God is beyond the world, he is above and beyond science; if, then, morality comes from and expresses God, it is placed beyond the grasp of our reason' (1925a:138).

But this deals just with religion in relation to theoretical reason. What about its relation to practical reason, as in Kant's second *Critique*? God is inaccessible via theoretical reason. Traditional arguments attempting such a route are mistaken, as are traditional views that religion is the foundation of morality. On the contrary, it is morality that is the foundation of religion, the pathway to it. It is through ethics and practical reason that we can infer, as beliefs we must postulate, the immortal soul and God.

Durkheim's line on autonomy in the moral education lectures suggests adherence to theoretical, and rejection of practical, reason. So does a brief allusion to Kantian practical reason in lectures of 1909 (see 1968c/1975b, 2:18–19). So does the discussion paper on moral facts:

> Kant postulates God, since without this hypothesis morality is unintelligible. We postulate a society specifically distinct from individuals, since otherwise morality has no object and duty no roots. Let us add that this postulate is easily verified by experience ... Between God and society lies the choice. I shall not examine here the reasons that may be advanced in favour of either solution, both of which are coherent. I merely add that from my point of view this choice leaves me quite indifferent, since I see in the divinity only society transfigured and thought about symbolically.
>
> (1906b/1924a:74–5)

What sort of society? And what else might God, taken metaphorically, be about?

The immortal soul and God, as Kantian postulates, concern the ethical importance of hope. If we drop them as literal beliefs, to look for something they symbolize, it is not enough just to go on about society. We must bring in hope. We must then look to see if there are secular substitutes for the immortal soul and God that, like them, offer hope.

Let us deal with the immortal soul first and tackle God later.

The immortal soul in Australia

The immortal soul gets short shrift in *Suicide*. Durkheim dismisses it as an 'illusion' (1897a:228). He is more expansive and more sympathetic in *The Elementary Forms*. Belief in the immortality of the soul is a way of 'rendering intelligible the continuity of the collective life' (385). This concludes the section on the immortal soul in the chapter of *The Elementary Forms* devoted to the soul itself (Book II, Chapter VIII). The essential change of attitude on the subject can be found in an earlier lecture course on religion and its origins (1907f/1975b, 2:65–122). These lectures are the first public sign of such a change. They are of general interest as one of the main preliminaries to *The Elementary Forms*. But their long section on the soul is the only main preliminary to the chapter on it in the book, and they contain one of the best statements of Durkheim's overall approach:

> The *raison d'être* of religious conceptions is above all to provide a system of notions and beliefs which allow the individual to represent

to himself the society of which he is part, and the obscure relations which unite him with it.

(1907f/1975b, 2:99)

We read this again, almost word for word, in *The Elementary Forms*:

> Religion is above all a system of notions through which individuals represent to themselves the society of which they are members, and the obscure but intimate relations which they maintain with it.

(323)

Indeed, let me begin with a comment on Durkheim's overall approach, to do with particular beliefs we might think bizarre as literal beliefs.

It is striking how ready he is, as a first move, to try to make sense of them as literal beliefs, in terms of a larger system of beliefs of which they are part. That is, it is striking how ready he is to try out an 'intellectualist' line, before also seeing them, in a further move, in terms of a hidden, underlying symbolism.

Evans-Pritchard, in the star case of the Nuer, dismissed Littlejohn's attempt at just such a literal, structuralist-cum-intellectualist line, and insisted – albeit without going in for secret symbolism – on a metaphorical interpretation of 'twins are birds' (Evans-Pritchard 1970: Littlejohn 1970). But Durkheim seems completely prepared to accept, as a literal belief, that one might be both man and pelican (1907f/1975b, 2:83). Later, it is how one might be both man and kangaroo (1968c/1975b, 2:20) – an example re-appearing in *The Elementary Forms* (355).

Another famous philosophical puzzle is the Yoruba 'soul in a box' case (Hollis 1967). There is a discussion, again in the 1907 lectures, of something more or less paralleling it. The discussion is a gem in miniature of Durkheim's whole approach. There is no need to invoke, like Frazer, *ad hoc* psychological explanations of the idea that one's soul is locatable in an external object. It makes intellectual sense, as a literal belief, in terms of a wider system of beliefs – although, in turn, the wider system itself also makes sense as a symbolic way of thinking about the nature of individuals and the social world (1907f/1975b, 2:110).

So it is not just that, as earlier remarked, Durkheim refrains from rubbishing beliefs, such as in the soul, as all incoherence and contradiction. He actively looks for an internal rationale, in their own terms and even as literal beliefs. But it is not to insist on a system of clear, fully worked out, tightly interlocking ideas. Instead, he emphasizes an essential vagueness, and a main concern is with how a network of beliefs can involve change, development, variation.

It is also part of his basic interpretive strategy – of looking for an internal rationale – that although this is at bottom the same in 'religious' as in 'scientific' thought, there are important differences that involve, as it were, logical style. Account must be taken, in trying to understand 'religious' ideas and find a coherence in them, of their logical style. This tends to represent resemblance or relatedness between things by fusing it into an identity, to represent difference or distinctness by polarizing it into an opposition, but also to come up, then, with unity in dualism – not a bad description, it could be said, of a clear tendency in Durkheim's own style of thought.

There is a perhaps surprising example in *The Elementary Forms* of his determination to look for a logic of beliefs. After discussing totems, souls, spirits and immortality, he comes to God. This is to come to the problem, in the Australian case, of an apparent contradiction of a belief in God with the network of the other beliefs. Durkheim nonetheless insists on looking for some sort of rationale connecting them. This insistence is the more remarkable since it throws away an opportunity to instantiate one of his own fundamental arguments, that there can be religion without God. Leading anthropologists of the time considered God – whether because inconsistent with autochthonous Australian beliefs, or for other reasons – a foreign import (for a discussion, see Hiatt 1996:100–19).

There is also a very different kind of example. After trying but failing to make sense of beliefs as literal beliefs, Durkheim is ready, before looking for a secret symbolism, to see them as metaphorical – that is, as *metaphorical*, rather than literal, *within the network of people's own beliefs themselves*, and not just in terms of a hidden social symbolism, obscure to the natives, but brought to light by the more knowing anthropologist. It is once they are understood as metaphorical rather than literal beliefs within the network, that they are then further interpreted in terms of a secret symbolism. The case is complex, involves Durkheim in a long discussion, and has to do with conception (353–67). It centres on the teaching that new-born children are animated by a soul coming from ancestors of a mystic time, and concerns conflicting accounts of how this might happen. Durkheim sees these as 'different metaphors', all expressing the same fundamental, literal belief (364).

It might be as well to emphasize that he distances himself from the claim that it is at the same time an ignorance or denial of sexual intercourse's role in conception (358 n.2; for a discussion of the controversy, see Hiatt 1996:120–41).

Another comment concerns the difference between 'myths' and 'beliefs'. Durkheim is rarely, if ever, very interested in 'myths', in the sense of stories which can be spun and respun in many versions, and which have a more or less optional character. His preoccupation is with 'beliefs', in the sense of core, commonly held, obligatory convictions. Even so, and as in this case, myths and beliefs are related in that his talk of 'different metaphors' concerns myths as variable, literary stories that are expressions of the same underlying, literal belief. It is thus a way – and an important way – of looking for a logic in an apparent jumble and contradictoriness of ideas.

Or this is what it seems to me, more than it is a way of trying to reconcile conflicting ethnographic reports. It is true that in covering the ideas of three modes of conception described by Strehlow it can at the same time cover the mode described by Spencer and Gillen. But it can do so, given the agreements that also exist between their reports. It cannot paper over just any disagreement.

Conception connects with death and immortality, and Durkheim's discussion of ideas of these again runs into a relevant difference between the ethnographic reports. Here, however, he does not try to cope with the problem by invoking metaphor. Instead, as he says in a note, one of the reports could be correct and the other mistaken, or they could reflect local variations in beliefs (364 n.2). But in any case, and again given the agreement that also exists between the reports, his own basic interpretation remains intact.

Thus, as he says in the note, for Spencer and Gillen the soul of the individual, after death, returns to a place where it remerges with the soul of the ancestor; for Strehlow it goes to the isle of the dead where it is finally annihilated. But in both myths, while surviving for a time after death, the individual's soul does not survive for ever (ibid.). As he explains in the main discussion, it is the ancestor's soul that is immortal – indeed, eternal. It is a member of the stock of souls which have existed since a mystic beginning of things, which enter into individuals at conception, which in this new incarnation grow and decay as the individual grows and decays, which depart the body at death, and which as manifestations of the individual finally, and in one way or another, disappear.

It is not a long jump from all this to the symbolic point that it is group life and its continuity that we see represented in Australian ideas of ancestral souls, their immortality and their transient manifestations in individuals – 'Individuals die; but the clan survives' (384). In fact, it is so short a jump that the ideas may well involve some such understanding of them in the society itself, and the anthropologist does not have to dig very deep to discover a 'secret' symbolism. Similarly, the great divinity as the great serpent seems clearly and autochthonously phallic, despite all the complications, autochthonously, coming in (cf. Hiatt 1996:112–15). And far from requiring an externally imposed interpretation, perhaps Durkheim's concern with the 'hidden' and 'obscure' can remain a concern with ideas that are thought and felt autochthonously at different – literal through metaphorical to symbolic – levels.

There are, anyway, other points. Durkheim rightly argues against psychological appeal to a universal fear of death to explain ideas of the immortal soul. It might be that individualistic ideas of immortality are connected in particular cultures with a deep-seated, individualistic fear in them of death. But ideas of immortality, in the Australian case, are precisely not ideas of the individual's immortality. In whichever ethnographic account, they are ideas of the individual's eventual, total, bodily *and* psychic annihilation, so that he could hardly have hit on a better ethnographic example to see the soul as a symbolic representation of the group.

He also seems right to argue against a universal desire to enact morality beyond the grave, in a justice of deserts that punishes the wicked and rewards the good. Again, given Australian ideas of the individual's after-life, this cannot be an important motivation there – although of course, and as he is explicit, it could be an important motivation in other cultures, with their own particular ideas both of morality and of the after-life.

But this is in fact to concede – indeed, to emphasize – that things can work out in diverse, culturally specific ways. Ideas of the immortal soul might represent, in Australia, the continuity of collective life. Need they do so universally, as Durkheim seems to want to imply? Are there not cultures and traditions resisting this view, within which people work with highly individualistic ideas of an immortal soul – such as the Protestant tradition, within which Kant worked?

The immortal soul in the second *Critique*

A Durkheimian theme, from the 1907 lectures on, through *The Elementary Forms* and beyond, is that ideas of the soul concern a dualism of human nature. What exactly is the dualism? It seems as protean, in his many formulations, as the ideas of the soul he sees as symbolic reflection on it.

But this is why we can focus on them as concerned, as much as anything, with the self – whether an embodied self, or an individualized self, or a communitarian self, or the Kantian person. Thus in the 1909 lectures Durkheim says, after a reference to Kant, that the soul is the person (1975b, 2:18–19), while also going on to say that the soul is a fragment of an impersonal force, 'individualized' (ibid.:21), and that the soul is 'society and civilization, that is, the *conscience collective*' (ibid.:22).

In *The Elementary Forms* the soul is again, of course, society. But it is also, again, an impersonal force – mana – individualized (378). And it is also, again, the person.

The brief 1909 discussion of Kant, the soul and the person might have prepared the way for the longer, corresponding discussion in *The Elementary Forms*. This is at the end of the chapter on the soul, in a section on the person, especially the Kantian person. It is about a problematic which runs throughout Durkheim's work, from at least *The Division of Labour* on, but which is buried by all the commentary on the individual versus society. The problematic instead concerns the individual versus the person – the particular/distinct/'sensible' individual versus the general/universal/ 'intelligible' person – and was much debated at the time (see, e.g., Boutroux 1926:373–4; Seth 1894/1908:193–200). Thus the main text of *The Elementary Forms* goes from anthropology and the Australian soul to philosophy and the Kantian person, to drive home the importance of the universal. But it is then all offset and balanced in a concluding note, referring to *The Division of Labour* and driving home the importance of the particular, varied, distinct individual.

But the discussion of the person, before getting on to Kant, involves a discussion of Leibniz. It is a highly sympathetic treatment of his idea of the monad. This might seem curious, given the highly hostile treatment of the self as monad in *The Division of Labour*. There is a solution, however, to the mystery.

Again, there are two problematics at stake rather than just one – the problematics of the individual and the person, and of the individual and society. As in *The Elementary Forms*, Durkheim looks kindly on the monad *qua* representation of the person, or, as he so often says, the individual in general, in the abstract and as man. As in *The Division of Labour*, he is implacably opposed to the monad *qua* expression of a detached, atomistic, asocial self. He develops and defends what I have discussed elsewhere as an idea of 'the organic self' (Watts Miller 1996:Ch.4). This is a self with the attachment that is at the very foundation of ethical life. It is an attachment to others and to society as ends, not only adopted as one's own ends but deeply *rooted* (in a thematic Durkheimian metaphor) as such ends in one's character, and in an inter-*penetration* (another thematic metaphor) of selves. With their particular, diverse interpenetrations (with *this* rather than *that* other, etc.), organic selves remain particular, distinct individuals. But a concern of one's own for oneself (or for others) can never be a concern *simply* for oneself (or *simply* for others). Also, a modern universalizing ethic requires, as part of the attachments rooted in our character, attachment not, impossibly, to everybody as an individual, but to everyone as a person, and so, as well, to "the person" as a universal, abstract idea.

Let us now return to the immortal soul as a Kantian necessary moral postulate, and to the possibility, in republican ethics, of a secular substitute.

Kant's postulate seems driven by a need for commitment to the moral law, through the hope that it is not forever beyond our capacity to live up to and live by it. Why, if there is no hope of enacting the law, be committed to it at all, and, in despair, have the will to struggle on? Yet, for the limited, embodied and mortal human individual, there is the certainty of moral failure, of an incapacity not only to live up to the law throughout our lives, from the start and without faltering, but even to develop, by the end, anything like its full realization. Hence commitment to the moral ideal requires belief in an immortal soul, in some sort of continuing existence in which, as an individual, one can move towards and at last achieve a life in conformity with the law. Because of this belief, we can hope. Because of this hope, we can believe.

But belief in one's own immortal soul, to sustain hope for one's own eventual virtue, and so to sustain moral belief and commitment itself, might seem to express a highly individualistic, monadic view of the self. Certainly, in going on and on about autonomy, many modern -- and especially English -- philosophers do read Kant in a highly individualistic way. Also, in going on and on about autonomy, they rarely if ever bother with Kant's religious postulates of morality, or with working out what happens if a secular ethics ditches these. They tend just to assume, without argument, the 'secularizability' of ethics and of Kant.

So what is it that happens if, not only individualizing but also secularizing Kant, we ditch the immortal soul? It is to strip the limited, embodied and mortal individual of hope, to strip us, therefore, of an essential basis of commitment to the ethical life, and to leave the self alone in the universe, not just as a momentary, soon to be extinguished atom, but as an amoral, momentary, soon to be extinguished atom.

Nor will it do, as an escape from this conclusion, to fall back on freedom itself as one of the necessary moral postulates. A puzzle in Kantian commentary is what freedom is doing as a postulate when, as the principle of autonomy, it is the ethical foundation of things. Delbos, in the outstanding work of French Kantian scholarship of Durkheim's time, suggests a solution. It is that freedom as a postulate is what Kant discusses as "autocracy". It is a belief, a confidence, a hope in our power as limited, finite human beings to enact the foundational principle of autonomy, and thus live up to the moral law and its regard for everyone as a person (Delbos 1905/1969:400–1). But Delbos does not suggest that such a belief, confidence, hope can depend only on freedom postulated on its own, rather than on freedom, the immortal soul and God postulated together. Philonenko draws on Delbos to argue that 'autocratic' belief in virtue is about the need to overcome 'all the doubts that man can experience in regard to his freedom', but also that each of the postulates is a 'belief in the foundation' (Philonenko 1993, 2:172–3). Indeed, he is one of the few commentators nowadays not only to go into all three postulates, but to defend their coherence and necessity.

It is difficult to disagree with him if, as so far, we concentrate on the soul, and if, as so far, we concede a highly individualistic reading of the Kantian self. An immortal soul is very much needed as a postulate of morality, given the self as individualistic atom, incapable, without an after-life, of becoming anything like a fully autonomous person. As a distinguished commentator reminds us: 'Kant insists, in ways that some contemporary "Kantians" do not, that human beings have quite limited capacities to enact their autonomy' (O'Neill 1992:219).

But it is possible to ditch both the self as monad and the reading of the Kantian self as this. The way is then open to dispense with the immortal soul. Part of the secret is not merely to secularize, but to collectivize the hope it represents – the coming one day, and despite everything, of the republic.

Kant, immediately after announcing the principle of autonomy in *The Groundwork*, links it with the ethical ideal of a kingdom of ends. And he immediately describes this as a *Verbindung* (Kant 1785/1911:433), that is, as a union, so that we might talk of the kingdom (or the republic) as a union of persons. In the context of Kant's work as a whole, the ethical ideal does not read as if it is just a matter of an association, of an aggregate of individuals. Rather, it reads as an ideal of the person in a union of persons, an organic whole and network of ends in which each person is an end but society itself is also an end – for example, in the discussion that again leads up to talk of a *Verbindung* in the third *Critique*, the *Critique of Judgement* (Kant 1790/1913:373–5), and elsewhere, as noted by Onora O'Neill in her reflections on Kant on hope (1996:20 n.9).

Moreover, it is possible to go on to interpret it as a union of persons who not only cognize and *view* each other and society as ends but also, as in Durkheimian ethics, *feel* these as ends, in strong, deeply rooted sentiments of attachment to them. That is, it is possible in this, as in other ways, to de-atomize the Kantian self and convert it, more or less, into a Durkheimian, organic self.

But in the case of the organic self and the ideal of the person in a union of persons, an immortal soul is unnecessary (even if it remains an option) as a moral postulate. The Kantian postulates and the Durkheimian search for a secular substitute deal with a question that, again, contemporary analytical English ethics rarely, if ever, bothers to address. The question involves an empirical, sociological and psychological one, of an explanation of the *fact* that many or most of us are motivated to work in the cause of a good that, if ever realized at all, will only be so long after our deaths. It also involves justifying this motivation to a post-mortal moral concern, and indeed insisting on it as integral to the ethical life. The immortal soul is part of the Kantian answer, but can be dispensed with by the organic self as part of the Durkheimian answer. Given the organic self's identity and attachments, there can be commitment to a collective rather than just individualistic ideal, unrealizable until long after we are dead. And the commitment can be sustained by a collective rather than just individualistic hope that there will be a coming, one day and despite everything, of the republic.

There is often criticism of Durkheim's optimism. The criticism is naïve if it ignores the demoralization of accepting that evil will inherit the earth and forgets the ethical importance of hope. There seems, anyway, a strongly pessimistic streak in him, to do with an 'internalist programme' that seeks, in a social world, a dynamic that is at once a source of its ideals *and* its ills. Thus the monad is not a mere philosophical illusion, but an expression of a real tendency. The modern world is not the Australia of *The Elementary Forms*. It generates, as part of its individualist human ideal, its own individualist pathologies, and, as part of a cult of man, an egoistic and anomic cult of the self that threatens to undermine it.

God

Let us turn, now, to God. It has already been noted how there was controversy over whether ideas of God were, in the Australian case, autochthonous or a foreign import. In siding with the autochthonous view, Durkheim passed up the opportunity to cite another example of a religion without God. Instead, he was more impressed by the need to understand ideas of God in terms of some internal dynamic logic at work in Australian religious beliefs themselves. What happens when, in his chapter on ideas of God, Durkheim moves on to their interpretation in terms of a secret symbolism?

Towards the end of the chapter, and after associating ideas of a great God with rites of initiation which involve a tribe as a whole, he states two main conclusions. A very general conclusion is: 'wherever the tribe acquired a livelier sentiment of itself, this sentiment was naturally embodied by some personage, who became its symbol' (420). Another, more particular conclusion is: 'In order to account for the bonds uniting them to one another, no matter what clan they belonged to, men imagined that they were all descended from the same stock and that they were all descended from a single father, to whom they owed their existence, though he owed his to no one' (ibid.). But in both passages, as well as in the chapter as a whole, he emphasizes God as a symbol of positive feelings of attachment and of a shared identity. To appreciate this emphasis in *The Elementary Forms* it helps to go to his other work.

The early article on the French Revolution (1890a/1970a:215–25) is the first time that Durkheim clearly refers to the modern secular ethic as a religion – not a sort of religion, or like a religion, but a religion. Tied up with this, it is also the first time that he sees religion, not as a traditional force crystallizing the past, but as a dynamic force, ushering in a new, socially creative vision of things. Indeed, it is the first time, too, that he hints at collective creative ferment. But although the revolution involved a religion, which had its martyrs and apostles, and which stirred up great things, there is no mention of its having had a God.

The first time in which man becomes the new God for man is in *Suicide* (1897a:379). Man is this again in the intervention on the Dreyfus Affair (1898c/1970a:265). There is also discussion of a cult of man, transferring sacrality from God to the human person, in the 1898–9 lecture course on moral education (1925a:11). Thus a question is who is God's secular Durkheimian replacement – man or society? The answer is and must be both. In traditional worlds, God is at once the source and the centre of the sacred. In the modern world, society is the source of the sacred while man is the centre of the sacred. As in the later discussion paper on moral facts, 'society consecrates man' (1906b/1924a:77). Something like this has to be the answer. It is impossible for a society to define and constitute itself just through the very idea of society, and without bringing in other ideas, such as of liberty, egality, fraternity, etc. Hence God, as a central constitutive idea of traditional societies, has to be replaced by other constitutive ideas, which define a society and enter into its very description – such as ideas of the individual and man, the constitutive ideas of our basic modern identity. It is impossible to take Durkheim seriously when, as also in the discussion paper, he seems to reduce God to a metaphorical expression of society, replaceable by secular, literal talk of society itself. This might work in the case of God's replacement by society as the *source* of the sacred (perhaps the point of the remark). It cannot work in the case of God's replacement as the *centre* of the sacred – which must be ideas, not of 'society' as such, or that just come from and express our particular, actual social world, but that help to create, constitute and drive reform of it. Put another way, the modern human ideal must be an ideal *both* of the person *and* of a particular (albeit universalist) society – the republic of persons.

If we now move on to another aspect of things, the course on moral education stresses an irreducible dualism of 'duty' and 'the good', in which 'the good' has to do with positive feelings of attachment, 'duty' with negative feelings of respect and constraint. This is repeated in the paper on moral facts, but with the difference that a parallel dualism, of negative respect and positive attraction, is also stressed in regard to the sacred. A lecture of the same year provides God with a job description in similar terms, as a stern lawgiver who must be obeyed and as a loving figure offering solace, comfort, happiness and hope. But God is also a source of a shared identity, and as society enlarges we all become His children, while as society secularizes sacrality is transferred from God on to man (1906e/1975b 2:10–11).

The emphasis, in *The Elementary Forms*, on God as symbol of a shared, general, even universal identity can be amalgamated with God as symbol of the good and of a positive love and fellow-feeling. But the Durkheimian picture is incomplete without God as symbol of duty and of a negative respect, awe and reverence for the moral law. This done, can God as a Kantian postulate just be replaced with man as the sacred centre, society as a sacred source?

The answer is 'no'. Kant's God has a job to do which cannot be done by Durkheim's secular republican substitute. It is to arrange the realization of the highest good – the *summum bonum consummatum*.

The highest good is all the happiness consistent with virtue. Virtue is man's work, not God's, a struggle to enact our capacity for autonomy, respect the authority of the moral law and realize an ethical commonwealth governed by it. There are also kinds of happiness that again are man's work, not God's. These, as discussed elsewhere (Watts Miller 1996:230–1), are the happiness intrinsic to virtue, and a happiness compatible with it. But all the happiness consistent with virtue includes, as well, contingent happiness – that is, a happiness completely outside our control, that comes to or escapes us completely independently of our own efforts and virtue. It is not, by definition, man's work.

Thus the highest good of all the happiness consistent with virtue is coherent, with its component of contingent happiness, as something for which we may *hope*. And it may be coherent, as Kant claims, as a hope that requires us to postulate God to arrange it. But one wonders how it is coherent, as he also claims, as an end – *Zweck* – in the sense of a consciously striven-for ideal (Kant 1788/1913:125). How can we adopt, as an end, something we recognize as wholly beyond our control – the contingent happiness Kant especially has in mind in discussing the highest good of all the happiness consistent with virtue? Hence the consciously striven-for ideal of a republic cannot be a secular substitute for the hope, of contingent happiness, that Kant especially has in mind in arguing for God as a necessary moral postulate, being the only power able to make good the hope and arrange a union of virtue with all the happiness consistent with it.

Yet all is not lost if, like Durkheim, we want to get from a kingdom of ends to a republic of persons. In the first place, while continuing to hope for contingent happiness, we can just see and accept it as nature's work, not God's – and not man's. It is beyond the task of struggling for the republic except insofar as this is also a struggle to limit the power over our lives of 'accidents' and contingencies of nature, a struggle, as Durkheim puts it, for autonomy in regard to nature (1925a:130–1).

In the second place, giving up on God and the immortal soul gives up on only one of the general bases of hope in Kant, the religious postulates. We can still turn to the other, the philosophical history.

It is true that English analytical ethics nowadays, as well as ditching religion, ditches the philosophical history. But this is par for the course. Blindness to the moral importance of hope extends all the way through, whether in the case of the religious postulates or in the case of the philosophical history. It is wrong, indeed deeply irresponsible, to dismiss the religious postulates without trying to find an adequate secular substitute for their offer of hope. And it is wrong to dismiss Kantian philosophical history without bothering to try to rework it in a more convincing version.

As reworked in a Durkheimian internalist programme, it is not a story of the coming of utopia, but of a society with its own characteristic, 'normal' forms and patterns of malaise. And we can hope for the republic because we see its realization written into modernity's dynamic even though, written into the dynamic too, are the pathologies that block and might collapse it. But belief in the human ideal is itself an essential, active part of the dynamic, helping to drive it on. There is therefore good reason for optimism. To sustain belief in the human ideal, we need to have hope in the coming, one day and despite everything, of the republic. As with the immortal soul and God, so with the philosophical history and the dynamic of the modern human ideal. We can hope because we believe. We can believe because we hope.

The Australia of *The Elementary Forms* contains some of the most important answers if we ask how, to get to a universal ethical republic, we can entrench not only belief but hope. Let me finish with a brief word on one of the answers. This concerns the theory of the sacred – but also Kant's linkage of morals with aesthetics, and Durkheim's attention to style (cf. de Lannoy 1996).

It is, amongst other things, a constative–constitutive theory. That is, in order to state and constitute something as a core conviction, and so in order to entrench it as a core hope-cum-belief, it is necessary to state it in the right register, the register of the sacred. This must have the right emotive force, operate in the right semantic field and involve the right deployment of rhetoric and symbolism. God is as much as anything poetry. So, in a modern secular ethic-cum-religion, is Man. Neither can be replaced, without loss of *meaning*, by talk in the wrong register, a register of the prosaic and the profane. Durkheim's sensitivity to the point, in touching on the sacred, is evident in the style itself of *The Elementary Forms*. With the sacred, there is an intertwining of beauty, truth and the good.

6

THE CULT OF IMAGES

Reading Chapter VII, Book II, of
The Elementary Forms

Giovanni Paoletti

This paper can be considered as an essay of analysis of a Durkheimian text.[1] The use of the word essay immediately points to its two major limitations. Although the text presents some specific features which facilitate its abstraction from *The Elementary Forms*, the abstraction is at least in part arbitrary. The connections between Book II, Chapter VII and the rest of the book will be referred to only indirectly. Second, the very analysis of the text thus isolated has some limitations because of lack of space. Some themes of the chapter, for example the theory of symbolism and the cult of images, will be dealt with more thoroughly than others, such as the notion of social effervescence or the controversy with Lévy-Bruhl about primitive mentality (see Chs 11 and 2 respectively).

Apart from that, the analysis is developed in a systematic way, with several rubrics (argumentative structure, lexicon, sources, position in Durkheim's thought), with the aim of providing a reconstruction of Durkheim's theory of social symbolism. Finally, we will try to show the connection between this theory and the theory of *représentations collectives*, and its relevance to sociological methodology.

The argument

Chapter VII of Book II, with its forty-nine pages, arranged into six sections and an introductory section, is the longest chapter of *The Elementary Forms*. It immediately appears as the keystone of the whole structure of the book. If we consider the formal division of the work into five parts (Introduction, three Books, Conclusion), it is exactly in the middle. The argumentative style of the chapter, which is distinctly generalizing and theoretical, distinguishes it from the chapters immediately preceding and following, recalling or anticipating the tenor of the Introduction and the Conclusion. On the other hand, in contrast to the Introduction and the Conclusion, this chapter deals only marginally with the sociology of knowledge. It brings to an end the analysis of the major totemic beliefs, after which we will meet only secondary notions – soul and gods – or the ritual dimension of totemism. This is therefore a crucial moment in the formulation of Durkheim's notion of religion. After about two hundred and fifty pages, it gives substance to the introductory, formal and phenomenal definition of religion in Chapter I of Book I.

The line of argument of the chapter is quite uneven, which means that single episodes, especially the description, through the case of the *corrobbori*, of the formation of social effervescence, can be more readily extracted from their context. Nevertheless, it is possible to detect a common core to which all issues can be related. It is the discovery, previously documented with several references to ethnographic literature (158–9), that totemism is not the worship of animals or plants, according to the well-known definition by McLennan, but of the symbols that represent them. They are 'the centre of the cult' and the source of religious attitudes, taken towards totemic species (294/205–6).[2] Such a factual 'discovery' corresponds exactly to the methodological principle, stated at the very beginning of the book, on which the sociological study of religion is founded: 'one must know how to go beneath the symbol to the reality which it represents and which gives it its true meaning'.[3] What is initially asserted about religion in general appears to be particularly true of totemism, the elementary form of religious life. Every religion is a system of symbols, and totemism in particular is a religion of the symbol, of the emblem.

This first assertion is followed by three questions. The first is simply the application of the above-mentioned methodological principle: 'the totem is above all a symbol ... But of what?' (ibid.). Durkheim already has the answer to this question, an extremely important answer, and he briefly expresses it in a few polished lines within the first section. The reality which must be perceived beyond the symbol is society itself, the clan, of which the mana is just a hypostatized *représentation* (argument of double symbolism: see Pickering 1984:236–8). The obvious conclusion is that acknowledging the symbolic nature of religion allows the sociologist to recognize the objective reality which religion, as a human institution, cannot but have. Introducing the notion of symbol raises two further questions, the answers to which are not so obvious. They are in a way the price Durkheim has to pay in order to found the sociological study of religion on symbolic interpretation. Question Two is first expressed at the end of section I itself (295/206) and is then proposed again in a more specific version at the beginning of section V (329/230). It is about the form of the totem/symbol: why is society represented through symbols? Question Three is eventually to be found in section IV (322–3f./225f.). It asks about the objective foundation of symbols: what proves that the religious exaltation, which follows social effervescence, is not merely a sort of delirium?

It takes Durkheim forty pages – sections II to V – to answer these questions. The answer to the second question (sections II, III, V) is the most complex one, and is arranged in three parts. First Durkheim explains the conditions of possibility of the expression of society through symbols ('how has this apotheosis been possible?' (295/206)). Such conditions are both specific characteristics of society in general (section II), and a particular feature of Australian society (first half of section III). In order to describe the general characteristics, Durkheim in essence develops arguments that were previously, thoroughly presented in *The Rules of Sociological Method* (1895a), illustrating the authority (both physical and moral) and the imperative force which makes the relation between society and its members like that between god and worshippers. The particular dynamics of Australian societies, on the other hand, consist of the alternation between concentration and dispersion in the rhythm of collective life, which regularly leads to the effervescence of the *corrobbori*.

Second, Durkheim tries to detect the origin of symbolism ('how did it come about that it [the apotheosis] took place in this fashion?' (ibid.)). It is the most difficult part of the question, but also the most logically relevant. The answer, or rather the attempt at an answer, which we will be specifically analysing, covers the second half of section III and the first half of section V. Finally, Durkheim inquires (second half of section V) about the specific form of totemic symbolism: why just animals or plants? The reason, in contrast to the answers given to previous questions, is simply factual: animals and plants are at the same time the most easily represented things and the most familiar to the members of the clan.

The answer to the third question, about the degree of reality of the symbols, covers the whole of section IV. It therefore strangely interrupts the line of argument. Section V begins exactly where section III ended, and readers could well omit section IV without impairing their comprehension. Even from a logical point of view, the insertion of this section arouses some difficulties. Although section I deals briefly with the question of double symbolism, it had already stated what the objective foundation of symbols was. Why should this topic be taken up again? In the résumé by Paul Fontana of Durkheim's course on religion given in 1906–7, the position of what was to become section IV appears more justified (1907f). Durkheim simply wanted to present new arguments against the empiricist theories of the origins of religion, as corollaries of the previous argument. Between 1907 and 1912 he added a new discussion, which became all important, about the objectivity of symbols, as shown in the well-known pages about the 'well-founded delirium' and the 'essential idealism' of religion. This reveals that Durkheim was not satisfied with his own solution to the problem. In our opinion, the extension of section IV is due to the difficulties inherent in the Durkheimian conception of objectivity (analysed in another essay to be published shortly[4]).

Finally, there is the last section, section VI. As often happens in the final sections of the chapters of *The Elementary Forms*, its subject is in part independent and more philosophical – the relationship between the primitive classifications and the classifications of modern scientific thought. It is connected to the essay of 1903, 'De quelques Formes primitives de classification' (Durkheim 1903a(i)). Although the section had been written beforehand, the topic had acquired new interest after the publication of Lévy-Bruhl's first anthropological work, *Les Fonctions mentales dans les sociétés inférieures* (1910). Nevertheless, it is also largely connected with the rest of the chapter, since it derives issues and examples from his theory of symbolism. Moreover, it again criticizes the main controversial reference of the chapter (and of the whole book), that is, empiricist theories of religion. Such criticism is not just a well-delimited *pars destruens*, but is rather a theme that runs through the whole chapter. Consequently, section I, which contains the first challenge to empiricism and the introduction of the theme of symbolism, briefly sums up the whole chapter in both its critical and constructive aspects.

As a matter of fact, Chapter VII of Book II finds its thematic unity and coherence of argument in the theory of symbolism. Such a theory therefore represents a crucial moment in Durkheim's conception of religion, although (together with Chapter VII itself) it has not always received adequate attention from scholars. Pickering, while relating the notion of symbol to the broader one of *représentation*, concentrates on trying to understand what are the object and the extent of reality in symbolism, i.e., on the first and the third questions of Chapter VII. This has been done with worthwhile results, but it inevitably neglects the second question about the form of the symbol (Pickering 1984:Ch.15). On the other hand, the question is central in Prades' analysis of the chapter (1987:232–6). The analysis is, however, merely sketched. Yet the contrast with our reading is, for that very reason, even more evident, as he mentions those parts pertinent to the conditions of the possibility of symbolism, while he almost eliminates those about its origin. We have already asserted the relevance of the second question. In taking it into consideration, we simply follow Durkheim's suggestion: 'Given the idea of the totem, the emblem of the clan, all the rest follows; but we must still investigate how this idea has been formed' (329/230).

The lexicon

Thus, in the analysis of the theory of symbolism, we assume that the notion of symbol in *The Elementary Forms* cannot be completely included in those of *représentation* or 'ideal', typical though these are of Durkheim's last works. It is clearly related to them, but it seems to retain its own specific features. Chapter VII should, first of all, prove – or disprove – this hypothesis.

Initially, we need to ascertain whether it is possible to give a definition of symbol in accordance with the text. The analysis of the lexicon of the chapter shows that this term is often and irregularly used as an alternative to 'emblem' or 'image'. They all belong to the same semantic area.

The word 'image' occurs in *The Elementary Forms* with two different meanings: one is related to the sacred, while the other, which is less frequently employed, is philosophical. When the word is used with the former meaning, the reader is struck by the close connection between the image and the sacred, even before it is explained: 'the images of totemic beings are more sacred than the beings themselves' (189/133). The philosophical recurrences reveal that images are some form of sensible *représentations*, which are flexible, indefinite, and subject 'to the free creativity of the mind' (545/381). They are a function of the moment and they submit to the laws of association (618/433; 206/145). The faculty of imagination is mentioned in the text especially in relation to the first meaning: it fulfils the 'metamorphosis' (or 'transfiguration') through which tangible things become symbols of society (270/190; 304/212; 544ff./381ff.; 590/412). This is the connection between the sacred image and the symbol. Through imagination, the images as inner-conscience acts (philosophical meaning) become visible objects that can be shared by the community of believers (religious meaning).

Emblem is the most specific of the three terms under consideration. It is comprehended by the other two – the emblem is a sort of symbol, a partic-ular image (331/231) – it makes their meaning specific. Its own meaning is established in relation to the coat of arms (158/113): the emblem is the sacred image which is engraved, carved, tatooed, in one word, repeated, as a membership mark. Repetition increases the visibility of the image and its power to mark the sacred and it emphasizes its collective nature: 'the emblem is everywhere before the eyes of individuals' (338/140).

The word symbol also has two meanings, and in this case also, the philo-sophical one occurs less frequently. Thus, any system of *représentations* can be defined as symbolic, whether it belongs to a religion or to science. A given reality, or reality *tout court*, has to be translated in terms which can be assimilated by thought. The symbolic form can be a form of thought, but also, in a broader sense, *the* form of thought.[5] Such a use of the word, which is based on a sort of epistemological nominalism, is certainly not original for it is documented by the *Vocabulaire de la philosophie* by Lalande and can be found, for instance, in Spencer.[6]

The word symbol is nevertheless employed with a different and narrower meaning – one on which Durkheim founds his theory of symbolism. A sort of incidental definition of the term is in section I: 'the totem is above all a symbol, a material expression of something else. But of what?' (294/206). As the expression of something else, the symbol has the function of trans-lation, which is present in the philosophical meaning. Not only that, it *materially* expresses something else. Such a connection with matter seems to be related to the etymological meaning of the word: the object (*sumbolon*) divided into two parts to allow identification. How is that to be understood?

The course on religion of 1906–7 offers a different version of the same sentence: the totemic beings and the totem 'are the symbol, the visible image of something else. But of what?' (1907f:94). Materiality and visibility are associated, as if the material substratum of the symbol were the screen on which to project the image. Moreover, the material nature of the symbol makes it different from conventional signs, such as linguistic ones, whose meaning is independent of the physical substratum of communication. Since the context or the denotation is the same, a sign or a word will keep the same meaning every time each is repeated. On the other hand, the substratum makes the symbol an individual entity; it is a *thing* before it is a concept. Symbols participate in the nature of the object on which they are grounded (339/237). Matter as *principium individuationis* as the heritage of Aristotelian tradition meets and agrees with the Durkheimian notion of social reality. The symbol as a material expression cannot be reduced to a convention. It is at first sight opaque to individual reason. It opposes the subject from the outside and it obliges him to yield to its concrete individuality. This is what, in our opinion, Durkheim means when he talks about the minimal part that the essential idealism of the social realm or domain leaves to matter (326). Matter, deprived of all its qualities, is reduced to the mere function of individuation of symbolic *représentation*.

The symbol is a material, that is, an individual image. It belongs to vision, rather than to language. In terms of the Hegelian opposition, which Durkheim must have known, symbol is opposed to allegory (*logos*) because of its concrete and immediate nature. Nevertheless, this does not mean that it is merely a function of sensation. Durkheim had already stated it as a matter of fact, before raising the theoretical question in Chapter VII.

> These facts prove that if the Australian is so strongly inclined to symbolise his totem, it is in order not to have a portrait of it before his eyes which would constantly renew the sensation of it; it is merely because he feels the need to represent the idea which he forms of it by means of a material and external sign, no matter what this sign may be.
>
> (179/127; cf.333/232)

In this case we can also clearly see Durkheim's customary dislike of the empiricist theory of knowledge. The symbol gives rise to the paradox of an image whose aim is not perception. Individual sensations do not constitute the components or the ground on which the symbol is based, but a means to reach something else.

Instances can be found in *The Elementary Forms* which seem to confirm our interpretation. The *churinga*, which can be considered as the symbol *par excellence* of totemism, are but 'pieces of wood or bits of polished stones, of a great variety of forms', on which the totemic diagram is carved or engraved (168/119). Among the instances of modern symbols, more or less explicit, which are mentioned in Chapter VII, the case of a collector's stamp is quite significant (325/227). It shows not only the immense disproportion between intrinsic and acquired value, which a banknote also exhibits; but it contains too the idea of a unique piece, of an individuality that cannot be replaced, which causes a sort of fetishism even stronger than that of money.

The most relevant instance, however, which is repeated as many as seven times in Chapter VII alone, is that of the flag.[7] Its appropriateness has been questioned by Firth, who asserts that the feelings of a modern citizen towards the national flag cannot be considered as deep and homogeneous as are the feelings of the clan members for their symbols (Firth 1973:339f.; 357; 364f.). This objection, however, is not to the point. It is evident from the text that Durkheim does not refer to national flags in general, but to military ones.[8] They correspond perfectly to the given definition of symbol. They are sacred objects in the Durkheimian sense of the word, when the number of rituals and prohibitions is considered which surround them.[9] As with the *churinga*, they are sacred because of the image they represent. Above all, they are individual and irreplaceable entities. Any army corps of importance has its own flag, and to that flag soldiers owe their special respect and devotion. Such flags represent only indirectly the nation. First and foremost they are the 'sacred ark' of that particular corps.[10]

The explanation and its sources

The symbol is a material, individual, visible image (German, *Sinnbild*) of something else. After defining the word, we turn to its explanation which, in the argument of Chapter VII, corresponds to the second question: why does society represent itself by means of symbols? Durkheim deals with the origin of symbolism in sections III and V. Briefly, his explanation is as follows. First, the symbolic value, according to a 'well-known' psychological law, is derived from a shift of feeling from its complex cause (the clan) to a concrete object (the totemic image) which, being simple and visible, makes it easier to conceive (314–6/219–21). To allow such a shift, the symbol has to be pre-existent. Second, and as a consequence, Durkheim tries to go back to the ultimate reason for the existence of the symbol itself. It is *useful* for the cohesion of a group, *necessary* to the communication and communion among individuals, *indispensable* for the permanence of collective feeling (329–31/230–1). To conclude: 'social life, in all its aspects and at every moment of its history, is made possible only by a vast symbolism' (331/231).

Being thus divided into two stages, the argument gives the impression of circularity. The psychological law of the shift of feeling implies the existence of symbols. On the other hand, some of the reasons for symbolism which are given later, such as the permanence typical of the symbol as compared with the feeling itself, echo the explanation in section III.

In fact, if we analyse the two passages into their conceptual elements, we realize that they can be largely superimposed. The relation between social reality and its symbols is defined by a number of oppositions, from which, we can assume, the reason for symbolism is derived. According to section III, the oppositions are the following (the first term refers to society):

(1) complex/simple. 'The symbol can be something simple, definite and easily representable, while the thing itself . . . is difficult to hold in the mind' (314/220): 'The clan is too complex a reality to be represented clearly in all its complex unity by such rudimentary intelligences' (315/220): or, what is closely related, abstract/concrete, 'an abstract entity . . . some concrete object' (314/220).

(2) invisible/visible. 'The primitive does not even see that these impressions come to him from the group . . . Now what does he see about him? . . . The numerous images of the totem' (315/220).

(3) fleeting/permanent. 'The sentiments experienced fix themselves upon it [the image of the totem] . . . It continues to bring them to mind and to evoke them even after the assembly has dissolved' (316/221).

Compared to section III, section V contains one further opposition and has one opposition less:

(2) invisible/visible. 'By expressing the social unity in a material form, it [the emblem] makes this more perceptible (*sensible*) to all' (329/230).

(3) fleeting/permanent. 'without symbols, social sentiments could have only a precarious existence' (330/231).

(4) internal/external. 'Individual minds cannot meet and come into communion (*communier*) except by coming out of themselves; but they cannot externalize themselves except in the form of movements. When . . . these movements have once taken a stereotyped form, they serve to symbolize the corresponding *représentations*' (330/230–1).

This simple system of oppositions reveals that Durkheim's argument moves at two levels, an epistemological one and an ontological one. The epistemological level is centred on the dichotomy (1) complex/simple, and it is therefore developed in section III. The answer which is here given to the second question (why has society been represented by means of symbols?) is: symbols make what is complex simple and, therefore, easy to conceive. The ontological level is centred on the opposition (4) internal/external, which is the core and the novelty of section V. The different point of view leads to a different answer to the same question: symbols allow the individual to go beyond the self and social life to begin.

The analysis clarifies the division of the argument into two phases treated in separate sections, at least as far as concerns substance. Section V goes deeper and further than section III, inasmuch as the level of being logically precedes the level of knowledge. This proves to be true even with the two oppositions which sections III and V have in common. Opposition (2), 'invisible/visible', is of an epistemological nature, and is in fact a central theme in section III, while in section V it is coherently secondary to the ontological argument. 'The emblem is not merely a convenient procedure for clarifying the sentiment society has of itself: it also serves to create this sentiment' (329/230). Opposition (3), fleeting/permanent, which in itself is neutral, is interpreted epistemologically, or rather subjectively, in section III, where the image has the function of 'bringing to mind' and 'evoking' feelings (316/221), and it is interpreted ontologically in section V ('without symbols, social sentiments could have only a precarious *existence*' (330/231: our emphasis)). In the system of oppositions we find once more both the features which define the symbol, and the reason for the symbol. The symbol is an image, since it makes the invisible visible. It is a simple image, since as it makes the complex comprehensible. It is concrete, so that feelings can fix on it. It is a thing, because there is no society without exteriority.

But why has such an analysis been necessary? An impression of circularity is created by the fact that the arguments of the two sections partly coincide. Might we consider it to be the result of an imperfect exposition, or even a confusion, by Durkheim? It may well be, but we must also consider such complication to indicate a theoretical problem. This doubt arises from the fact that, after all, even oppositions (1) and (4) are not perfectly distributed between the two sections. An echo of opposition (4), internal/external can also be found in section III. 'However, he [the primitive] must connect these sensations to some external object as their cause' (315/220). The material nature of symbols is pointed out in section V – 'actions and reactions which are themselves possible only through material intermediaries' (330/230). This recalls the opposition, abstract/concrete, which is in turn closely connected in section III to the opposition (1), complex/simple. Durkheim in fact seems to have employed the same materials for the two parts of his explanation. Could this also imply that the two parts are closely related one to the other?

We can put aside this question for a while and note first that sections III and V differ at least as concerns originality. Indeed, in section II! the formation of symbolic value is presented as a particular instance of a general psychological law. 'In fact, it is a well-known law that the sentiments aroused in us by something spontaneously attach themselves to the symbol that represents them' (314/219). In the psychological literature of that time, this law has a name, which Durkheim evidently takes for granted at this point but mentions in passing later on – the *transfert de sentiments* (transference of feelings). This law had been formulated by James Sully and then by Théodule Ribot, before Freud gave the notion of *transfert* the meaning which it now has:

> In its more general form . . . it consists in the *direct* investment of emotion in an object which in itself does not arouse emotion. The transference does not consist in removing the emotion from the original event to give it to another one, but in a movement that generalizes and spreads the emotion like a drop of oil.
>
> (Ribot 1896:175)[11]

In such terms the law was well adapted to accounting for the dynamics of social feelings aroused by association, as well for the contagiousness of the sacred. Durkheim, as we know, states that if the symbol is simpler than the cause of feeling, the transference is all the more thorough and obvious. However, even this is not altogether new. In a text by Pikler and Somló, which Durkheim quotes in a note, we find the thesis that totemism is explained by the fact that primitive man uses a simple sign to indicate the whole group (294; cf. 263; Pikler and Somló 1900:7ff.; and see Van Gennep 1920:98–9). Further similarities with the content of Chapter VII can also be found in a work by the Italian criminologist Ferrero, in his *I simboli* (1893:79), which was translated into French in 1895. We do not know whether Durkheim was acquainted with it, but the text was probably quite widely read. It is mentioned in Lalande's dictionary under the heading Symbol, and is quoted by Ribot in *La Psychologie des sentiments*. When dealing with emotional symbols, Ferrero uses the argument of the permanence of the symbol relative to the feeling. But, above all, he develops a proper theory of emotional arrest based on the power of symbols to express simply and materially realities that are too complex, abstract or transcendent to rouse human emotions (Ferrero 1893:Ch.VI). Ferrero uses the same instances as Durkheim, only without relating them one to the other. Sacred images, which symbolize the divinity, and the flag, which symbolizes the mother-land or society. About the flag he writes:

> The social feeling, or love for the motherland, becomes extremely complex when it no longer concerns small tribes, but large societies ... It is an emotion which cannot but result from the association and the fusion of an extraordinary number of states of conscious-ness, which must inevitably gather around an abstract idea, the idea of the motherland. Nowadays, man, because of his mental devel-opment, is not able to feel such a complex emotion, and he therefore replaces it with a simpler one, which has the symbol as its centre. The flag, which can be seen and touched, rather than the moth-erland, becomes the object of love, whose image can be easily evoked ... A very complex emotion is brought to the level of ordinary feel-ings by putting between it and man a material symbol, where the emotion stops.
>
> (ibid.:98–9)

However, explaining symbolism according to a psychological law is hardly original. In a Durkheimian perspective it is also a methodological mistake, because it gives a psychological explanation of a social fact. This further justifies the reformulation of the argument in section V. The law of trans-ference is replaced as *explanans* by the theory of collective *représentations*, so that the rule 'explain a social fact with another social fact' is strictly observed. The theory is central in the final stage of Durkheim's thought. Section V therefore leads us to consider, albeit in broad terms, the theory of symbolism presented in Chapter VII, and its place within Durkheim's sociology.

The place of *représentations collectives* in Durkheim's work

The notion of *représentations collectives* appears in a central position in the onto-logical argument of section V. It gives the opposition 'internal/external', on which the argument is founded, an original character. Durkheim starts from a traditional idea of language according to which signs serve to express consciously individual inner states. Through association and social effer-vescence, individual inner states gain uniformity and become parts of a whole. Consequently, the signs that express them should be the same or, at least, they should be similar to one another – 'the same cry ... the same word ... the same gesture' (330/230–1). Yet the collective sign does not simply express a homogeneous state of consciousness, it reacts on it, helping to create it. The relationship between internal and external elements is reversed – 'But it is quite another matter with *représentations collectives*' (330/230). What is external does not express or follow, rather it generates or precedes what is internal.[12] If our reading is correct, the material nature of symbols is closely related to the new importance of the external element. In terms of the semiotic theory to which Durkheim here refers, the moral unity formed through association cannot be the object of communicative exchange, because it is the immediate content of a lived experience which is not controlled by individual consciousness. The group is a whole, and as such it cannot perform any communicational exchanges: it can only assert itself and become aware of itself. It does that by means of an external reality, (the 'material intermediaries' of 330/230), which reflects its image like a mirror. Here is the reason for the symbol. 'It is by . . . performing the same gesture in regard to *the same object* that they become and feel themselves to be in unison' (ibid. Our emphasis).

We do not intend to deal here with the complex theory of *représentations collectives*, but we shall briefly point out the theoretical implications that are relevant to a correct understanding of Chapter VII. First of all, the theory clarifies the relationship between sections III and V, and not only, as mentioned above, in the sense that it makes it possible to overcome the drawbacks of a psychological explanation of symbolism. On a deeper level in fact, it provides an answer to the question that we formulated and left aside in the previous section, namely, how to account for the close connection between the two parts of the explanation. We have seen that they are to be placed on different levels, an epistemological one and an ontological one. Now, from an interpretation of social reality in terms of *représentations collectives*, it follows that the level of knowledge and that of being, though distinct, are connected and closely related. On the one hand, social reality is indeed, by definition, 'essentially made of *représentations*' (1897a:352). On the other hand, the *représentation* of social reality conditions the formation of reality itself. Not only does it express it, it also creates it. This shows, in our opinion, a close relation between the arguments of the two sections: symbols express the complex social reality in a simple way, making it comprehensible to individuals (section III, epistemological argument, opposition (1), complex/simple); on the other hand, such comprehension is an essential stage in the formation of society, because it is a way, or perhaps *the* way, in which individuals transcend their inner dimension and are involved in an external reality which is beyond them (section V, ontological argument, opposition (4), internal/external).

Second, the connection between symbols and *représentations collectives* sets us a problem regarding the development of Durkheim's thought. It is known that the notion of *représentations collectives*, though the term already occurs in Durkheim's early writings, was given a proper theoretical formulation in 1898 (Durkheim 1898b). Subsequently, it became one of the main instruments in the analysis of the favourite themes of the later Durkheim – religion, ethics, knowledge. Is it possible to mark a similar course for the theory of symbolism? Thorough research apart, a brief survey will suffice here. There is evidence of the theme of symbolism in connection with religion just after 1895 – the year which ideally represents the beginning of Durkheim's sociology of religion – both in *Leçons de sociologie* (1950a:188–9, 220) and in *Suicide* (1897a:352ff.). Yet the hints appear to be incidental while, quite significantly, there is no mention of symbols, emblems, sacred images in the first theoretical text that deals only with the sociology of religion (1899a(ii)). It is therefore a terminus *ante quem non*. By contrast, the theory of symbolism is quite developed in the course on religion of 1906–7 (1907f). There we can find all the arguments that will be used to explain symbolism, except for the ontological one. As already suggested, Durkheim could have introduced it in section V of Chapter VII (together with the theory of collective *représentations*) to resolve the difficulties of a merely psychological explanation of symbolism.

We might still ask ourselves what elements enriched Durkheim's thought between 1899 and 1906? Here is a possible answer. At the end of section II of Chapter VII, Durkheim concentrates on an important historical example of the deification of society, namely, the French Revolution. A point of reference is the work by Albert Mathiez (1904).[13] Durkheim must surely have known it since it explicitly refers to the innovative definition of religion he gave in 1899. Such definition allowed Mathiez to appreciate the religious nature of revolutionary cults. However, Mathiez extended it to other characteristics of religious phenomena. He mentioned 'the general overexcitement of sensibility' which accompanies their formation, as well as the immediate crystallization of beliefs 'into material objects, symbols, which are at the same time signs of gathering for believers and kinds of talismans' (1904:12). The idea is the same as Durkheim's. Moreover, Mathiez's formulation is similar to the one given by Durkheim in the course of 1906–7 (Mathiez 1904:29): Revolutionary symbolism was formed 'as by chance ... with a remarkable spontaneity', choosing 'the emblems most suitable to show their hopes and to serve as signs of gathering' (1907f/1975b, 2:100). There was 'the need for a sign of gathering', that the clan 'had to create spontaneously, urged by a sort of immediate need' (ibid). When giving, in *The Elementary Forms*, the preliminary definition of religion, Durkheim seemed to have left aside Mathiez's suggestions. However, they may have induced him to re-evaluate in Book II the religious and social function of symbols.

We can conclude our analysis by broadening the context further and connecting the theory of symbolism with another theme of Durkheim's sociology, namely the definition of social facts. This procedure is apparent in section V. In it, after trying to explain the origin of symbols, Durkheim cites *The Rules* to assert that the objectivity of symbols is the visible illustration of the exteriority that defines social facts (331/231). Our analysis of the theory of symbolism confirms that there is a close relation on this point between the two works. The relationship between social life and social facts is described in Chapter II of *The Rules* using the same terms that Durkheim later employed in formulating the oppositions between society and symbols in Chapter VII of Book II (as seen above). As to the dichotomy internal/external, we simply refer to the passage from *Les Formes élémentaires*, which has just been cited. The other dichotomies are not less documented:

(1) complex/simple. 'Its [sociology's] facts are perhaps more difficult to interpret because they are more complex, but they are more readily accessible (*faciles à atteindre*)' (Durkheim 1895a/1901c:39/t.1982a:72).

(2) invisible/visible. 'Social life may possibly be merely the development of certain notions, but even if this is assumed to be the case, these notions are not revealed to us immediately. They cannot therefore be attained directly, but only through the real phenomena (*réalité phénoménale*) that express them' (ibid.:36/69–70).

(3) fleeting/permanent. 'Thus social life consists of free-ranging forces (*libres courants*) which are in a constant process of change and which the observer's scrutinising gaze does not succeed in fixing mentally . . . Yet we do know that social reality possesses the property of crystallising without changing its nature' (ibid.:56/82).

Social reality derives from the dialectic of the terms of the oppositions, between social life on the one hand and social facts (as in *The Rules*), or symbols (as in *The Elementary Forms)* on the other. An equivalence between symbols and social facts seems to follow. So how should we interpret it? Are symbols included in social facts or vice versa? We do not need to comment on the obvious fact that symbols *are* social facts, that is, they are objects for sociological observation. But not so obvious is the other possible sense of the equivalence, according to which social facts would be symbols, in the exact meaning of the word symbol, given by *The Elementary Forms*. Nevertheless, their features are the same: social facts are external, objective, concrete. Although they are not strictly individual entities, that is things, they must be dealt with 'as things' (*comme des choses*) (ibid.:20/60). Yet, for whom are they symbols? There is only one possible answer: for the sociologist. To compare scientific research to the procedures of the symbolic transfiguration of reality may seem a paradox. Nevertheless, Durkheim constantly asserts that even scientific objectivity derives from society, of which symbols are in their turn a necessary condition. The perception of social facts contributes to the formation of society in the same way as does the perception of a symbol. As is well known, correct sociological observation does not have for Durkheim a purely speculative function, but an essentially practical purpose. The understanding of society through the study of social facts represents a moment of awareness, therefore, an increase in the cohesion of society itself. The assumption on which our analysis is based (see section above, The lexicon) seems therefore to be twice confirmed: not only is it the case that symbols in their proper meaning cannot be reduced to *représentations*, but also, scientific (or at least sociological) *représentations* are not possible without resorting to symbolism (see section II). The sociologist's job, in terms of Chapter VII, thus appears to be a sort of modern cult of images, another way of representing society – 'that fleeting reality which the human mind will perhaps never grasp completely' (ibid.:58/83) – accompanied perhaps by less effervescence and more awareness.

Notes

1 My grateful thanks to Paola Volante, who patiently helped with the translation from the Italian.

2 I follow, in general, Swain's translation of *Les Formes élémentaires* (rather than Fields' more recent and freer translation) in which I have made a number of necessary changes.

3 This argument, with its over-hasty explanation for the animal form of the totem, is weak, as was thoroughly proved by Van Gennep (1920:79–81).

4 *Durkheim e il problema dell'oggettività. Una lettura filosofica delle Forme elementari della vita religiosa* (forthcoming).

5 See 319 n.1. About the relationship man/nature, 'We undoubtedly have a different conception of this unity and relationship than the primitive, but beneath different symbols, the truth affirmed by us and by them is the same.' Again, a collective *représentation* 'could not be completely inadequate to its object. Without doubt, it can express this object through imperfect symbols; but even scientific symbols are never more than approximate' (625/438).

6 'The interpretation of all phenomena in terms of matter, motion and force is nothing more than the reduction of our complex symbols of thought to the simplest symbols; and when the equation has been brought to its lowest terms, the symbols remain symbols still' (Spencer 1862, II, Ch. XXIV:194).

7 See pp. 294, 315, 325, 326, 328, 332, 338; see 175–6, Durkheim 1907f:97.

8 (315) 'The soldier who dies for his flag'; (325) 'We know what the flag is for the soldier'; (326) 'the soldier who falls while defending his flag'. But on this subject see Mergy 1996.

9 It cannot be touched, damaged, moved without a ritual procedure, it must be saluted, etc. See Firth 1973.

10 In the French army, for instance, according to the rule of Napoleon I, even to the present day, the different corps (battalions, regiments) must have a force of at least 1,200 soldiers to have the right to a flag.

11 Durkheim quotes *La Psychologie des sentiments* in his sympathetic analysis of another work by Ribot, *La Logique des sentiments*.

12 This pertains to the definition of social facts as a result of association (see the excellent analysis by Borlandi 1995): the reading of II, 7 confirms Borlandi's suggestion of a strong continuity in the definition of social facts in Durkheim's thought following the *Rules*.

13 Mathiez's book was analysed in *L'Année sociologique* by Mauss in 1905.

7

DURKHEIM AND SACRED IDENTITY

Kenneth Thompson

Introduction

This chapter argues that it is possible to read Durkheim's *The Elementary Forms of Religious Life* as a contribution to a general theory of ideology. It can be seen as sketching out processes of symbolization and imaginary *représentations* of the underlying social relations into which individuals are inducted. However, when we turn from the general theory of ideology to the analysis of particular ideologies in modern social formations, we have to engage in some imaginative elaboration of ideas that are only briefly or implicitly touched upon in *The Elementary Forms*. In particular, Durkheim's ideas on such signifying forms and practices as clan, totem, soul and tattooing will be examined.

Durkheim's sociologism and his theory of ideology

The ethnography of Durkheim's *The Elementary Forms of Religious Life* was criticized from an early stage, but that was the least original part of the book. What was more controversial was the alleged extreme 'sociologism' of its main theses, which was a criticism levelled at his earlier works. To the Catholic Simon Deploige, writing in the *Revue néo-scolastique* in 1907, Durkheim's sociologism derived from German social realism. To which Durkheim replied that the characteristics that Deploige criticized were derived not from German thought but from his reading in 1895 of Robertson Smith's work. To the Protestant Gaston Richard, Durkheim's alleged sociologism lay in his denial of the freedom and contribution of the individual. In general terms, by referring to his sociologism the critics implied that Durkheim was claiming an epistemological and methodological monopoly for his sociological analysis of the most fundamental features of human and social life, including religion and knowledge itself. To his supporters, his sociologism was radical but justifiable. According to Bouglé, in his Preface to the collection of Durkheim's articles entitled, *Sociology and Philosophy* (Durkheim 1924a/t. 1953b),

As Durkheim developed his researches, he saw that they not only led to a better understanding of the role and value of this or that particular moral rule or discipline but also to a new conception of the relations of mind, and even reason, with nature. An explanation of the dualism which is the particular characteristic of human kind began to take shape in his mind. Durkheim was not content to leave half-glimpsed the general conclusions to which he was moving, and thus was born what is nowadays often called 'sociologism': a philosophical attempt, that is, to crown the objective, comparative and specialized studies of sociologists with a theory of the human spirit.

(Bouglé, in Durkheim 1924a/t.1953b:xxxvi–xxxvii)

The articles which were reprinted in *Sociology and Philosophy* first came out in the *Revue de Métaphysique et de Morale* and the *Bulletin de la Société française de philosophie*. They are Durkheim's defence against criticisms of his sociologism and appeared before the publication of *The Elementary Forms* – a book which did not dispel the criticims. As Bouglé explained, the articles 'help to resolve a certain number of ambiguities to which the tendencies of this sociologism have been prone ... and show how it might be distinguished from materialism, organicism and social utilitarianism' (ibid.:xxxvii).

There is no doubt that in his earlier works Durkheim took pleasure in insisting upon the close relationship that appeared between the beliefs and the actual form of their social milieu. According to the size of groups, the density and mobility of the component individuals vary, the relationship between the collective and the individual minds varies and the beliefs which the former sanctify become less effective and finish by giving place to the cult of individualism. Thus 'social morphology' helps us to understand this process of evolution. Once formed, collective *représentations* combine, attract and repel each other according to their own particular psychological laws. Durkheim is very concerned to point out that men's religious ideas, and all the more their scientific notions, are very far from being simple reflections of the social forms themselves. He was thus very far from wishing to impose upon sociology explanations of a materialistic tendency.

(Bouglé in ibid.:xxxvii–xxxviii).

However, it can be argued that it is Durkheim's daring sociologism in *The Elementary Forms*, which accounts for the book's relevance to contemporary debates, particularly with respect to current discussions of cultural identity in late modernity (Hall 1992:274). The fruitfulness of this particular sociologism lies in the combination of social determinism with a space reserved for some autonomy and even causal significance for cultural factors. Similarly, with respect to methodology, *The Elementary Forms* suggests that the most fruitful combination might be one which combines social morphological analysis with a cultural structuralism. But it must be admitted that it was the claimed structural-functionalist character of *The Elementary Forms* that brought the book into prominence in post-war sociology.

As I have argued elsewhere, there are different views about which aspects of the theoretical legacy from *The Elementary Forms* have been most influential in sociology, particularly with respect to the analysis of ideologies (Thompson 1986:31). To some extent the different views reflect judgements concerned with placing more emphasis either on Durkheim's functionalism, or on his embryonic cultural structuralism, later to be developed by Lévi-Strauss and other structuralists. The neo-Durkheimian functionalism, exemplified in the works of Talcott Parsons, suggested that the routinized features of society express motivational commitments that people have internalized through socialization and that the norms which govern behaviour are an expression of shared values and beliefs (the collective *conscience*). By contrast, structuralism sought to delve below the surface phenomena of social life to discover underlying relations whereby it is ordered, in a way similar to that in which combinatory elements are uncovered in linguistics.

Both perspectives can claim to develop central insights derived from *The Elementary Forms*. The functionalist line of development has generated studies of boundary-maintenance through which ideological communities preserve their unity by defining deviance from normative behaviour and mobilizing negative sanctions against such negative behaviour. The study of the Salem witch trials by Kai Erikson provides a good illustration of this (Erikson 1966). In contrast, structuralism has developed the idea of social classification within symbolic codes, as in the work of Mary Douglas on purity and pollution (Douglas 1966), and has extended the idea of decoding to all kinds of symbolic *représentation*, giving rise to the semiological studies of Barthes and others (Barthes 1967; 1972). And although Althusser rejected the label of structuralism for his approach, it is possible to draw parallels between Durkheim's discussion of how religious *représentations* position people and give them an identity and Althusser's thesis that 'all ideology has the function (which defines it) of constituting concrete individuals as subjects' (Althusser 1971:160).

Although Althusser's reputation has waned in recent years, there was a moment when his influence had some beneficial effects on sociology, if only in prompting interesting parallels between his analysis of ideology and the implications of similar elements in Durkheim's *The Elementary Forms* (Thompson 1986; Strawbridge 1982). Although the theory of religion in *The Elementary Forms* was based on studies of totemism in pre-industrial societies, Durkheim clearly intended it to have a wider applicability. Both Durkheim and Althusser portray ideology as a universal dimension of social life. This universality derives from the socially cohesive function of ideology, which provides a mythical or imaginary *représentation* of the underlying social structure or system of social relations. As both Durkheim and Althusser believed, it is not just a matter of a cognitive explanation of those relations, whereby this function will increasingly be taken over by social science to the detriment of ideology or religion. Rather, ideology acts in such a way as to reproduce the social order by symbolically representing it as a unity in which the individual subject has a place. At the same time the symbols operate so as to generate a sense of identification and commitment. Thus the individual is hailed or constructed as a subject within a symbolic discourse, and it is these symbolic discourses which constitute ideological or imaginary communities. The task of sociological analysis, therefore, is to decode the system of symbolic *représentations* (which are not free-floating, but embodied in material things and practices), and where possible to reveal their referents in the order of social relations.

This broad outline of a Durkheimian general theory of ideology, viewed as a universal social dimension, is adequate as far as it goes. It sketches out the processes of symbolization and the imaginary *représentations* of the real conditions of existence – the underlying social relations into which individuals are inducted, and which exist independently of our will. However, when we turn from the general theory of ideology in *The Elementary Forms* to the analysis of particular ideologies in modern social formations, we have to engage in some imaginative elaboration of ideas that are only briefly or implicitly touched on. In particular, it is interesting to examine Durkheim's ideas on such signifying forms and processes as clan, totem, soul and tattooing, with a view to applying these ideas to the analysis of equivalent phenomena in late-modernity or post-modernity. Although Durkheim's analyses in *The Elementary Forms* were in the main devoted to apparently unitary or 'elementary' social formations, there are some suggestions that the same analysis might be applied to modern social forms.

Clan, totem, soul

Debates about post-structuralism and post-modernity have in common concerns about fragmentation – social fragmentation deriving from threats to the unity and primacy of the nation state from such developments as multiculturalism and globalization; and fragmentation of personal identity. Durkheim's discussions of the clan, totemism, and personality in *The Elementary Forms* are directly relevant to these concerns.

Just as he chose to focus on totemism as the most elementary form of religion, so too Durkheim focuses on the clan because it is the form of society most dependent on symbolic *représentation* for its social construction and reproduction, rather than on political authority, territoriality, or consanguinity:

> Moreover, the clan is a society which is less able than any other to do without an emblem or symbol, for there is almost no other so lacking in consistency. The clan cannot be defined by its chief, for if central authority is not lacking, it is at least uncertain and unstable. Nor can it be defined by the territory it occupies ... Also, owing to the exogamic law, husband and wife must be of different totems ... Therefore we find representatives of a number of different clans in each family, and still more in each locality. The unity of the

group is evidently, therefore, only in the collective name borne by all the members, and in the equally collective emblem reproducing the object designated by this name. A clan is essentially a grouping of individuals who bear the same name and rally around the same sign. Take away the name and the sign which materializes it, and the clan is no longer even representable.

(333–4/232–3)

In other words, the clan is far from being a unitary, material-physical society. It is a social formation that depends heavily on the symbolic *représentation* of 'difference' from the Other(s). This makes Durkheim's analysis of it particularly instructive for sociologists studying contemporary social formations of late-modernity or post-modernity in which cultural distinctions are increasingly central, ranging from ethnicity to life-style groupings and 'affective communities' (cf. Hebdige 1989).

In addition to the signification of difference, intrinsic to symbolization associated with the clan, Durkheim's discussion of the soul in *The Elementary Forms* sheds some light on cultural processes involved in social reproduction. The reproduction of the clan beyond the life-spans of its individual members is then accounted for by members through a belief in the soul, which Durkheim in turn interprets through a kind of DNA theory of culture, or what he calls a 'germinative plasm':

In fine, the belief in the immortality of the soul is the only way in which men were then able to explain a fact which could not fail to attract their attention; this fact is the perpetuity of the life of the group. Individuals die, but the clan survives. So the forces which give it life must have the same perpetuity. Now these forces are the souls which animate individual bodies; for it is in them and through them that the group is realized. For this reason, it is necessary that they endure. It is even necessary that in enduring, they remain always the same; for, as the clan always keeps its characteristic appearance, the spiritual substance out of which it is made must be thought of as qualitatively invariable. Since it is always the same clan with the same totemic principle, it is necessary for the souls to be the same, for souls are only the totemic principle broken up and particularized. Thus there is something like a germinative plasm, of a mystic order, which is transmitted from generation to generation and which makes, or at least is believed to make, the spiritual unity of the clan through all time. And this belief, in spite of its symbolic character, is not without a certain objective truth.

(384–5/268–9)

Soul equals personality

Durkheim states that 'The idea of the soul was for a long time, and still is in part, the popular form of the idea of personality.' He then goes on, in a footnote, to anticipate modern conceptions of the divided self and fractured identity, insisting that this equation of the soul and the personality does not imply the unitary nature of personality:

> It may be objected perhaps that unity is the characteristic of the personality, while the soul has always been conceived as multiple, and as capable of dividing and subdividing itself almost to infinity. But we know today that the unity of the person is also made up of parts and that it, too, is capable of dividing and decomposing. Yet the notion of personality does not vanish simply because of the fact that we no longer think of it as a metaphysical and indivisible atom. It is the same with the popular conceptions of personality which have found their expression in the idea of the soul. These show that people have always felt that the human person does not have that absolute unity attributed to it by certain metaphysicians.
>
> (386 n.1/269–70 n.1)

This can be related to changing conceptions of identity. As Hall puts it:

> Three very different conceptions of identity can be distinguished in modern social theory: those of (a) Enlightenment subject, (b) sociological subject, and (c) post-modern subject. The Enlightenment subject was based on a conception of the human person as a fully centred, unified individual, endowed with the capacities of reason, consciousness and action, whose 'centre' consisted of an inner core which first emerged when the subject was born, and unfolded with it, whilst remaining essentially the same – continuous or 'identical' with itself – throughout the individual's existence. The essential centre of the self was a person's identity.
>
> (Hall 1992:275)

What we tend to regard as the typical sociological subject is mainly elaborated by symbolic interactionism. It is reflected in the growing complexity of the modern world and the awareness that the inner core of the subject is not autonomous and self-sufficient. It has been formed in relation to 'significant others', who mediate to the subject the values, meanings and symbols – the culture – of the worlds the subject inhabits. In this perspective, the subject still has an inner core or essence that is the 'real me', but this is formed and modified in a continuous dialogue with the cultural worlds 'outside' and the identities which they offer.

The post-modern subject, which in some ways was anticipated by Durkheim, is conceptualized as having no fixed, essential or permanent identity. Identity is formed and transformed continuously in relation to the ways we are represented or addressed in the cultural systems which surround us. It is historically, not biologically defined. The subject assumes different identities at different times; identities which are not unified around a coherent 'self'. In so far as there is a sense of a unified identity it is because we identify with certain socially derived narratives of the self and an ideology of individualism (including, in one version, the cult of the individual).

According to Durkheim, 'the notion of person is the product of two sorts of factors'. The first of these is impersonal (i.e. social): 'it is the spiritual principle serving as the soul of the group' and 'it is this that constitutes the very substance of individual souls'. It is in and through this that communicative consciousness is possible – it is the shared element. By contrast with this 'spiritual' constituent of the person, in order to have separate personalities there has to be a differentiating and individualizing factor. 'It is the body that plays this role' (386/270).

However, for Durkheim, 'not only is the individual contribution strictly confined to the corporeal, the phenomenal. In addition, this is an insignificant aspect of personality' (Lehmann 1993:113). The social soul 'may well take from the body the outward form in which it individualizes itself, but it owes nothing essential to it . . . Individuation is not the essential characteristic of the person' (388/271). Durkheim follows Kant in declaring the body not only secondary to the soul, but actually the enemy of the soul it houses. To do so, he renounces the individual aspect of personhood and constructs it as exclusively socially given:

> So it is not at all true that we are more personal as we are more individualized. The two terms are in no way synonymous: in one sense, they oppose more than they imply one another. Passion individualizes, yet it also enslaves. Our sensations are essentially individual; yet we are more truly persons the more we are freed from our senses and able to think and act with concepts. So those who insist upon all the social elements of the individual do not mean by that to deny or debase personhood. They merely refuse to confuse it with the fact of individuation.
>
> (389–90/272)

The final way in which Durkheim effects a mediation between social determinism and individualism is through his concept of the cult of the individual. Firstly, he reconciles the collective consciousness with individualism on the grounds that the two are not incompatible because individualism becomes the active content of the collective *conscience*. Thus individuals are merged, identified, and unified on the very basis of individual distinction, difference and autonomy. Individualism becomes the collectivizing religion (or ideology) of the modern, individualized collectivity:

> This is how it is possible, without contradiction, to be an individualist while asserting that the individual is a product of society rather than its cause. The reason is that individualism itself is a social product, like all moralities and all religions. The individual receives from society even the moral beliefs which deify him.
>
> (1898c/t.1969d:28 n.1)

Tattooing and body symbolism

The most elementary form of individual appropriation of collective symbolism discussed by Durkheim is that of tattooing. It is elementary because it seems to have made an 'early appearance without calculation or reflection', was produced 'almost automatically' and men were led by 'an instinctive tendency, as it were, to paint or cut upon the body, images that bear witness to their common existence' (332/232). However, as with sacred forms in general, Durkheim does not suggest that tattooing dies out in modern society. Not only was it widely used by the early Christians and then later by pilgrims in Italy, he also cites the example given by Lombroso in *L'Homme criminel* of members of an Italian college tattooing themselves before separating in order to record the time spent together. Other examples given are soldiers in the same barracks, sailors in the same boat, and prisoners in the same jail. 'Its object is not to represent or bring to mind a determined object, but to bear witness to the fact that a certain number of individuals participate in the same moral life' (333/232).

The resurgence of tattooing in modern society suggests that it continues to bear witness to a shared moral identity, where the moral life may be 'deviant' or be that of a minority. The reference to prisoners suggests that. Durkheim might have been interested to have found that there has even been a resurgence among similar groups to those he reported on. According to the *Independent* newspaper (11.6.95), 'One hundred years after vanishing, apparently for ever, the full facial tattoo of Maori men is making an unexpected reappearance in New Zealand, a sign of a resurgence of Maori consciousness ... Today, the sight of a young man with full *moko* in a busy street brings home the differences that have resurfaced in a country which, for a hundred years, convinced itself it was on the road to social and racial uniformity.'

Since the mid-1960s, it is said, tattooing has undergone what some have called a renaissance (Sanders 1988:401). The tattoo acts as more than simply what Goffman calls a 'mark of disaffiliation' (Goffman 1963:143–7). In some cases it symbolizes membership in subcultures (e.g. motorcyclists, youth gangs) centred around socially disvalued or law-violating interests and activities. The stigmatized social definition of tattooing and the negative responses tattooees commonly experience when 'normals' are aware of their stigma, may also precipitate identification with a subculture in which the tattoo is of primary significance. Within the tattoo community, consisting of those who positively define their unconventional mark, the tattoo acts as a source of 'mutual openness' (ibid.:131–9), providing opportunities for spontaneous appreciative interaction with others who are also tattooed (Sanders 1988:425; Goffman 1963:23–5).

Contemporary ethnographies of tattooees or 'body modifiers' (i.e. permanent modifications include tattooing, branding, scarification and piercing; temporary modifications include body painting, cosmetics, hair styling, costume, ornamentation) or intentional body marks 'serve as a sacred chronicle to the individual's spiritual commitment' (Myers 1992:295). As Victor

Turner aptly concluded, 'It is clear that the body, whether clad or unclad, painted or unpainted, smooth or scarred, is never religiously neutral: it is always and everywhere a complex signifier of spirit, society, self, and cosmos' (Turner 1967:274–5). Or as one American practititioner of genital piercing was quoted as saying:

> I know we are kin to those secret souls of so many cultures before. I know that this urge to pierce, to feel, to tattoo, to express with our very bodies in such primitive ways, is deep in the genetic memories, constant and strong as the tides. The chord it strikes resonates strongly for some of us, affecting our psyches, our spirits, our libidos.
>
> (Myers 1992:295)

Until recently it might have been assumed by sociologists that tattooing was simply part of a passing fashion, rather than a necessary aspect of religious culture or the stratification system. But, as Durkheim perceived, it is still the case that, for example among young men, tattooing is a mark of social membership within an urban 'tribe'. However, the sociology of the body and cultural analysis of body symbolism has been relatively underdeveloped in sociology until recently. It was left to anthropology to develop Durkheim's ideas. For example, the question of the body as a classificatory system has been fundamental to the anthropological vision of Mary Douglas (Douglas 1966). The central theme of her work is the human response to disorder, in which may be included risk, uncertainty and contradiction. The response to disorder takes the form of systematic classification: the creation of ordered categories which both explain disorder and restore order. And the principal medium of classification has been historically the human body itself (Turner 1991). Although Douglas does not provide an explicit explanation of why the body rather than some other alternative medium is the principal code, we may assume that she is following Durkheim's explanation that the body is the most ubiquitous, natural and unreflectively available source of allegories of order and disorder. Douglas was able to use the idea of the body's boundaries as a metaphor of the social system to explain a wide variety of cultural patterns (from Old Testament dietary rules to modern organizational behaviour) and, at the same time, she made the cultural analysis of the body a central issue in anthropological theory.

It may be that anthropology, rather than sociology, developed the theory of the body because in pre-modern societies the body is such an important surface on which the marks of social status, family position, tribal affiliation, gender and religious condition could most easily and publicly be displayed. Certainly, in pre-modern societies, the body was a more important and ubiquitous target for public symbolism, through such practices as tattooing, decoration and scarification (Polhemus 1978). The use of such body symbolism was also associated with the fact that in pre-modern societies status differences of an ascribed nature (e.g. between age cohorts and sexes) were both more rigid and more obvious. In modern societies, although there are still some rituals which employ the body as a mechanism to display a change in status, for example in degradation ceremonies (Garfinkel 1956), such ritualism is less prevalent or important. Bodily displays relating to status groups (dress, posture, cosmetics) are still crucial for indicating wealth and life-style, but it is not obvious how these would correspond to the sacred symbols of pre-modern societies. Nevertheless, it can be shown that in some cases in late-modern or post-modern social formations there are parallels. In order to make an argument for such a parallel it is necessary to re-examine the theoretical basis of Durkheim's use of the sacred–profane dichotomy.

Sacred and profane

Elsewhere I have proposed a neo-Durkheimian reconceptualization of the processes previously designated by the concept of secularization, stressing Durkheim's formulation of the binary opposition of the cultural principles of the sacred and profane, and the formation of symbolic communities (Thompson 1990). I suggest that the opposed principles and processes of sacralization and profanization (including mundanization) should be seen as in an ongoing dialectical relationship. The 'sacred' is that which is socially transcendent and gives a sense of fundamental identity based on likeness (kinship), constructed and sustained by difference or opposition over and against: (1) the alien Other (which may be another culture that threatens takeover or some other danger to the maintenance of its identity); (2) the mundane/profane i.e. the world of everyday routine, particularly economic activity and its rationality. Community (*Gemeinschaft*) is based on symbolic unity – it is an imagined likeness with limits or boundaries that separate it from a different, alien other. It contrasts with the functionally-specific relations and instrumental rationalities characteristic of societal associations (*Gesellschaft*).

My critique of secularization theories is that they too easily assume a continuing, long-term decline in the activity of the principles of community and the sacred as sources of identity. An alternative thesis would be that the tensions produced by modernity stimulate assertions of total identity grounded in experiences of the socially-transcendent produced by symbolic community. The symbolic community is held to be of ultimate or sacred significance because it sustains a sense of total identity, as opposed to the partial roles and fragmented identities produced by the processes of rational–functional differentiation of modern social systems. There is also the possibility that a symbolic community may not so much represent an attempt to resist fragmentation as provide an assertion of difference and opposition to integration into a whole in which a particular group would occupy a subordinate position.

Both these responses have been discerned, for example in the case of young Rastafarians in Britain, who adopted body symbols such as dreadlocks and the whole 'rude boy' style (see the interpretative analysis by Hebdige 1979). Perhaps the most important point to make here in relation to Durkheim's original discussion of clans and totems in *The Elementary Forms*, is that the

Rastafarian case reveals the multi-accentual character of symbols – that they can articulate a variety of meanings and positions, depending on how the elements are combined and accented. As Durkheim pointed out, symbols do not have fixed meanings. They operate as part of a chain or pattern of signifiers. Such a chain or pattern, as Durkheim explained, does not 'confine itself to translating into another language the material forms of society and its immediate vital necessities'. The ideas and images 'once born, obey laws all their own. They attract each other, repel each other, unite, divide themselves, and multiply without all these combinations being not commanded and necessitated by the condition of the underlying reality' (605/424).

The example of Rastafarian body symbolism can be connected with Durkheim's reason for choosing to focus on the clan and totemism, on the grounds that 'the clan is a society which is less able than any other to do without an emblem or symbol' and that cannot be 'defined by the territory it occupies'. In other words, it depends on symbolic *représentation* of difference from the Other. Further, it is related to the concept of living in a diaspora – of being related to diverse groups of people dispersed over space and not confined to a territory. The modern diasporas spawned by international migrations call into question the current significance given to national boundaries and definitions of citizenship – legal and cultural – in western nation-states. It is ironic that in Durkheim's own France, in recent times the apparent danger has come not from cultural division due to conflict between traditional religion (Catholicism) and civic ideals of the Revolution, as he implied, but from Islam and transnational multiculturalism. The recent furore over Muslim girls who wear scarves (or *chadors*) to school is emblematic of the fact that western nation-states are finding it increasingly difficult to construct culturally unified 'imagined communities'. This is perhaps the most urgent problem facing the west at the present *fin de siècle*. But it is Durkheim's own pioneering work on cultural analysis of clans, totems and body symbolism in *The Elementary Forms*, itself written as an attempt to grapple with problems presented at the *fin de siècle*, that offers some of the tools for analysing these developments. (It is, therefore, doubly ironic, that Meštrović's book claiming to re-apply Durkheim's ideas to the coming *fin de siècle* should have taken as its case-study the Catholic cult of the Virgin Mary in Yugoslavia, whilst confining its one reference to Bosnia-Herzegovina to the statement that it is predominantly Moslem and 'definitely pre-modern' (Meštrović 1988:152).)

Sacred identity and new social movements

One final area of theoretical development which could be claimed as an insufficently acknowledged descendant of Durkheim's pioneering work on symbolic processes and sacred identity, is the theory of new social movements (see especially the work of Alberto Melucci 1989 and 1996). Melucci claims that in the new social movements of contemporary society, 'collective action is focused on cultural codes, the form of the movement is itself a message, a symbolic challenge to the dominant codes' (1989:60). They bestow collective identity through collective emotional experience.

Contemporary movements assume the form of solidary networks entrusted with potent cultural meanings . . . Social movements too seem to shift their focus from class, race, and other more traditional political issues toward the cultural ground. In the last thirty years emerging social conflicts in complex societies have not expressed themselves through political action, but rather have raised cultural challenges to the dominant language, to the codes that organize information and shape social practice.

(Melucci 1996:4, 8)

In many ways they surpass instrumental action directed towards the state and constitute a sphere of symbolic activity and collective identity that is quasi-religious in the sense indicated by Durkheim in *The Elementary Forms*. Although ostensibly Durkheim took his understanding of such phenomena from ethnographies of cultures he felt were the most elementary – that of the Australian aborigines as described by Spencer and Gillen, that of the ancient Semites by Robertson Smith, and that of the contemporary Kabyle tribe of colonial Algeria by French researchers. Further, in the back of Durkheim's mind was the French Revolution, which he referred to several times as the prototypical example of a socially revivifying, effervescent movement imbued with an idealized (ideological) collective identity (300ff./210ff.). The Revolution demonstrates, he said, that the emotional essence of religion is not related to gods, or creeds, but rises out of spontaneous mass actions and the collective passions these generate (305ff./214ff.).

In this he was following the image of the revolutionary movement's enthusiasm propounded most notably by the great romantic historian Jules Michelet who, five years before Durkheim's death, wrote in a highly Durkheimian manner of revolutionary fervour overwhelming individuals and transporting them into transcendent realms of community.

There are no longer any mountains, rivers, or barriers between men. Their language is still dissimilar, but their words agree so well that they all seem to spring from the same place – from the same bosom. Everything has gravitated towards one point, and that point now speaks forth; it is the unanimous prayer from the heart of France. Such is the power of love. To attain unity, nothing could prove an impediment, no sacrifice was considered too dear.

(Michelet 1967:444)

The Elementary Forms was animated as much as Michelet's work by an implicit faith in the equalizing and energizing experience of symbolic community (Lindholme 1990:30). Participants feel a surge of renewed vitality when they are part of the ecstatic group. Each one is borne along by the rest. They feel themselves to be part of the larger truth of the timeless and potent community, which stands above the individual's limitations and morality, self-interest and personal weakness. Only the sharing of *communitas* can give an inner sense of higher purpose, and this is as necessary in the modern world as in the pre-modern:

> All that matters is to feel below the moral cold which reigns on the surface of our collective life the source of warmth that our societies bear in themselves.
>
> (Durkheim 1919b:104/t.1975a:187)

Durkheim located the new creative effervescence and new ideals as likely to arise within the working class movements. He told the Conference of Free Thinkers and Free Believers of 1913–14 that: 'One can go further and say with some precision that it is among the working classes (*les classes populaires*) in particular that these new forces are in the course of formation' (1919b/ t.1975a:187; cf. Pickering 1984:479–80). Of course, for a long time the labour movement spoke the language of the French Revolution and dreamed of a return to the community and solidarity of corporations. But these idealistic elements waned under the pressures of bureaucratization, consumerism, etc. The brief uprising of 1968 marked a watershed. Since that time the growth of new social movements has been discontinuous with the political tradition of the labour movement. Most of the revitalizing new social movements today are not class-based, but they are often concerned with symbolic community and identity that is sacred, because it transcends the mundane and separates itself from the profane Other. The most formidable of these are the ethnic movements which, combinining with cultural elements such as religion, language, custom and dress codes, expose the fragility of 'organic solidarity' based on civic and economic contractual ties. Globalization provokes localizations and particularizations of identity, rather than representing a progressive evolution from national patriotism to world patriotism and a dying out of ethnicity, as Durkheim predicted in *Professional Ethics and Civic Morals*:

> As we advance in evolution, we see the ideals men pursue breaking free of the local or ethnic conditions obtaining in a certain region of the world or a certain human group, and rising above all that is particular and so approaching the universal. We might say that the moral forces come to have a hierarchic order according to their degree of generality or diffusion.
>
> (1950a/t.1957a:74–5)

Durkheim's foundation of cultural analysis rested on his assertion that, once set in play, symbols are free to develop according to their own 'laws'. Hence, as ethnicity becomes more a 'symbolic ethnicity' (as Herbert Gans called it) and is not a reflection of morphological factors (whether territory or biology), it is more akin to the symbolically united 'totemic' clan as a sacred collective identity. It is to these social and symbolic formations of *fin de siècle* late modernity that the methods of Durkheim's 'religious sociology' should usefully be applied, rather than to an increasingly nebulous civil religion of the nation-state or a secularized 'cult of man'.

8

RESCUING DURKHEIM'S 'RITES' FROM THE SYMBOLIZING ANTHROPOLOGISTS

Malcolm Ruel

'Beliefs' and 'rites', Durkheim claims, are the 'two fundamental categories' by which religious phenomena are 'naturally arranged'. The distinction is indeed fundamental to both the arrangement and argument of *The Elementary Forms*. Beliefs are characterized as 'states of opinion', and consist in *représentations*, rites as 'specific modes of action' (50/36). Yet in the immensely important influence that Durkheim has exerted in the ensuing anthropological study of religion, this basic distinction has somehow become obscured so that *représentations* and modes of action have become merged in what has become the orthodox view of ritual whereby it is both defined and largely interpreted as symbolic action. Thus in a telling essay Asad opens his discussion with the assertion: 'Every ethnographer will probably recognise a ritual when he or she sees one, because ritual is (is it not?) symbolic activity as opposed to the instrumental behaviour of everyday life' (Asad 1993:55) and his confidence in posing the rhetorical question is extensively supported by the writings of anthropologists (e.g. Lienhardt 1961; Beattie 1966; Leach 1966; Turner 1967; Firth 1973; Lessa and Vogt 1979:220ff; and many others).

Two accounts need to be offered to elucidate this situation: the first to explain the process by which Durkheim's careful distinction has been in this way gradually subverted, the second to re-examine what is really entailed in Durkheim's treatment of rites as a distinctive category of religious fact, 'determined modes of action'.

I

The first account must start with Radcliffe-Brown who in seeking an explanation for those elements of Andamanese culture that interested him, notably their ceremonial customs, myths and legends, seized upon the method of sociological explanation being developed by Durkheim and his associates to provide what was essentially a functional account of prescribed cultural forms (see Radcliffe-Brown 1933: Preface and Chs V and VI). The very

particular reading that Radcliffe-Brown gave to Durkheim is apparent
in his definitive Henry Myers Lecture, 'Religion and Society' (reprinted in
Kuper 1977). Here he directs our attention away from 'the religions of other
peoples ... as systems of erroneous and illusory beliefs' (ibid.:103) and
suggests rather 'that in attempting to understand a religion it is on the rites
rather than on the beliefs that we should first concentrate our attention'
(ibid.:105). Drawing support on this point from Robertson Smith and the
significance of ritual in Chinese and other recorded ancestral cults, he turns
eventually to Durkheim and *The Elementary Forms*. He recognizes Durkheim's
aim 'to establish a general theory of the nature of religion' (ibid.:115) but
shortly adds 'it is not possible to discuss this general theory' (ibid.) and so
deals with only one part of Durkheim's work, 'his theory that religious ritual
is an expression of the unity of society and that its function is to "re-create"
the society or the social order by re-affirming and strengthening the sentiments on which the social solidarity and therefore the social order itself
depend' (ibid.). He then embarks upon his own revised account of Australian
totemism, which does not shy away from adducing notions implicit within
the ritual,[1] but which he uses to confirm Durkheim's theory:

> The two kinds of totemic cult are the demonstration, in symbolic
> action, of the structure of Australian society and its foundations in
> a mythical and sacred past. In maintaining the social cohesion and
> equilibrium, the religion plays a most important part. The religion
> is an intrinsic part of the constitution of the society.
>
> (ibid.:119)

One should not be misled by the reference to 'religion' in the last two
sentences, for what Radcliffe-Brown is referring to is in fact the totemic
ritual that he has been describing. The central thrust of his argument is
indeed to substitute ritual for religion, and then to treat ritual as though it
were religion. And this is effected by focusing upon the symbolism implicit
within (or adduced from) the ritual. Religion becomes ritual; ritual becomes
symbolic action (as in the quotation above); and 'beliefs' are side-lined, made
secondary to ritual, with religious 'doctrines' a special derivation, 'the result
of certain social developments in societies of complex structure'.[2]

By the time this Henry Myers lecture was given (1945) social anthropology in Britain had been established as an essentially empirical, fieldwork-
based study. Radcliffe-Brown himself asserted it as 'the natural science of
society' and although Malinowski's 'science of culture' was less rigorously
pursued as a positivist science, the structural-functionalist (or simple functionalist) orthodoxy rested upon basically behaviourialist assumptions. What
was important was what people actually did; the conclusions to be drawn
were to be the practical effects ('functions') of the observed patterns of behaviour (cf. Leach 1957). These assumptions lent further weight to the attention
given to ritual as something that could be directly observed – 'religion in
action' as Radcliffe-Brown called it. This in turn lent weight to the view
that gained wide acceptance that within religion rites are primary and beliefs

a secondary and variable derivation. Oddly, this view, although it was certainly Radcliffe-Brown's, has on occasion been ascribed to Durkheim.[3]

We have seen that the identification of ritual as symbolic action was clearly made by Radcliffe-Brown but it was not until social anthropology detached itself to some extent from its behavioural and positivist aims that the symbolist interpretation of ritual began fully to take hold. The movement from 'function' to 'meaning' can be dated to the late 1950s and 1960s, with John Beattie's *Other Cultures* as a significantly representative text. In this book, presented as an introduction to social anthropology (the first of a wave of introductory texts), Beattie gives carefully balanced weight to 'function' and 'meaning'. He is less radical than Evans-Pritchard, whose Marett Lecture a decade earlier had mounted a stronger attack on the positivist orthodoxy of Radcliffe-Brown, but by this time Evans-Pritchard's views appeared less heretical (as he himself was to note, 1962:46) and Beattie's pairing of 'meaning' with 'function' – the semantic with the instrumental – effected a kind of compromise. Meaning was 'in', but function was not excluded. It was on this basis that Beattie developed an elaborated account of ritual as symbolic action, 'expressive acts' misconceived by the actors as having causal effectiveness (1966; 1970). Around the same time Leach was asserting his own definitional distinction between ritual as expressive or communicative action versus instrumental action that seeks directly to secure an effect, so detaching ritual or the expressive aspect of behaviour completely from religion (and incidentally making it so general and abstract as to remove ritual from its empirical accessibility to become subject only to analytical account).[4]

Victor Turner stands as the writer who illustrates most forcefully this study of ritual as symbolic action–observable occasions to be analysed at all possible levels for their putative or adduced meaning. His contribution to the developing anthropology of religion has been immense, but it is also subject to the limitations of his time. Through his own academic mentor, Max Gluckman, Turner stood very much within the main anthropological tradition leading from Radcliffe-Brown and Durkheim.[5] His first book – his revised Ph.D. thesis – is an exemplary structural–functional study of Ndembu society, that records the importance of ritual within the society and gives an account of its function (to re-assert situationally the moral unity of persons and social groups fractured by structural conflicts and disunity) that was fundamental to all his later work, even that which took him into psychology and neuro-physiology.[6] We have an extraordinarily rich account of Ndembu rituals, coupled with a methodologically elaborated account of the way in which the symbolism of rituals can be analysed, but the account of anything that could be called Ndembu religion is perfunctory in the extreme – a page or so listing beliefs in an otiose high god, the existence of ancestor spirits or 'shades', the intrinsic efficacy of certain animal and vegetable substances and finally the power of witchcraft (Turner 1968:14–15). Yet Turner's description of the actual Ndembu rituals makes it clear how thoroughly implicated the ancestors are in the organization of the ritual cults and in the whole process of affliction and cure. If Ndembu religion focuses upon the achievement of wholeness (both social and personal) through a process of conflict and suffering, as Turner fleetingly suggests,[7] the ancestors, who have passed through this process and are the continuing cause of their descendants' afflictions, are integrally involved in the conceptual system that underpins the manifold rituals – beliefs that, *pace* Turner, are far from 'simple and, indeed, naïve' (cf. ibid.:15); however, these interconnections between idea and action, belief and ritual, are given no sustained attention by Turner, intent as he is throughout upon unpacking the 'meaning' of ritual symbols and adducing ever more diffuse accounts of what the performance of ritual effects. It is wholly characteristic that the one passage of Turner's early work that is concerned with religious ideas is a comparison of Ndembu insights with those of the Christian story, and that its theological interpretation as 'pure act-of-being' derives from the study of a single ritual (*Chihamba*) considered solely in terms of its integral symbolism (Turner 1962, reprinted 1975).[8]

II

A very different line of influence from Durkheim is evidenced in the work of E. E. Evans-Pritchard. His debt to Durkheim is plainly evident in *Nuer Religion* (1956), one of the first major monographs on religion by a British social anthropologist. During the time that this was published he was promoting the translation and publication of essays by Durkheim and his colleagues, and in his introduction to one of these volumes, he concluded on a personal note: 'I would, though with serious reservations, identify myself with the *Année* school if a choice had to be made and an intellectual allegiance to be declared', having already asserted (only four years after the publication of *Nuer Religion*) 'I am convinced that no field study of totemism has excelled Durkheim's analysis' (Evans-Pritchard 1960:24). Yet Evans-Pritchard puts Durkheim's sociological analysis to a very different use from that of the tradition stemming from Radcliffe-Brown. 'The problem of symbols' is one of the two problems that Evans-Pritchard identified as central to his account (the other being that of diversity in unity, 'the problem of the one and the many') and a named chapter is devoted to it (Evans-Pritchard 1956:Ch.V). Essentially, however, it is treated as a problem of Nuer conceptualization: 'What meaning are we to attach to Nuer statements that such-and-such a thing is *kwoth*, spirit?' (ibid.:123). His answer ('which is not . . . simple') follows Durkheim's insistence upon the social grounding of conceptual categories, that 'the conception of Spirit has . . . a social dimension' (ibid.:143) being 'refracted' by the social contexts of Nuer experience.

Evans-Pritchard draws here upon the first major section of Durkheim's treatment of religion in the *The Elementary Forms* – that which concerns beliefs, 'states of opinion, [which] consist in *représentations*'.[9] It is notable that when, in parallel with Durkheim, he comes to treat in the latter half of his book the major Nuer rite of sacrifice, Durkheim's theoretical influence is much less manifest.[10] The rite of sacrifice is presented as 'an enactment of their most fundamental religious conceptions' (ibid.:197), but the analysis is set within the context of the relationship of Nuer to God rather than their relationship to society. This is, of course, consistent with Evans-Pritchard's criticism of Durkheim, his 'serious reservations', that 'it was Durkheim and not the savage who made society into a god' (Evans-Pritchard 1956:313; cf. 1965:57, 63). It is also consistent with the dissatisfaction Evans-Pritchard felt at Durkheim's account of ritual, 'the central and most obscure part of Durkheim's thesis, and also the most unconvincing part of it' (Evans-Pritchard 1965:61).

If we reject (as did Evans-Pritchard) Radcliffe-Brown's reading of Durkheim, is there anything that we can draw from Durkheim's treatment of ritual that avoids the confusions of adducing symbols or *représentations* too readily from it? Two general points need to be made at the outset.

First, Durkheim's use of the term religious 'rites', his 'negative' or 'positive cult', is at once more general and less clearly delimited than the anthropological category of 'ritual'.[11] When he writes of a 'cult' he may refer to a set of formal prescriptions (thus in the negative cult) but he also uses the term more inclusively to include a cult as a congregation of worshippers as well as the object or being that they worship. Book III of *The Elementary Forms* is in effect concerned with the major classes of ritual (negative prescriptions, sacrifice, imitative rites, representative or commemorative rites) but its title, 'The Principal Ritual Attitudes', is more diffuse than that of Book II, 'The Elementary Beliefs', although it is intended no doubt to treat the fundamental classes of ritual action in the same way as Book II treats the fundamental categories of religious thought.

Second, and following on from the last point, Durkheim, unlike his nephew Marcel Mauss, was very much a systematic thinker, someone who assimilated a wide range of topics and findings to a single underlying argument. As Talcott Parsons has observed, he 'possessed to a remarkable degree the faculty of persistence in thinking through the consequences of a few fundamental assumptions' (Parsons 1937:302). These assumptions have often the character of a perception or intuitive understanding of a complex empirical fact. In the case of his work on religion, this fundamental assumption concerns the interdependence of social life and religious values or, in Durkheim's own terms, society and those *représentations* that define and sustain it. As Parsons himself discusses the point, the equation that Durkheim makes between society and religion is better expressed, not as 'religion is a social phenomenon' but as 'society is a religious phenomenon', so 'emphasizing not the material aspect of religion but the ideal aspect of society' (ibid.:427). Or, as Ernest Gellner has expressed in a comparable view, 'at the core of [Durkheim's] thought there lies not the doctrine of worshipping one's own society, but the doctrine that concepts are essentially social and that religion is the way in which society endows us with them and imposes their hold over us' (Gellner 1970:49).

It is, I would argue, entirely to misunderstand Durkheim's theoretical exploration of the relation between religion and society if one ignores the fact that he approaches this relationship first and foremost at the conceptual level. This is not to say that he treats religious ideas out of relation with religious (social) actions: he is very much concerned with their action setting. 'Religious ideas are ideas in relation to action, not merely to thought'

(Parsons 1937:431; the 'merely' is critical). But the primacy is still given to the religious ideas, 'beliefs', *représentations*.[12] To collapse Durkheim's equation into religion = symbolic action = ritual, as Radcliffe-Brown and his successors have done, is to miss the really significant perception that religious ideas are socially grounded, where these ideas are the expressed ideas of the actors, the members of that society, not the values, assumptions or symbolic 'meanings' that can be adduced for them.

The much used quotation from Durkheim, that 'social life, in all its aspects and in every period of its history, is made possible only by a vast symbolism' (331/231), needs to be understood in its own context. This is a consideration of the role of emblems – actual material *représentations* – in Australian totemism and thus potentially all religions. The emphasis is on the objectivity of the emblem, on its role in unifying diverse actors and in representing therefore collective sentiments:

> A clan is essentially a gathering of individuals who bear the same name and rally round the same sign. Take away the name and the sign which materializes it and the clan is no longer even representable. Since the group is possible only on this condition, one thus understands both the institution of the emblem and the part it takes in the life of the group.
>
> (334/233)

'Emblematic symbols' (as Durkheim describes them at one point) are actual objects or classes of object that serve to represent particular groups: they are not the free-floating 'integrative' cultural symbols that unify members of an ill-defined society.

Bearing in mind that it follows and does not precede Book II on 'The Elementary Beliefs', how then should we read Book III on 'The Principal Ritual Attitudes'?

The first point to make is that much of what Durkheim has to say in general terms about the function of cultic practices has already been said in Book II. Thus in his summary statement of why religion ceases to be 'an inexplicable hallucination', 'a fabric of errors', but is rather 'a system of ideas with which the individuals represent to themselves the society of which they are members ... ', he immediately goes on to add that the practices of the cult:

> are something more than movements without importance and gestures without efficacy. By the mere fact that their apparent function is to strengthen the bonds attaching the believer to his god, they at the same time really strengthen the bonds attaching the individual to the society of which he is a member.
>
> (323/226)

Much of Book III is then an elaboration of this basic argument in respect of the various classes of ritual (ritual proscriptions, sacrifice, imitative and commemorative rites, etc.) that Durkheim detects as presaged within Australian totemic practices and that are found in their fuller forms elsewhere. The procedure essentially parallels that of Book II, in which all recorded classes of religious belief can be seen as extensions of the totemic principle.

This assimilation in Book III of a variety of data and theoretical discussions to the general theme (including notably Robertson-Smith on sacrifice and Durkheim and Mauss' earlier discussion of primitive classification) has something of a portmanteau inclusiveness. There is an odd alternation between argument at the level of physical causality – for example, the consequences of the heightened emotionality of a crowd – and an insistence upon the importance of governing ideas – commonly, the consciousness that a group must have of its own identity. The tension between Durkheim's empiricist methodology and his epistemological concerns, that Parsons in particular has demonstrated (1937), is especially evident in this Book, not least in his derivation of the principle of causality from imitative rites. The psychologism of his argument at crucial points – that the performance of ritual *induces* certain attitudes or sentiments – has also rightly been much criticized.[13]

To turn to the more positive aspect of Durkheim's theory: in discussing the origins of the totemic principle he makes much play with the notion of force, even to the extent of identifying the two: 'totemism is the religion, not of such and such animals or men or images but of an anonymous and impersonal force ... This is what the totem really consists in: it is only the material form under which the imagination represents this immaterial substance, this energy diffused through all sorts of heterogeneous things, which alone is the real object of the cult' (269/188). This force, which is further identified with the idea of mana, is experienced as real and not merely metaphorical (270/190). It is a moral power (271/190), a power that Durkheim attaches to ritual actions as well as to religious ideas: 'When someone asks a native why he observes his rites, he replies that his ancestors always have observed them, and he ought to follow their example ... he feels himself morally obliged to act thus; he has the feeling that he is obeying an imperative, that he is fulfilling a duty' (271/190). The sacred as *the* religious idea is thus partnered by the rite as a category of action. The former is an imperative of thought, the latter of behaviour. Both are derived by Durkheim from the same imperative, the moral power of society:

> This is the original matter out of which have been constructed those beings of every sort which the religions of all times have consecrated and adored ... If the sun, moon and the stars have been adored, they have not owed this honour to their intrinsic nature or their distinctive properties ... If the souls of the dead have been the object of rites, it is not because they are believed to be made of some fluid and impalpable substance, nor is it because they resemble the shadow cast by a body ... [etc.] ... they have been invested with this dignity only in so far as they contained within them something of this same force, the source of all religiosity.
>
> (284–5/199–200)

The passage illustrates both the strength and the weakness of Durkheim's argument. Within any culture certain categories of thought and of action acquire a particular imperative and much of that imperative has the force of a social sanction. But is that their only force? And can they all be reduced to this one common element?

The first chapter of Book III, 'The Negative Cult and its Functions: The Aesthetic Rites', is that which carries forward most clearly Durkheim's central positive argument. Although doing so negatively, religious interdictions serve to define, to separate out, to categorize: 'the religious interdiction necessarily implies the notion of sacredness . . . In a word religious interdictions are categorical imperatives' (430/301). And the argument is carried forward to suggest the widespread significance of categorical oppositions that was to be much drawn upon by later anthropologists: 'There is no religion, and, consequently, no society which has not known and practised this division of time into two distinct parts, alternating with one another according to a law varying with the peoples and the civilizations' (440/308). The system of interdictions when applied to behaviour enforces an asceticism, a rejection of the profane that often implies an acceptance of suffering: 'In order to serve his gods, [the worshipper] must forget himself; to make for them a fitting place in his own life, he must sacrifice some of his own profane interests. The positive cult is possible only when a man is trained to renunciation, to abnegation, to detachment from self, and consequently to suffering' (451/316). Such asceticism does not serve religious ends only but is 'an integral part of all human culture' (452/316).

In treating the categorizing effects of the negative cult Durkheim refers to the need to distinguish two aspects of the sacred, 'the auspicious' and the 'inauspicious' sacred, and this polarization is taken up again at the very end of the last substantive chapter of Book III, 'Piacular Rites and the Ambiguity of the Notion of Sacredness'. Here is developed an account of the two kinds of 'religious forces', the pure and the impure, 'the beneficent guardians of the physical and moral order, dispensers of life and health and all the qualities that men value', versus 'the evil and impure powers, those productive of disorders, causes of death and sickness, instigators of sacrilege' (584f./409). The two classes oppose each other, yet they 'are not two separate classes, but two varieties of the same class, which includes all sacred things' (588/411). The point is developed from Robertson Smith and has an obvious and an illuminating relevance to many religions, but Durkheim's attempt to assimilate it to his general theory is far from satisfactory. The two aspects of the sacred, the 'propitious sacred' and the 'unpropitious sacred' are offered as *représentations* of the two different states of collective well-being and ill-being. But how can they be *représentations* when the actual situations themselves (the fact that they are 'well' or 'ill') must depend, by prior argument, on the recognition of certain common values? And while they may be said to oppose each other, do the two conditions not include certain substantive qualities – the totemic principle enshrining order, say, versus corpses and menstrual blood – that are more than merely formal opposites? And what, at this stage of the argument, do we make of an 'ambiguous sacred' when everything has previously depended upon its clear differentiation from the profane, the everyday. For all its empirical relevance, Durkheim faces a logical problem similar to the theological one of accounting for evil in the face of an all-powerful beneficent god, and his final sentences do little to resolve matters:

> However complex the outward manifestations of the religious life may be, at bottom it is one and simple. It responds everywhere to one and the same need, and it is everywhere derived from one and the same mental state. In all its forms, its object is to raise man above himself and to make him lead a life superior to that which he would lead, if he followed only his own individual whims: beliefs express this life in *représentations*; rites organize it and regulate its working.
>
> (592/414)

This easy appeal to a single unifying 'need' – orderly life in society – simply will not do. The difficulty is to draw out of Durkheim's all-encompassing argument that which is valid and that which is not.

Much hinges upon the way Durkheim uses the term 'sacred', which would seem at once to have a distinct empirical reference (those things that are especially revered, the gods, places or objects of worship) but which also operates as a logical category that mediates between religion and society, ready as it were to be the vehicle for the moral force of society. Religious beliefs are sacred ideas. Rites are actions accorded sacredness. What fits and is valuable in this formulation is the discriminating effect that the notion of sacredness entails. It is helpful to ask of any society or culture whether certain ideas – categories or names of beings, particular qualities or values – are 'set apart', to be distinguished from others. So similarly, we may ask whether certain types of activity, or actions, are subject to special prescription, institutionally enjoined, 'ritualized'. It may well be that the very ordering of a society, and of the values that the members of that society recognize, are dependent upon such a discrimination, such a categorization. But the question has to be open-ended, empirically answerable. Religions, for all their interpenetration with the societies in which they exist, focus upon different qualities, conditions or objects. The 'sacred' is not everywhere the same.

I have argued throughout this account that ritual cannot be treated independently from religious ideas (Durkheim's 'beliefs') and that to take Durkheim as doing so is to misunderstand him. I would add that the collapsed treatment of ritual as 'symbolic action' often leads to a situational and piece-meal interpretation of ritual that departs further from Durkheim's unifying view of religion ('a cosmology at the same time as it is a speculation upon divine things' (12/9). A religion, as he points out (57/41), cannot generally be reduced to one single cult but 'rather consists of a system of cults' (as is the case for Australian totemism). To 'rescue' Durkheim's contribution to the study of ritual one has to reassert his fundamental perception that rites are specially categorized actions – actions that carry a special significance

– that are given the moral force of prescription: they are the 'done things' inherited from the ancestors or the past, having been 'found to be good'. They carry thus, as Durkheim puts it, a 'religious force'. Beyond that, the attempt to formulate a more general 'theory of ritual' would seem unwise, despite Durkheim's intention to do just that. This does not mean to say that generalizations about ritual are impossible, but that they need to be related to the particular objects of ritual, its role within a religion, or the processes by which certain acts become ritualized. And for all those questions one has to focus upon particular societies or cultures, of whatever extension.

Notes

1 E.g. 'These rites imply a certain conception, which I think we can call specifically a religious conception, of the place of man in the universe' etc. (in Kuper 1977:117).
2 In Kuper 1977: 126, from the summarized points of the argument, where its general drift becomes plainly evident.
3 E.g. by La Fontaine (1985:21, 24). Pickering (1984:362–79) discusses at some length the issue of whether Durkheim accords primacy or parity to beliefs over ritual and comes to the conclusion that whereas 'Durkheim for a number of reasons wants to assert parity of status between ritual and belief, he secretly awards first prize to belief' adding that by belief one must understand *représentations*: 'So, if the first prize is given to *représentations*, ritual comes a close second' (ibid.:379). There is something very odd in the devaluing of Durkheim's attention to 'the elementary beliefs' when so much space is devoted to them in the *The Elementary Forms* and so much of Durkheim's argument is directed towards a sociological account of what he describes as the 'secondary subject of research: the genesis of the fundamental notions of thought or the categories' (639/v).
4 It is of course Leach's distinction that Asad picks up in the sentence quoted above p. 105, that nicely captures the assumptions that were at this time too easily made.
5 Turner makes passing acknowledgement to Durkheim throughout his work, referring, for example, to his 'Durkheimian background' (1985:121) or setting out in some detail how 'in many ways my methodology is Durkheimian' (1974:183).
6 The early formulation will be found in Turner 1957:316. Its development as a theory of liminality was first made in an essay (1967:IV) and this was later elaborated in *The Ritual Process* (1969). Its psychological and 'neurosociological' extensions are found in the posthumous collection of essays, *On the Edge of the Bush* (1985), that also has an informative biographical 'Prologue: from the Ndembu to Broadway', written by his wife, Edith Turner. The situationality of the early formulation, linked as it was to the notion of 'social dramas', was later re-stated in terms of regular process – the 'ritual process' whether social or psychological – but its reference remained circumstantial and empirical, focusing on what was to be observed and/or experienced.
7 'In the idiom of the rituals of affliction it is as though the Ndembu said: "It is only when a person is reduced to misery by misfortune, and repents him of the acts that caused him to be afflicted, that ritual expressing an underlying unity in diverse things may fittingly be enacted for him"' (Turner 1968:22).
8 Cf. Sperber's criticism of Turner for his 'cryptological' view of ritual symbols, based on the assumption that to reveal their 'hidden meaning' was to explain them (Sperber 1975:18ff).
9 'We are not asking what Spirit is but what is the Nuer conception of *kwoth*, which we translate "spirit". Since it is a conception that we are inquiring into,

our inquiry is an exploration of ideas. In the course of it we have found that whilst Nuer conceive of Spirit as creator and father in heaven they also think of it in many different representations (what I have called refractions of Spirit) in relation to social groups, categories, and persons' (Evans-Pritchard 1956:143).

10 Interestingly, however, it is still evident in Evans-Pritchard's descriptive classification of the rite and in identification of its piacular aspect.

11 This is in accord with the fundamental difference between Durkheim's category of social facts and the anthropological concern with the domain of customary behaviour or culture. The two categories certainly overlap, but where they do not there is a significant difference.

12 Both Parsons (1937) and Gellner (1970) are absolutely clear about this, as also is Pickering in his extended discussion of the same point, see note 3 above.

13 One needs to be clear about the grounds of such criticism. It is not that (following Durkheim's own methodology) social facts need to be explained sociologically, but that no *general* account of the effects of ritual is possible that ignores the variant cultures within which the ritual is performed and its possible variant effects for different classes of person within the one society. For example, Heald has shown the important psychological concomitants of Gisu initiation, but these relate to the special values of Gisu society and only to men (Heald 1989). A single ritual can have a very different significance for the different classes of participant actor (e.g. Nugteren 1995) and as Leach long ago pointed out, ritual can be as much a matter of discord as of unity (e.g., Platvoet 1995).

9

DURKHEIM'S BOURGEOIS THEORY OF SACRIFICE

Ivan Strenski

Two theories of sacrifice?

Years ago, Lukes observed how ragged the edges of Durkheim's thought sometimes were. Seams appear where one wanted smooth transitions, untidy threads dangle, and some things just never knit together at all. Durkheim's account of sacrifice in *The Elementary Forms of Religious Life* seems one of these rather badly stitched up items. Doubtless the best treatment of the genesis of Durkheim's thinking about the nature of religion in *The Elementary Forms* is still that of Robert Alun Jones (See Jones 1981:184–205; Jones and Vogt 1984:45–62). Of his many insights, I find the most intriguing is that *The Elementary Forms* advanced two theories of sacrifice, but the two theories are never knitted together. I want to devote my attention here to why Durkheim gradually accepted the theory worked out by Hubert and Mauss in their *Sacrifice: Its Nature and Function*. He thus abandoned a view which originated with William Robertson Smith. In doing so, I want to revise Jones' reading of *The Elementary Forms* as a conversation with Robertson Smith, and therefore, indirectly with the German liberal Protestant theologian, Albrecht Ritschl.

Sociologists have tried to discredit Jones' historical work because of their own theoretical interests. Jones has, I believe, been successful in undermining these attempts to de-historicize Durkheim's thought. My argument turns instead on whether Jones has got the historical context quite right. To wit, I believe that Jones has not given sufficient space to the background Durkheim shares with French Christian and Jewish religious liberals or modernists of his day, even though it was Jones himself who urged us to study such religious modernists (Jones and Vogt 1984:57). Accordingly, I believe we need to give more attention to Hubert and Mauss, partly because it is through them that the Catholic modernists, such as Loisy, as well as the great Indologist and Jewish modernist, Sylvain Lévi, exerted their influence on the development of Durkheimian thought about sacrifice and religion (ibid.:48–50; 55). While Durkheim undoubtedly 'converses' in his imagination with the likes of Robertson Smith, but less so (and I personally think not at all) with Albrecht Ritschl, he also inhabited a world in which religious liberalism had tremendous influence both in theological and political circles. It is just that world which I therefore would like to connect to the pages of *The Elementary Forms*.

Smith and Jones

Jones does not believe we can draw a direct line of influence from Ritschl to Robertson Smith to Durkheim. More 'typical', Jones says of Durkheim's relation to Robertson Smith, is its 'dialectical' character. 'Questions are posed and alternate answers critically evaluated, as the proper means to ultimate philosophical truths' (Jones 1981:185). Certain general features of Durkheim's approach to religion may be linked to Robertson Smith, for 'magic is opposed to religion as the individual is opposed to the social': the sacred is marked by ambiguity (ibid.:192) and 'contagiousness' (ibid.:185), totemism is connected to the celebration of a communion feast (ibid.), religion is conceived dynamogenically, as a locus of forces (Jones and Vogt 1984:47f.; 55), religion is really a practice, and therefore we should attend to its practices such as ritual and ethical behaviour, and to its pragmatic functions (ibid.:55). The spiritual life is at bottom simply the moral life: only within a social environment can our moral natures be realized (ibid.).

Robertson Smith, and initially Durkheim, saw the origins of sacrifice in a joyous alimentary, sacramental communion linked with totemism. In *The Elementary Forms*, Durkheim of course demonstrated this pattern from Australian ethnographic materials, but tellingly in Robertson Smith's methodological style of 'the one well-conducted experiment' (see Pickering 1984:68). As for the totemic aspect of sacrifice, Jones has noted how quickly controversy gathered round it. Numerous critics, among them Hubert and Mauss, variously sought to sever the links between alimentary communion, sacrifice and totemism. Such sacrifices, if they did occur, were either not accompanied by a communion meal, or were early in an evolutionary scheme (Jones 1981:191–6). Despite such objections by his closest confederates, Durkheim persisted in asserting that the *intichiuma* was a 'totemic sacrament and the evolutionary origin of sacrifice' (ibid.:196) long after it had been shown that no necessary connection prevailed between totemic belief and alimentary sacramental communion in Australia or elsewhere.

There is, however, another problem with making Robertson Smith the major source of Durkheim's thinking about religion.[1] Much of what is attributed to Robertson Smith can be found in Durkheim's review of Jean-Marie Guyau's *L'Irréligion de l'avenir* (1887b). There Durkheim upholds Guyau's affirmation that religion is a social fact (1887b/t.1975a:24), that it must be therefore studied sociologically (ibid.:33f.), and that sociability is the determining cause of religious sentiment (ibid.:35f.). Durkheim also praised Guyau for emphasizing the importance of ritual and practice in religious life (ibid.:26–7; 30f.) even if he felt Guyau was too intellectualist in these matters (ibid.:34f.). Finally, religion is above all a 'practical' affair, says Durkheim, like morality. In fact, religious prescriptions have an 'obligatory nature' and thus morality is at the heart of religion (ibid.:34).

All the religious modernists of Durkheim's day held positions Jones wishes to link exclusively with Ritschl and Robertson Smith. Both Jewish and Christian religious modernists stood for certain closely related fundamentals – the primacy of science and morality; non-theistic, impersonal conceptions of the focus of religious life; the belief in social evolution and the possibilities of progressive reform; religious pragmatism as against religious propositionalism, literalism and ritualism; and the adoption of symbolist modes of interpreting religious doctrines and scriptures (Strenski 1997:Ch.3). It is thus doubtful that we can lay those characteristics of religion, which Durkheim shared with his French religious modernist contemporaries, at the door of any one particular thinker – least of all Albrecht Ritschl, whose name never occurs in the entire Durkheim corpus. By contrast, the French religious modernists, Albert Réville, Jean Réville, Alfred Loisy, Auguste Sabatier, Louis Germain-Lévy, Salomon Reinach, Israel Lévi, Sylvain Lévi and the American Jewish liberal, Morris Jastrow, wrote articles and books that were reviewed and debated by the *équipe*. Indeed, the only reference I can find to Ritschl in works of the Durkheimian nucleus of Durkheim, Hubert and Mauss is in Mauss' 1904 criticism of Ritschl's reduction of religion to little more than, in Mauss' words, a 'tissu de sentiments mystérieux', making of him a German analogue to Auguste Sabatier – a figure whom the Durkheimians criticized (Mauss 1904/1968–9, 1:95). We also know that Durkheim was aware of positions adopted by religious liberals and modernists of his time, especially his conversation partners in the Société Française de Philosophie and in the Union pour la Vérité. And one cannot forget Durkheim's celebrated contribution to 'Le sentiment religieux à l'heure actuelle' where his address to the 'libres croyants' portion of the gathering was, in effect, his gospel to religious liberals (1919b). In the midst of these affinities, we should bear in mind of course that Durkheim was above all concerned to displace the religious modernists with his own *sociologie religieuse* (Strenski 1997). The Durkheimians were jealous of sharing the stage of social or religious reform with plausible competitors, such as the religious modernists; it is clear from their severe attacks on their chief competitor for the role of Robertson Smith's intellectual representative in France, Salomon Reinach (Hubert 1909). The Durkheimians even relished polemics with modernist religious thinkers in sympathy with their programme. In a letter of 1898, Hubert revealed how he delighted in the mischief his and Mauss' work on sacrifice would cause the religious powers of the day. Writing to Mauss, Hubert said:

> . . . we are condemned, my dear fellow, to make religious polemics. We shouldn't miss a chance to make trouble for these good, but badly informed, souls. Let's stress the direction of our work, let's attend to our conclusions – so that they be pointed, sharp like a razor, and so that they be treacherous. Let's go! I do love a battle! That's what excites us![2]

With attitudes like these, plus their own ambivalences as 'scientists' or ideologues for a new *morale*, it is small wonder the Durkheimians tried to keep religious modernists at arm's length. In terms of sacrifice, this meant that although Durkheim considered, and in part accepted, some of Robertson Smith's views about sacrifice, he did not accept all of them.

Hubert, Mauss and Sylvain Lévi

Thus I want to argue that instead of focusing on Durkheim and Robertson Smith, we ought to cast an eye at the positions Durkheim was *beginning* to take on sacrifice in *The Elementary Forms*. Why not see what new 'fabric' Durkheim was beginning to stitch, however imperfectly, to the older, badly worn cloth in which he had up until that time wrapped himself? Instead, therefore, of assuming the overriding importance of Robertson Smith's thought about sacrifice, why not pursue the sources of key notions such as sacrifice in the larger religious modernist context to which Jones frequently and rightly refers? I suggest then that we need to shift attention from what may in fact have been a nearsighted ethnographic focus on totemism (because of the desire to link Durkheim with Robertson Smith), and recapture more of Durkheim's own farsighted sociological priorities in *The Elementary Forms*. There Durkheim, while registering his interest in totemism, actually distances himself from it in the interests of a general sociological programme. Thus he justifies the study of totemism as casting light on man in general and more specifically on 'the man of to-day, for there is none whom we are more interested in knowing well' (2/3). Then allaying fears that he has strayed into primitivist exotica by taking up with totemism and primitive religion, Durkheim adds that he is not going to study a very archaic religion 'simply for the pleasure of telling its peculiarities and its singularities'. Rather, Durkheim promises to keep faith with his interests in the big sociological issues:

> If we have taken it [totemism] as the subject of our research, it is because it has seemed to us better suited than any other to lead to an understanding of the religious nature of man, that is to say, to show us an essential and permanent aspect of humanity.
>
> (ibid.)

Let me put my case positively first by proposing a re-reading of the crucial second chapter of Book III of *The Elementary Forms*. I believe the whole of *The Elementary Forms* must be read as a treatise on the sacred, which is to say as well, a treatise on society. *The Elementary Forms* is both about the social aspect of religion and the religious aspects of society. For Durkheim, there is no sacredness, no sense of obligation, no respect, no authority, no energizing force moving human beings to concerted action, outside the force generated by society. So also there is no society without a sense of sacredness – of boundaries, moral force, proscriptions, inspiring ideals, respect and so on.

This interest in the social and sacred is why, I submit, Durkheim devoted the bulk of the discussion of the positive cult of Chapter II of Book III to developing the idea that sacrifice sustains the gods, rather than, as Robertson

Smith would have it, the other way round. If sacrifice literally makes the gods, it in effect produces the sacred. Here it is worth looking more closely where Durkheim really stands in Chapter II of Book III on whether sacrifice *creates* the sacred or whether the sacred is a natural and pre-existent condition of certain things which sacrifice only revives (481/337; see Jones 1981:197f.). Regarding the *Intichiuma*, Durkheim indeed broadly takes up Robertson Smith's view of sacrifice as alimentary communion, and not as a ceremony of renunciation (481/337). Accordingly Durkheim says, as Jones rightly notes, first in killing and eating the totemic animal, the devotees communicate with the 'sacred principle residing in it' (ibid.). Or, they fulfil the 'object of this communion' by seeking 'periodically to revivify the totemic principle which is in them [the totemic animals]' (482/338). Both these imply that the sacrificial victim is already sacred, although it needs to be revived from time to time.

Now, I think Durkheim is far less firm on whether the sacred is in things already or whether it needs to be produced. In the conclusion of the very paragraph in which he declares the pre-existence of the sacred, Durkheim tellingly adds in respect to the *Intichiuma*: 'the only difference we find here is that the animal is naturally sacred while it *ordinarily* acquires this character artificially in the course of sacrifice' (482/337. Our emphasis). Here, therefore, is an exception which proves the rule. Durkheim in fact accepts the position of Hubert and Mauss as to what '*ordinarily*' prevails. It is sacrifice which makes the sacred – not the other way round, as in the exceptional case of the *Intichiuma*, as related by Robertson Smith, where the sacred totemic principle already resides in the victim.

But this is not even the gravest difference between Durkheim and Robertson Smith on the nature of sacrifice and its relation to society and the sacred. Indeed, as Jones himself freely admits, on various points the position articulated by Durkheim directly opposed what Robertson Smith believed about sacrifice. My claim is that these are differences so fundamental to Durkheimian thought that it makes little sense casting them constantly in the light of a conversation with Robertson Smith. I have in mind a view internally related to the issue of the creation or prior existence of the sacred. Indeed, in some sense, it is the same point seen from another perspective. It is crucial to Durkheimian thought that sacrifice makes and sustains the gods. This means, it can be argued, not only that *ritual* sacrifice is prior to a *belief* in the existence or *mythology* of the gods, but that sacrifice has a prior existence to that of the gods. It actually causes the gods or the sacred to exist. Durkheimian ritualism is simply another way of expressing Durkheimian sociologism, since in Durkheim's time rituals were understood to be pre-eminently social.

There is no other way to make sense of the claims made in Chapter II of Book III than to assume that Durkheim actually departs from Robertson Smith's position. First, sacrifice does not entail the presumed existence of a personal divinity, but is 'independent of the varying forms in which religious forces are conceived' (551/385). Second, the gods depend on men, such as by being fed through the offering of food in sacrifice: they are sacred only because men believe in them (551/386). This dependence of the gods upon men, covering a whole range of activities, is linked by Durkheim directly with a critique of Robertson Smith – the gods would die without their cult (555/388). Durkheim notes that linking the religious with social dynamics means that the gods cannot do without worshippers any more than society without individuals (555–6/388–9). And, as we all know, the gods need worshippers and sacrifice, because the reality of the gods *is*, for Durkheim, society. If then it is the case that Durkheim's position on so fundamental a matter as the role of sacrifice in relation to the existence, creation or pre-existence of the sacred cannot be likened to that of Robertson Smith, then we must inquire elsewhere, outside of the context of conversation with Robertson Smith.

More on the context of *The Elementary Forms*

The context just referred to can be supplied by reference to the studies Hubert and Mauss were making in preparation for the publication of their rightly famous *Sacrifice: Its Nature and Function*. Indeed, in re-reading Book III, Chapter II of *The Elementary Forms* in the light of their essay, it is tempting to say that Durkheim is really in conversation with them and the traditions of scholarship which they represented, just as much as he was in dialectic relation with the writings of Robertson Smith. This then means that Durkheim was, in effect, in conversation with Sylvain Lévi, a distinguished Jewish scholar and a religious modernist.

Mauss referred to Sylvain Lévi as his 'second uncle' (Mauss 1935:537) and 'guru', and with good reason. Mauss credits Lévi for giving him a completely 'new direction' to his 'career' (ibid.:535; 537). By any standard, Sylvain Lévi (1863–1935) was one of the most distinguished Indologists of his day.[3] Encouraged by Ernest Renan, himself a former student of the Indologist, Eugène Burnouf, to take up Indology, Lévi eventually succeeded Bergaigne in the chair of Sanskrit at the Ecole Pratique des Hautes Etudes, Fifth Section. By 1894, he was elevated to the Collège de France in Sanskrit Language and Literature, where he continued until 1935 (see Strenski 1997:Ch.5). In 1896, after having worked with Durkheim in Bordeaux, Mauss moved to Paris to study Indology and to do his doctorate with Lévi on prayer as an oral ritual. His influence on Mauss seems significant either as a source of certain notions or as someone who confirmed trends already under way among the Durkheimians. I believe that Sylvain Lévi had much to do with the development of the late Durkheimian concept of the sacred as positive, impersonal and material, which I have just discussed. For Sylvain Lévi as for the Durkheimians, this sacred was at once radiant with the highest ideals of the society from which it was born and bound to actual ritual performance. As Mauss said in his studies with Henri Hubert and Sylvain Lévi: 'the ultimate aim of our researches (is) the sacred'; it was also the 'highest reward of our work on sacrifice' (Mauss 1900b:293–5).

Also, as early as 1892, Sylvain Lévi decided on a social approach to religion, which was as much as four years before he met Mauss. Against the prevailing psychological and theological trends of thought dominating the Fifth Section, Lévi pressed strongly for a social approach as the methodological principle for studying religion in general. As Sylvain Lévi says 'history of the church is therefore the necessary introduction to the study of religion; it is the centre around which gravitates or from which radiates the active imagination of the faithful' (Lévi 1892). By this route, Lévi seems to have formed or at least confirmed Mauss' devotion to the collective, concrete and embodied approach to religion, which by 1896 was typical of the Durkheimians. Sylvain Lévi's emphasis on the collective and concrete were congenial to the Durkheimian agenda for the study of religion in at least two other ways – the study of ritual and the idea of the sacred.

When Mauss arrived to study in the Fifth Section in 1896, Durkheim's *équipe* was a year or so from being formed, and plans for *L'Année sociologique* were just being made from Durkheim's provincial post in Bordeaux. Moreover, in 1896, Sylvain Lévi was doubtless in the midst of researching and perhaps writing his classic of two years hence, *La Doctrine du sacrifice dans les Brâhmanas* (1898). In commenting on their own work on sacrifice, Hubert and Mauss mention Lévi's masterpiece of Indology, *La Doctrine du sacrifice dans les Brâhmanas* saying that 'we have greatly drawn upon it' (Mauss 1900b:293–5). Mauss further elaborates this in commenting on Lévi's course on the Brâhmanas.

> [It] was personally destined for me. His *Idée du sacrifice dans les Brâhmanas* – his chief work – had been made for me. From its first words, it delighted me with a decisive discovery: 'the entry into the world of the gods'; there, right under our noses, was the starting point of the labours which Hubert and I realized in *Sacrifice*. We were only bearing witness.
>
> (Mauss 1935)

The sacred was thus far from being what it was for the religious liberals of the day – an idea or private mental state. It was instead something one might even call palpable, material and bodily. 'Electricity' is how Sylvain Lévi spoke of it. Citing Lévi with approval, Mauss agreed that sacrifice and the forces it liberated were socially embodied. Sacrifice thus 'was a mechanical action, which acts by means of its own deep-seated energy. It has its abode in the act, and finishes with the act' (Mauss 1900b:353).

Lévi's interpretation of sacrificial ritual could also contribute to the positive and non-theistic idea of the sacred – an idea subsequently made famous by the Durkheimians (Lévi 1898:293–5). In particular, he showed how Vedic and Brahmanic sacrifice assumed that ritual itself actually produced the gods. This meant, first of all, that the definition of religion could be separated from a belief in the existence or even the idea of God.[4] So potent is the sacrifice, that even if gods are relevant, those very gods are 'born' of sacrifice, are 'products' of it. Behind the figure of Prajâpati, a major Hindu creation deity, is the sacrifice: 'Prajâpati, the sacrifice is the father of the gods ... and its son'.[5] Further, instead of the idea of the gods defining religion, the notion of an impersonal sacred power behind the gods and empowering them took over. For Sylvain Lévi, this power – the *brahman* of Indian thought – is a property of sacrificial ritual itself. It is an 'impalpable and irresistible power which is released . . . like electricity'. As with Hubert and Mauss' notion of the sacred as dangerous, Lévi reports that 'the force of sacrifice, once released, acts blindly; he who does not know how to tame it is broken by it' (ibid.:77).

But why did Durkheim think Lévi was right?

Having linked the thought of Lévi with Durkheim's view of sacrifice in *The Elementary Forms* via that of Hubert and Mauss, we are now in a position to deepen our understanding of this affinity by asking why Durkheim thought that Lévi was right.

At the outset we know that Durkheim's theoretical logic made it natural to embrace Sylvain Lévi's contention that sacrifice created and sustained the gods. Durkheim had always seen ritual as social. Thus, in so far as Durkheim pursued sociological explanation of religion in terms of the social, ritual would be well placed to play a major role. This is of course the same issue evident in Durkheim's indecision in Book III, Chapter II, to wit: whether the victim in sacrifice was already sacred, or was only made so by the sacrifice.

Now while Durkheim may already have been hospitable to 'causal ritualism', one cannot be sure that it appeared in his work before Hubert and Mauss' study on sacrifice of 1899. As early as his review of Guyau (1887b) – two full years before Robertson Smith's *Lectures on the Religion of the Semites* – Durkheim concurs with Guyau that ritual was a privileged mode of religious life: 'Cult is religion become visible and tangible' (Durkheim 1887b/t.1975a:26). But whether this implies that ritual sacrifice 'made the victim sacred', as Hubert and Mauss were to argue, is not clear. Yet, when Durkheim was ready to incorporate the causal ritualism of Hubert and Mauss, he had in Sylvain Lévi's work a factual basis for such a claim from a historian of religion of impeccable credentials. For this, one only had to turn to Buddhism and Brahmanism, the subjects of Lévi's special scholarly expertise. Note in particular Durkheim's citations of Lévi's teacher, Abel Bergaigne, and in particular the Vedicist's claim that:

> 'The sacrifice exercises a direct influence upon the celestial phenomena' says Bergaigne; it is all-powerful of itself, and without any divine influence . . . More than that 'the sacrifice is so fully the origin of things *par excellence*, that they have attributed to it not only the origin of man, but even that of the gods'.
>
> (47–8/34–5)

Further, why did Durkheim think he was right to rehabilitate the gift theory of sacrifice (as had Hubert and Mauss) and indeed to promote it over Robertson Smith's alimentary communion?

Part of an answer lies again in the requisites of Durkheim's theoretical logic. However, the stronger reason for Durkheim's resort to the modified gift theory of Hubert and Mauss can be found in Durkheim's participation in the political world-view of the bourgeois idealism of the neo-Kantian social ethics epitomized by Renouvier and Hamelin. Because it rests in good measure on individualist assumptions, exchange theory simply fits the bourgeois values which the Durkheimians themselves never surrendered despite their curiosity about the extremist politics and economics of their day. The reputation of the Durkheimians for societism and/or collectivism apart, their position on the relation of the individual to the group was, as we know, considerably nuanced. In 'Individualism and the Intellectuals' (1898c), Durkheim celebrated the sacredness of the individual, and in so doing recommended individualism. Yet we also know that Durkheim boosted individualism by brilliantly appealing to the social and traditional historical values of individualist Republican France. Philosophical rationalists close to Durkheim, like Octave Hamelin, also produced similar moral formulae. This long-standing good friend of Durkheim noted, for example, that the first duty we have to others is to ourselves. Put otherwise, Hamelin argued that in order to give of oneself one must first have a self to give. This is to say that although the philosophical rationalists whom Durkheim knew and admired were eager to assert the vital place of altruism in moral life, they, like him, also clung to profoundly bourgeois social values. They held fast to the sacredness of the human individual – just as Durkheim himself always did, even while developing his sociologism.

How then does Durkheim's rehabilitation of the gift exchange approach to sacrifice in Book III, Chapter II, fit against this backdrop? Quite simply, to the extent the sacredness of individuals is placed at the centre of social life we may expect exchange to appear as the typical way relationships are articulated and even created among people. This is so because to the extent individuals are sacred, they have ontological integrity and thus can be real actors. Exchange is one of the ways individuals may perform sacrifice. Much the same implication arises, if one views the relation of individualism and exchange theory in reverse. To the extent one thinks of human relations in terms of such transactions as exchange, one will think of the relations established as between and/or among individuals. This follows trivially from the fact that exchange requires an 'other' and assumes the plural parties in an exchange. This is precisely what we find in Hubert and Mauss' *Sacrifice: Its Nature and Function* and later in Mauss' *The Gift* where the sacredness of the individual is coordinated with the logic of sacrifice and gift. The victim protects the *sacrifier* and sacrificer from having to give up themselves; prudence in giving of oneself is encouraged, while the perfection of self-giving is viewed by Hubert and Mauss as an ideal, never reached but held up as a model. As if proposing a theory of sacrifice tailor-made for members of the bourgeoisie that they were, Hubert and Mauss say:

> In any sacrifice there is an act of abnegation since the *sacrifier* deprives himself and gives ... But this abnegation and submission are not

without their selfish aspect. The *sacrifier* gives up something of himself but does not give up himself. Prudently, he sets himself aside. This is because if he gives, it is partly to receive. Thus sacrifice shows itself in a dual light; it is a useful act and it is an obligation. Disinterestedness is mingled with self-interest.

(Hubert and Mauss 1899:135/t.1964:100)

Thus the Durkheimians are very far from the fantasies of communion and altruistic selflessness sometimes associated with them. They are socially attuned, but committed to the integrity of the individual at the same time.

So the seams along which Durkheimian thought is stitched together, and which we have exposed, stand out once more for all to see. What theorists will eventually make of this fact is a matter yet to be seen. As a historian of Durkheimian thought, I am more than satisfied for the moment to have understood how a significant part of one of the greatest books in the study of religion and culture was put together.

Notes

1   This point is missed, for example, by Margit Warburg in her article, 'William Robertson Smith and The Study of Religion' published in 1989 (*Religion*, 19:55). Warburg's shortcomings have been amply noted by Heinz Mürmel (1994).

2   Letter of Henri Hubert to Marcel Mauss, n.d. 1898. I thank Marcel Fournier for this citation. See also Marcel Fournier and Christine de Langle, 'Autour du sacrifice: lettres d'Emile Durkheim, J. G. Frazer, M. Mauss et E. B. Tylor', *Etudes durkheimiennes/Durkheim Studies*, 3, 1991:2–9.

3   Born in Paris of Alsatian parents, Lévi was educated in the rather conservative Jewish learning of the time. Although Lévi was poised to continue Jewish studies in Paris, he instead chose Oriental studies. Deciding upon an area specialty, however, proved to be more difficult. Sylvain Lévi sought the advice of Ernest Renan, himself a former *élève* of the Indologist, Eugene Burnouf. Renan had a special affinity for Indian studies, in no small part because he tended to follow German fashions of thought, one of which was the so-called 'Aryanist' movement. The Aryanists were not only great promoters of the glories of Indian civilization, but more insidiously, scholarly anti-Semites, as was the young Renan in his own way. Nevertheless, Renan confided to Lévi that the resident Sanskritist, Abel Bergaigne, had no students at the time, and that he would therefore eagerly welcome an opportunity to take Lévi as his *élève*. By way of such a series of accidents, at the age of nineteen, Lévi began what would prove to be an illustrious scholarly career.

After finishing with Bergaigne, Lévi was unable to find a suitable academic post in his field. But the leadership of the same rather conservative rabbinic school in Paris where he had done his own seminary training was eager to have Lévi on their faculty. So when they offered Lévi a position teaching traditional seminary subjects, partly out of a sense of obligation to his Jewish faith, he accepted. After several years teaching seminary students, Lévi eventually succeeded Bergaigne in the chair of Sanskrit at the Ecole Pratique des Hautes Etudes, Fifth Section. By 1894, he was elevated to the Collège de France in Sanskrit Language and Literature, where he continued as a professor until 1935.

4   Lévi says that the *nature* of the religion revealed in the *Brâhmanas* is constituted by sacrificial ritual. Thus sacrifice 'is God and God *par excellence*'. Further, sacrifice 'is the master, the indeterminate god, the infinite, the spirit from which

everything comes, dying and being born without ceasing' (Lévi 1898:Ch.2). This
was noted as well by Mauss (1900b:353).

5   Lévi 1898:27. See also p.38, where sacrifice is identified as the life source of the
gods, p.54, where it is said to save the gods, p.76, where the superiority of sacrifice to the gods, in particular, Indra, is asserted. Lévi in effect argued for what
Renou calls the 'omnipotence' of ritual (see Louis Renou, p.viii of the Preface
to Lévi 1898, 2nd ed., 1966, Paris: Presses Universitaires de France).

10

MEMORY AND THE SACRED

The cult of anniversaries and commemorative rituals in the light of *The Elementary Forms*

Werner Gephart

Introduction

Although I would have liked to present a lecture on *Les Formes élémentaires de la vie religieuse* as a contribution to an anniversary, it is difficult to find a historical date in Durkheim's intellectual biography which would correspond to this conference seen as part of a commemorative ritual. Nevertheless an international congress about *Les Formes élémentaires* is in itself an interesting case to be considered because it contains elements which are important to the aspect of memory we shall be raising here. There exists a holy scripture, rules of interpretation, even an organizational framework which pertain to Durkheimians spread all over the world but centred in Oxford. Now we meet here in the common exercise of reading and re-reading the holy text. Of course it is still unclear whether or not the mood of effervescence will spread and impregate our individual consciousnesses with an emergent collective spirit of sociological awareness, which according to Durkheim should be the effect of a commemorative ritual.

The sociological problem I would try to analyse, using *The Elementary Forms*, is very simple to explain, but much more difficult to resolve. Collective memory has recently become one of the most debated questions in public life. Most of us realize how difficult it was to remember recently D-Day in order to commemorate it with due regard. Not long ago France lived through a period of intense reflection, fear and commemorative rituals at the time of the bicentenary of the Revolution, during which it was even necessary to invent a ministry for the organization of collective memory! In Germany discussions never end about the insoluble question of constructing a moral as well as an aesthetically valid memorial for the Holocaust in Berlin. And at lower levels of social life we find, for example, problems over celebrating the real or merely fictional birthday of a city – problems concerning the myth of the origin and identity of the city.

My question is whether these different events have something in common that makes them a specific *fait social*. And second, whether a reading of Durkheim's works on the sociology of religion, and especially *The Elementary*

Forms, will help us to understand the forms and functions of collective memory. To this end I shall first briefly show how his analysis of religion is embedded in a more general conception of the elementary forms of social life. Second, I want to argue how collective memory may be theorized in the light of this paradigm. And, third, I will demonstrate how local anniversaries and national festivities can be interpreted in the light of the sacred character that collectivities attribute to their history in the course of commemorative rituals.

A model of the elementary forms of social life

The community of scholars who interpret Durkheim's work is not very clear about the essence of his theory. Some, such as Parsons and his followers, still see him as a representative of action theory. Others make him the founder of a normative paradigm, or try to identify him with organicism, while symbolic interactionists try to claim him as one of themselves. It would be too easy to criticize all these interpretations as calculated errors or unintended misinterpretations as a result of personal theoretical interests. Quite simply I would maintain that such interpretations are wrong insofar as they try to encapsulate Durkheim under only one of the aforementioned headings.

Of course there is the problem that Durkheim did not develop any systematic categorical concepts, such as we are accustomed to find in the work of Max Weber. However his use of general concepts, culminating in those of *Les Formes élémentaires*, is impressive. One can point to the symbolic representative dimension, the normative aspect, its social organization and the interactional facet of social life.

I now comment on the four ways of interpreting Durkheim mentioned above.

(1) Labelling Durkheim as an action theorist is of course completely wrong or misleading (see especially Parsons 1937). Though it is true that in the *Rules of Sociological Method* he speaks of social facts as a *manière de faire*, this does not represent more than a *façon de parler* (1895a/1901c:19). He rejects explicitly any explanation of action by intentional behaviour – as in his study of suicide. In addition, he refuses explanations based on purpose.[1]

(2) It is precisely the problem of contingency that leads him to the normative solution of the problem of order in social life. Starting with the reception of Wundt (1887c:49–58), 'Le cours de science sociale' at Bordeaux (1888a) and the anomic type of division of labour (1893b: 343ff.), Durkheim develops his general idea of structuring the social world by norms.[2] This view connects him with Foucault's formulation of the realm of normativity (see Gephart 1995). But it would be wrong to reduce Durkheim to this normative conception of social facts, which understands Durkheim, like Weber (Gephart 1992), as part of a sociology born out of the spirit of law and jurisprudence.

(3) What we now call social structure was treated by Durkheim under the heading of *organisation sociale* (1903a(ii)(2):316). To reduce Durkheim's

theory to the morphological factors of social life and to give it an organizational foundation, is to overlook the very different dimension of symbolism, which is not to be grasped through functionalism or organicism.

(4) Together, the cognitively reducing qualities of symbols and their ability to focus on collective feelings, give social symbols the fundamental meaning for social life that they are seen to possess in *The Elementary Forms*. My point is that the theoretical significance of Durkheim is not centred on the analysis of action, nor on structures or institutions as such, nor on symbols or communication, but that his theoretical originality lies in interlacing interaction, social organization, normative regulation and symbolic *représentation* under the general heading of or, if you prefer, in the name of social life. This means saving the vitalist orientation of his theory of effervescence without dissolving the structures of social life. As I see it, this is the secret of Durkheim's analysis. The programme is neither a search for the loss of society (cf. Tiryakian 1979:97–114), nor a mere look at the non-rational preconditions of social action, but a *recherche des formes élémentaires de la vie sociale*[3] one of which forms, we would claim, is collective memory.

Collective memory seen within the Durkheimian paradigm of social life

Collective memory is unfortunately not an explicit concept or a well-defined topic which Durkheim dealt with directly. But it seems to be very close to what he defined in *The Division of Labor* as the *conscience collective*. It means: 'l'ensemble des croyances et des sentiments communs à la moyenne des membres d'une même société [qui] forme un système déterminé qui a sa vie propre' (1893b/1902b:46). On the other hand, in *The Elementary Forms* (Book III, Chapter IV), Durkheim deals with rituals and directly refers to *rites commemoratifs*. Combining the definition of the *conscience collective* and the reference to *rites commemoratives*, we shall try to conceptualize certain aspects of collective memory. I hope this goes beyond the Durkheimian legacy in *Les cadres sociaux de la mémoire* by Maurice Halbwachs (1925). The inner link between history, memory and the construction of sociality in primordial communities lies in the belief about their common origin. The myth of origin is therefore one of the most powerful means of establishing a community's unity. At a very basic level we find, therefore, a close connection between mechanisms of collective memory on the one hand, and institutions guaranteeing the collective identity in social life, on the other. Memory as one aspect of the diffuse *conscience collective* may be analysed with regard to the elementary forms of social life which we recognize as central characteristics of the *conscience collective*.

(1) On the symbolic level it is important to know how commemorative symbols work. Heroes, holy events, material signs may evoke the past and stand for the group's bond with its history. Destruction of these symbols is almost destruction of the group itself. Taking away the history

means cutting off social life from its sources. On the other hand, what we can observe in a revival of nationalism is exactly the struggle for those symbols which represent the past of a community, in other words a claim to a specific collective identity.

(2) In a normative dimension it is interesting to observe – and thereby to understand, memory as a *fait social* – that those beliefs and convictions of a community which constitute its memory are more or less obligatory and normatively imprinted. It is not up to the individual to construct his collective past, for the specific identity of a community is necessarily constituted within a complex normative system. This is of course very clear for religiously-grounded communities where the myth of origin is a central component of religious *représentations*. But other elements of a people's history, such as the Shoah and its memory, can become constitutive of collective identities. That is why the denial of the Holocaust is regarded in the German criminal code as a criminal act directed against a community.

(3) The organizational aspect helps us to understand why the collective memory does not, so to say, simply work by itself but is shaped by values and interests, themselves transformed into different forms of social organization. Socializing agencies, such as schools, religious communities and 'ethnically-grounded' communities organize, more or less systematically, the transmission of their past from one generation to the other by structures of collective memory. Institutions specializing in the preservation of the past are dealt with in the French tradition as the multitude of *lieux de mémoire*, as Pierre Nora entitled them (1984–92). Such studies deal, for example, with memorial stones of the First World War, the national flag, education and the army, the Collège de France, the Académie Française, and so on. These places of memory stand between the real and the imagined, where the collective memory is concentrated through the agency of commemorative organizations which hold specific commemorative rituals.

(4) In his reading of Spencer and Gillen Durkheim makes the very important remark that nearly every ritual contains elements of collective commemoration. The central passage needs to be cited at length:

Everything unrolls in *représentations* whose object can only be to render the mythical past of the clan present to the mind. But the mythology of a group is the system of beliefs common to this group. The traditions whose memory it perpetuates express the way in which society represents man and the world; it is a moral system and a cosmology as well as a history. So the rite serves and can serve only to sustain the vitality of these beliefs, to keep them from being effaced from memory and in sum, to revivify the most essential elements of collective *conscience*. Through it, the group periodically renews the sentiment which it has of itself and of its unity; at the same time, individuals are strengthened in their social natures. The glorious memories which are made to live again before their eyes, and with which they feel that they have a kinship, give them a feeling of strength and confidence: one is surer of one's faith when one sees to how distant a past it goes back and what great things it has inspired.

(536–7/375)

The passage contains important elements for our analysis. The welding of history, identity, and memory as a central part of the *conscience collective*, which is periodically enlivened by rituals representing and creating the identity of the group. To them are added the effects of collective effervescence such that the glorified past leads on to new ideals and projects for the future.[4]

Commemorative symbols, norms, a commemorative social organization and rituals as specialized or non-specialized social interactions are at the basis of collective memory. Its relation to the sacred is obvious. Whether we start from the normative definition of religion in the second volume of *L'Année sociologique* (1899a(ii)), or whether we take the differentiation between the sacred and the profane[5] as the theoretical starting-point, the collective memory is not subject to discussion. Its reality is not to be contested; it is, so to say, invulnerable. Though the selection of certain material signs as sacred things is mainly arbitrary, there is no doubt that its collectively imagined past stands at the centre of what a community holds to be sacred. Religion is the symbolization of society and its forces, and they in turn depend on the vitalizing power of memory.

Ambivalent fields of collective memory and identity construction

Finally we look at some selected examples where this vitalizing power of memory and tradition may be studied.

Local memory

Among the many varieties of local self-representation, the anniversary of a city holds a special place. It recalls the foundation of the city, constructing its sometimes precarious identity by imagining the past. Anniversaries give a rhythm or pattern to local history and bring people together as a local community. They are collective events, organized around rituals of commemoration, and we can probably understand them as survivals of ancient local cults. As long as the city was primarily a ritualized community, the religious character of its festivals was obvious. The frontiers of the city were determined by sacred walls that could only be pierced by portals. Membership was defined as the community of all those who had the same protective gods and celebrated the same religious rituals. The stranger was defined as one excluded from its religious activities, one whose participation would desecrate the sacred ritual. The adoration of the local gods was the object of many common rituals, of public meals, sacrifices and calendrical cults. The anniversary of the city recalled the customs by which the gods were held within the boundaries of the city. Participation was for that reason obligatory (Fustel de Coulanges 1903).

Modern anniversaries seem at first glance very distant from such practices. The plural character of modern cities excludes the participation of all citizens. But even Rome knew the difference between *sacra pro populo*, which were celebrated by the magistrate and the priests without participation of the people, and *sacra popularia* celebrated by the people. We have of course a similar differentiation between mass activities and banquets for the notables of a city.

The anniversaries of the city of Düsseldorf can now be examined within the framework of the commemorative paradigm (see Gephart 1991:9–14). In 1888 the symbolic reference point was destiny and change, the glory and suffering of the city founded six hundred years before. Flags and garlands were laid at the monument of the emperor, erected specially for the occasion. Allegorical groups led the festive procession, symbolizing art, trade, industry and navigation. There followed a historical pageant, in which a battle was enacted, a mock castle was constructed and other local historical events were presented. Of course the banquets for prominent citizens were not open to the public and the festival committees lay in the hands of powerholders.

Fifty years later, in 1938, the anti-modernistic atmosphere was impressive and the justification of community feeling was not surprising. Nevertheless it is most irritating how close the Nazi organizers came to the idea of collective rituals, as is clear from the following:

> As in the case of all great community festivals, whether as here in the city or in the village, the most important thing is that members of the community should not just watch but get involved. It is certainly not always easy to achieve this, but it is necessary if we are to get away from the pure and simple 'amusement business', where we were merely the people who paid, and move towards genuine community festivals.[6]

The raising of collective feeling through community festivals was naturally the aim of the festival organizers who included a ceremony at the Schlageter Denkmal, the monument of a Nazi hero. Given those ideological interests I discovered nonetheless that the pure functionalization of an old tradition, in the form of those local anniversaries, did not fulfil the expectations of the *Gauleiter* (head of a Nazi administration district), because in a way the autonomous city was a counterforce to the processes of *Gleichschaltung* (being forced into line).

What can one say about the 1988 ceremony? I was in charge of the organization of a conferencee, which involved academic funding from the Thyssen steel company and the city administration. It was little more than a reflection on the importance of the city as Georg Simmel described it. The occasion also aroused 'reflexive' analysis of the emotional function of anniversaries, to which some responded with deep ambivalence. For the dialectic communal life does not always render desirable the ideals associated with such occasions.

That is why I read the following central passage of Durkheim with some ambiguity:

> A day will come when our societies will know again those hours of creative effervescence, when new ideas will arise and new formulae will emerge to serve for a while as a guide to humanity; and when these hours have been experienced, men will spontaneously feel the need to relive them from time to time in thought, that is to say, to keep alive their memory by means of celebrations which regularly reproduce their outcomes.
>
> (611/427)

The analysis of the anniversaries of the French Revolution by Pascal Ory, in his study *Une Nation pour mémoire 1889, 1939, 1989 trois jubilés révolution-naires* (1992), is impressive. But it is more important to uphold a distinction which was glossed over in the famous *Historikerstreit*. Collective identity, history and memory have related but different logics, which should not be homogenized for the sake of community-building at anniversaries. They have become, however, simultaneously the occasion for 'worship' and for rational scientific critiques.[7]

Remembering the Holocaust in Germany

Arno Mayer has exclaimed that he cannot 'reason with dogmatists who seek to reify and sacralize the Holocaust for being absolutely unprecedented and totally mysterious' (1994:446). This view parallels remarks of Siegfried Kohlhammer, citing Howard Jacobson, that there is a 'perverse sacraliza-tion' of the Holocaust (Kohlhammer 1994:505). Jack Kugelmass speaks in his fascinating study of Holocaust tourism about the birth of a cosmogenic time, or even a 'Holocaust-Religion' (1994:156), to cite the critical formula by Adi Ophir (1987).

In accordance with Durkheim's thought, I would insist that there is a reli-gious dimension in recalling the Shoa. This view, however, is highly ambivalent insofar as it is not really clear what commemorative community the rituals of the Holocaust in Germany should refer to. It is paradoxical and deeply tragic that, as seems well established, the power of Auschwitz has helped to create the state of Israel.[8] It remains uncertain what sort of identity-building has emerged for the German non-Jewish community, which has sons and daughters of 'willing executioners', as well as of those who resisted the régime.

At the symbolic level there are a lot of problems of adequate represen-tation, if representation is possible at all. The discussion about the Central Holocaust Memorial in Berlin is revealing. Neither the act of creating a monument in itself, nor creating a monument to compensate for horror and crime, seems to be reasonable. More convincing are the attempts at 'anti-monumentalism' which do not pretend to represent either events or structures, but only memory itself. I think of those reflexive and in this sense post-modern memorials where the disappearance of collective memory is displayed. The memorial 'mise en scène' in Hamburg-Harburg, realized by Esther and Jochen Gerz, is a most impressive example (Schmidt-Wulffen 1994:43–9). A column twelve metres high was covered with a lead sheath, on which passers-by were invited to scratch their names. The monument was continuously eroded during the period of this 'memorial action' until it literally dwindled into meaningful insignificance.

In the normative dimension, any denial of the Holocaust as an intended and nearly successful attempt to exterminate the Jews is subject to penal law. The legal construction of the Leuchter case was somewhat complicated. Even if the negation of victimship by Leuchter actually occurred, the charge could not be made to stick under the heading of laws to protect the honour of victims, since in a way Leuchter did not entirely deny the honour of Jewish people: what he did was to deny the dishonour of the executioners. He did not defame the relatives but he exonerated the reputation of criminals. Collective memory cannot be formed and preserve itself, as Arno Mayer notes in today's context of declining media attention, 'without organisation and orchestration' (1994:450). The dilemma over organization is obvious. Without a specific memorial day, for example, there would be no co-ordinated remembrance at all. At the same time empty ritualization is an obvious threat to the maintenance of memory! But why did not an organized public cult of commemoration emerge in Germany until now? It was not just a matter of disregard, ignorance or repression. Perhaps the answer has to do with the problem of building a collective identity by means of collective memory.

What sort of collective identity could emerge from that unimaginable catastrophe, given that the people responsible for it were not expelled but 'integrated' into a society that was rebuilding itself? This is the theoretical issue inherent in the famous historians' debate in Germany (Gephart 1990a). Habermas was very critical of those who thought that an understanding of the executioners' motives implied a moral sympathy with the criminals. 'Identification' therefore was looked on as highly dangerous.

But perhaps identification could be imagined differently, as a subtle reference to the potentiality for such behaviour in all of us, in the hope that we shall find ourselves unable to make the identification. Not self-accusation for a non-existing collective guilt,[9] as the self-declared 'disinfectors of the past' claimed to fear, but a highly sophisticated and moralized identification and rejection of the perpetrators might be the ground of a 'remembrance-community'. Sacralization of the memory could not be avoided as such, but it would have to gain its place in the utopian project of founding in Germany a civil religion of *Verfassungspatriotismus* (Constitutional patriotism).

Conclusion

Durkheim could not have thought the unthinkable. He could not have foreseen that his theory of solidarity producing commemorative rituals would one day have to be applied to a society with the most negative and unique content to its collective memory. Nor was such thought possible, at the time he wrote his book, for the famous analyst of collective memory, Maurice Halbwachs, who was murdered on 16 March 1945 at Buchenwald. An analysis of Durkheim's contribution to the sociological understanding of the ambiguities in collective memory is a good occasion to reflect on the tragic death of Halbwachs who, in his study of 1925, continued work on the legacy of *Les Formes élémentaires*.

Notes

1 For this refusal, see Durkheim's writing on Rudolf von Ihering which is no less important than his reading of Spencer in this respect. Cf. Durkheim 1887c:49–58.
2 This interpretation is developed in its diverse consequences for the competition between law and religion in Gephart 1993:321–418.
3 This interpretation is developed in Gephart 1990a:49–55. See also Gephart 1993:321–418.
4 Cf. 'A day will come when our societies will know again those hours of creative effervescence when new ideas will arise and new formulae will emerge to serve for a while as a guide to humanity.' (611/427–8).
5 Owing to the universalistic extension of Durkheim's notion of religion as defined by the pure differentiation of sacred and profane, the sacred can no longer be regarded as a substantialized concrete section of reality. See 50/37.
6 See *Düsseldorfer Stadt-Nachrichten*, Beilage der Düsseldorfer Nachrichten of 13 August 1938.
7 For interesting discussion of a vast debate, see Marie-Claire Lavabre 1994.
8 See, e.g. Friedländer and Seligman 1994.
9 It would be most interesting in this context to read the theory of Paul Fauconnet in his book of 1921.

11

EFFERVESCENCE, DIFFERENTIATION AND REPRESENTATION IN *THE ELEMENTARY FORMS*

William Ramp

Introduction[1]

In certain vivid passages in *The Elementary Forms*, Durkheim details a set of scenarios taking the following form.[2] A society of small, segmented groups spends a season engaged in mundane activities in isolated camps, perhaps following a few, low-key religious practices. But at given seasonal points, all congregate. Ritual assemblies build up in frequency and intensity, and on some occasions, certain everyday social rules are set aside (308/215). The difference between these two modes of social life is taken to parallel a religious distinction between the profane and the sacred (things, spaces, times). Durkheim describes the arousal of a liminal energy at times of heightened social intensity marked by frequent ritual assemblies, and does so with a verve distinct from the didactic severity with which he delineates categories and terms.[3] He refers to a contrastive violence needed to 'disengage' or shake loose an awareness of the sacred in participants (313–14/218–19); to totems as embodiments both of a sense of dependence and of enhanced vitality (314–5/219–20); to occasions on which 'passions moving them [participants] are of such an intensity that they cannot be satisfied except by violent and unrestrained actions, superhuman heroism or bloody barbarism'. This effervescence 'often reaches such a point that it causes unheard-of actions', gestures, cries, howls, rhythmic song and dance, contraventions of sexual mores, destructive actions: a point at which 'a man does not recognize himself any longer' (312/218). In piacular rites, there may be drinking of blood or fatal, self-inflicted wounds. Through this excitation, exhaustion and delirium, society consecrates things (557ff./390ff.).

In these passages, certain descriptive elements stand out. One set concerns expenditure, excess and exhaustion; a second, the violation or inversion of normal order and constraint, or the revaluation of the sacred (see Pickering 1984:354). The sacred may also appear ambiguously as an object of veneration and of horror; as in the instance of blood and its associated images of contagion.[4] A third concerns violence as a manifestation of intensity in piacular rites: 'the exceptional violence of the manifestations by which the common pain is necessarily and obligatorily expressed even testifies to the fact that at this moment the society is more alive and active than ever' (574/402). A fourth element involves the treatment of collective *représentations* as a kind of delirium adding another dimension to our normal sense-perception (324/227).

The language Durkheim uses to describe effervescence drives us to ask not only what social processes are at work on such occasions, but also what collective psychology they express.[5] Functionalist interpreters of Durkheim, of course, have had ready answers: effervescent assemblies bind individuals to the group; their intensity serves as a social glue. But the logic of these assertions merits interrogation. In what sense would excess, exhaustion, contradiction or violence serve as an adhesive? And what individuals are meant: individuals as social categories? Pre-social individuals? Individual groups within a larger social totality? To explore the narrative sense of Durkheim's description of effervescence, and to address these questions, we need to detour briefly through some other work by Durkheim (and by his associate, Marcel Mauss).

The logic of differentiation

Durkheim's accounts of elementary religious phenomena in *The Elementary Forms*, in discussions of the origin of property in *Professional Ethics and Civic Morals* (1950a), and elsewhere, exhibit a dialectic of totality and differentiation: one structured in terms of *représentation* and reciprocity.[6] But this dialectic also appears threatened by a heterogeneous excess – by a danger that energizes the differential order of social life. It is present in its highest forms of expression and haunts it with images of catastrophe. This danger wears a different face for different interpreters of Durkheim. North American sociologists – and we not only have Parsons to thank for this – have often represented him as a theorist of order *par excellence*, as someone concerned with the Hobbesian problem, that is, with the relation of the individual to society. It relates to the constitution of the person as *homo duplex*: self-interested and individual, yet (at least, ideally) also social and dutiful. In this light, Durkheim is said to express a horror of social disorder and moral breakdown. The problem with this interpretation is that its counterposition of individual agency and social constraint generates precisely the complaints first directed at Durkheim by Americans such as Gehlke (1915), before Parsons' and Alpert's exercises in rehabilitation. The allegation is that Durkheim commits the fallacy of misplaced concreteness, hypostasizing the social as an entity which not only stands over against the individual but eviscerates individual agency.

By contrast, Durkheim's own discussion of *homo duplex* (1914a) proposes a distinctive 'elementary' psychology – that 'the prototype of selfish drives is what we call improperly enough the instinct of self-preservation – in other words, the tendency of every living creature to keep alive. That tendency makes its action felt without our thinking of the pleasures that life might have for us.' For example, a suicidal person may struggle for life in the midst of the act because of an *élan vital* that is neither instrumental nor conscious – nor, therefore, in any real sense concerned with the individual as 'self'. For Durkheim, calculating, instrumental self-interest is a *social* phenomenon, only distantly related to this primordial will to life. He also postulates that humans are possessed of a second basic will: a will to sociability linked to the supplanting of instincts by morals. Again, by 'will' he means a basic compulsion, undefined and undelimited, and as such, straining against definition or limit. Regulation gives it form and meaning, as part of the conscious human subject, while also necessarily frustrating it. These compulsions to life and sociability are the 'givens' of human existence, form a substrate to the social and are not necessarily experienced consciously by individuals.

There is a Hegelian air to Durkheim's explanatory logic here (as in Mauss 1925/t.1990:81–2). Sociability binds us together but confronts us with otherness – other biological individuals, other groups, and the otherness of the environment in which we meet. While the postulation of an *élan vital* as part of this scenario might appear Hobbesian, neither individuality nor self-interest, as social categories, are said to predate the establishment of a social universe which provides their meaning. This consideration necessarily leads us to ask what significance Durkheim gave to the concept of an original social totality, given that in his descriptions of the social universe in its primordial forms, Hobbesian issues of regulation are less prominent than those attending the dual recognition of differentiation and totality.

In *The Division of Labour*, Durkheim's remarks on primordial social forms are framed by a quasi-evolutionary distinction between mechanical and organic solidarity: elementary forms of association are defined by a relative lack of internal differentiation, and by a low level of development of the division of labour (1893b/1902b/t.1984a:126–31). In such societies, members are said to be bound by a strong common consciousness and individuation is present only in rudimentary forms. Conversely, organic solidarity is characterized by a developed division of labour, by specialized subgroups and institutions with their own collective rules and values, by specialized individual roles, and by individualism as a social value. Durkheim later complicated this evolutionary schema (e.g., 1901a(i)), elaborating on cultural differentiations found in the simplest of social groups, and on the complex rituals, rules, laws and forms of exchange with which such differentiation is associated. For our purposes, we need note only two things about these various formulations. First, social differentiation is said to give rise to and to necessitate forms of exchange. Second, it entails the development of distinctive groups and individuals who none the less retain an essential relation to each other and to the social whole. This relation is not simply a matter of shared values, but of a social bond in terms of which each differentiated individual or subgroup sees itself not merely as a *part* of a larger whole but in some sense as *representative* of it. For example, the forms of contractual justice referred to in *The Division of Labour* are linked intimately to a representationalist solidarity: a contract is fair only if each party sees the other both as a co-participant in a larger social whole and as a representative element of that whole. This is the sociological insight that Durkheim brings to his appreciation of the necessity of 'equilibrium' in contractual arrangements (1893b/1902b/t.1984a: 316–22).

Représentation and differentiation

The concepts of *représentation* and reciprocity have profound significance in *The Elementary Forms of the Religious Life*, in *Professional Ethics and Civic Morals*, and in Durkheim's discussions of the nature of modern individualism and the evolution of punishment. Durkheim suggests that individuals come to exist as such – to have 'souls', and to be taken as sacred – to the extent that they *represent* the social totality as moral beings, and *enact* such a totality in their dealings with each other (see Pearce 1989:88–117). The existence of individuals as differentiated, conscious, moral entities, is predicated on their mutual relations in and through a shared sense of totality in which they exist representationally: as representatives of each other and of the social whole. Society, said Durkheim, is a structure of *représentations*. In English, it is easy to become tangled in questions of who or what represents or is represented. But for the Durkheim of *The Elementary Forms*, *représentations* in themselves are basic structural features of social life, and representational acts, in some important sense, designate their own terms. They also have substantive force. As early as *The Division of Labour*, Durkheim claimed that 'every strong state of the consciousness is a source of life', and that,

> a *représentation* is not a simple image of reality, a motionless shadow projected into us by things. It is rather a force that stirs up around us a whole whirlwind of organic and psychological phenomena.
> (1893b/1902b/t.1984a:53)

Durkheim's historical and ethnographic writings elaborate such themes. *Professional Ethics and Civic Morals* addresses the origin of categories of property, contract and individuality in ways which appear to indicate that these universals of Western culture had particular – almost accidental – origins. But Durkheim also asserts that these origins were necessarily collective and representational. Early forms of 'individual' property arose when certain males, in this instance, patriarchs of early Roman families, took representative roles in relation to the family group, began to act and to hold property in its name, and later extended rights of *représentation* to their sons, in the same instant restricting their own rights of life and death over their sons. Modern individuals owe their status and rights as property-holders to the fact that at a certain point in time *some* individuals came to represent *certain* social groups: today, *all* individuals in theory have such rights inasmuch as each represents the social totality – and all *other* individuals within the social whole (1950a/t.1957a:145–70).

But we now approach the core of the narrative – whether in elementary or advanced forms, *représentation* follows from differentiation. Likewise, exchange, reciprocity, forms of contract binding individuals or groups; all are predicated on differentiation. The prehistory of modern individualism, and of property, is marked by a process in which, in Durkheim's words, 'men' differentiated themselves both from the earth and from things – a process accompanied by another in which groups of humans began to distinguish themselves from each other, and in which men ritually set themselves apart from women (Gane 1983b). But exchange is both a consequence of differentiation and an affirmation of a social bond, and through it, of social totality. *Représentation* is a structure of recognition – of self, of other and of the social whole in which self and other have both place and meaning. *Représentation* entails a dual recognition: of differentiation and otherness, and of a *totality* enacted by self and other in the social bond. It is a totality carried within each person as a conscious and conscientious being. As particular inhabitants of a social universe, we recognize the presence of totality in whatever form. We recognize that we are 'no longer' subsumed in it but that we still form a differentiated part of it. We recognize particular others in terms of relations of affinity and likeness (kin) or complementarity, for example, sex roles). Moral regulation also entails a representational dialectic: the whole in the particular (society inculcated in the differentiated soul), and the particular in the whole (social totality enacted in ritual, or expressed in narrative form by particular members).[7]

The dynamics of effervescence: differentiation and de-differentiation

It is possible to argue that in some sense Durkheim conceived the social as an articulation of difference, as being inherently complex from the beginning. In this light, the distinction between mechanical and organic solidarity would appear less as an evolutionary one, for example 'primitive' versus 'modern', than as a distinction between possibilities inherent in all social life. This structural and arguably a-temporal emphasis also marks another aspect of Durkheim's evolutionary schema. The social bond in terms of which we represent ourselves, to each other and to the totality within which we have meaning, evokes a nostalgia for totality writ as origin; for a lost unity before differentiation, in which humans and nature, persons and things were one. But as an object of nostalgia, this totality does not pre-date its diffraction; it is in effect constituted by that event. The recognition of otherness and particularity which calls forth a nostalgia for a primordial unity thus could be said to express an essentially atemporal de-differentiating drive, and the idea of social totality, when construed as an *original* unity left behind but still depended on, could be characterized as an effect of a universal desire to transgress structures of differentiation in order to merge 'once again' with a primordial whole. Thus, specific forms of differentiation – defining those 'like me' but 'other' to me, and those both other to and unlike me – relate to social practices in which totality is perpetually re-enacted. For example, binding like to like while proscribing certain forms of alliance; allying the different, as by marriage or treaty, where their distinctiveness is maintained. In Durkheim and Mauss these enactments of totality take two primary forms, both of which may be ritualized. One is exchange, as in Mauss, where I both become part of the other and lose part of myself via the alienation inherent in the gift, and the other reciprocally becomes part of me (see Mauss 1925/t.1990:50; 66). The other is *représentation*, through which I am bound to an other in terms of a totality represented in our souls and expressed in recognition (523/366). We reproduce a totality sometimes reciprocally, and other times in concert.

Here again, the moral problem of *homo duplex* is represented quite differently from that of individualized self-interest pitted against the social good represented in the conscience. For Durkheim, the self-interested individual is clearly an effect of modern social and economic life. The primordial impulse behind anomic self-interest is not identical with it, and could take other forms, including extreme altruism. This force, which is identified as 'will' in what Meštrović (1989a) terms Durkheim's 'Schopenhauerian' moment, is an undifferentiated, unconscious and expansive will to life. This, when expressed in the face of the social and translated into social terms as 'self-interest', becomes in effect a will to death unless countered and complemented by a love of co-operation and duty. Like many of his contemporaries, Durkheim refers to a need to redirect basic energies, such as the sexual energy of adolescents, into an active enthusiasm for duty.

Effervescence and transgression: danger in the celebration of order

We now return to Durkheim's vivid and seemingly paradoxical references to collective rites and effervescence. In contrast to notions that effervescence simply functions to bind individuals together, Durkheim himself claims that the charged emotional environments of ritual assemblies *call individuals out of themselves*, imbuing them with a heightened sense of their participation in the collective, of being borne along by collective life, even of dying for the collective. Durkheim does assert that such assemblies reinforce social order by binding members more tightly, both to the social whole and more specifically to their social identities, though he tends to emphasize revivification over order *per se*. But there is an apparent paradox in saying that on ritual occasions, individual participants find themselves called out of the differential structures of ordinary social life to which, in the same instance, they are called to be loyal. To make sense of this apparent paradox, let us make the following propositions:[8]

(1) Ritual assemblies renew a collective loyalty to the social totality undergirding the normative order of everyday, differentiated and delimited existence. Such assemblies also renew collective energy by investing the particularity of social life with a sense of totality. The realm of the everyday and particular catches some of the fire of the collective and extraordinary when brought into proximity to it, as participants in

everyday life cross the threshold, temporal or spatial, of the event or assembly and are transformed in that act.

(2) However, in being called out of their particularity, and into identification with each other in and through the social whole, participants risk their differentiated existence along with the social distinctions and prohibitions which support it. Effervescence can be accompanied by saturnalian reversals of everyday rules and rankings, and in events such as piacular rites, by the death of participants, symbolically or in reality. In such rites, the death of the social itself seems to be portended and then ritually held at bay. Further, Durkheim acknowledges Hertz's point that the sacred is ambiguous. In being set apart, it may be venerated as emblematic of the social group and serve to protect the delimited structure of social life. But such setting-apart may also, perhaps unpredictably, generate a sense of revulsion. In a sense the sacred may come to be ritually expelled or excluded while remaining strangely attractive.

Thus Durkheim's discussion of effervescence, even in the context of established ritual occasions, seems somehow to hint at the possibility of something apocalyptic, even if more as a subtext than a foreground. Precisely at moments when totality is invoked most powerfully, when collective loyalty to a differentiated social order is renewed, the ordered social differentiation which generates a nostalgia for totality may be most threatened. One might argue that such occasions are distinguished by temporal and spatial thresholds precisely to contain this danger, and that effervescence most effectively reproduces a given order when it itself is subject to the distancing effects of nostalgia and remembrance (see Pickering 1984:389–90). But, as Durkheim himself noted of the French Revolution, the danger can be realized if effervescence becomes an occasion for destruction – destruction which may, or may not, be a threshold for creative renewal or revolutionary synthesis.[9] As we have seen, Durkheim's reserve slips in his description of effervescent assemblies, as he recounts examples of stressful activities in certain rites: jumping, shouting, groaning, weeping, self-mutilating, brandishing. While this physical excess can be explained functionally, the enthusiasm of Durkheim's description leads us in another direction. It is one to do less with some functional requirement for emotion than with the process of leaving self and limits behind, of dying to a differentiated existence. To use Georges Bataille's words, it means reversing the orders of homogeneity and heterogeneity. Death, as the end of the subject and of all things in relation to it, and destruction would be co-present with renewal, or danger with possibility, as it is in the later work on sacrifice and violence by Bataille and others (see, e.g., Bataille 1938; Baudrillard 1976; Girard 1978).

Reciprocity and *représentation*: the symbolic structure of differentiation

A similar thematic attends Durkheim's and Mauss' accounts of sacrifice, as ritual and non-instrumental exchange. They understand sacrificial gifts as vehicles of communication by which those who sacrifice recognize their difference from a deity embodying the social totality, and attempt to close the gap opened by that difference in order to forge a moral bond of *mutual* dependency with a god (491–500/344–50). Sacrifice is not only a form of exchange – a gift in return for recognition – but a substitute death by which those who sacrifice, through the sacrificial gift, symbolically die to their differentiated particularity. It thus involves both differentiation and de-differentiation, the destruction of particularity at the moment of its affirmation. Sacrificial expenditure symbolically bridges a divide between humans and gods, and between living and dead. Thus, in the context of collective assemblies, one might postulate that sacrificial rituals, too, could exhibit a dangerous instability.

Hubert and Mauss (1899) define sacrifice as a 'means of communication between the sacred and the profane worlds through the mediation of a victim, that is, of a thing that in the course of a ceremony is destroyed (1899/t.1964:97). They also refer to the 'ambiguity' of sacrifice: the victim's substitutionary role allows the one offering a sacrifice 'prudently to set himself aside'. In sacrifice, 'disinterestedness is mingled with self-interest'. Yet sacrifice is only possible when 'things exist outside the sacrifier which cause him to go outside himself' (ibid.:100–1). Sacrifice recalls 'frequently to the consciousness of the individual the presence of collective forces', while individuals through the sacrificial act 'confer upon each other, upon themselves, and upon those things they hold dear, the whole strength of society'. This strength, whether in the form of authority, protection, redress, expiation or the right of enjoyment, always involves forms of recognition in which god and people are bound by acts through which people represent to themselves their common relation to a deity who is in turn their reflection. The role of the sacrificial intermediary is not simply to allow survivors to enjoy their bargain, but to provide a 'rite of exit' by means of which participants in social life *may continue to live socially*. For Mauss, as for Durkheim, a dangerous force also inheres in other forms of exchange. In sacrifice, transgressing distinctions between sacred and profane carries the threat of death: in gift exchange, unbalanced reciprocity affects distinctions between subjects, reducing one party to an object of the other – an imbalance and a lack of recognition that must be redressed by war or endured as slavery. In unequal or denied reciprocity, it is the other's *social* existence that is denied – the effect of which is ultimately to deny the social existence of *both* parties, given that both are constituted socially in each other's image as representative of each other and as bearers of a common humanity. In a real sense, one who initiates an unjust exchange is already dead before revenge is taken, while ironically, revenge is an affirmation of the life denied: a deadly power when provoked. For Mauss, the denial of reciprocity, as an example of such provocation, is rooted in interest or status competition extending beyond the time–space boundaries of effervescent assemblies. But considerations of interest aside, the very existence of effervescence on any ceremonial occasion – and almost all exchange has a ceremonial aspect – could likewise, even on different terms, be said to call out the possibility of transgression and the power of death. This would be especially true of occasions when perils to the social order are ritually addressed.

In this latter sense, we can suggest that a compulsion – a legacy of social differentiation and individuation – can surface in effervescent assemblies when ceremonial is joined to excess. It is also seen in a compulsion to dissolve limits, differentiation and particularity, expressed variously as a will to die in or for others, perhaps to kill, or perhaps to give or to take too much, thereby potentially denying life to self or others, and provoking a confrontation with the *élan vital* and the will to sociability. Such transgressions threaten those *représentations* of social totality articulated in the codes they breach or invert. Effervescent assemblies are in this light ambiguously dangerous arenas, in which social relations governing differentiation and the order of *représentation* are affirmed, and in which 'the social logos inscribes itself deliriously' on the bodies of participants (Gane 1983b:236). Heightened emotions also invoke a will to transgress the very limits set by this order. For Durkheim, 'emotion' refers specifically to an infusion of *collective* energy which takes individuals out of their particularity.

But transcendence becomes transgression only when a desire to merge or die in the ecstatic moment, or to violate boundaries constituting individuals, groups or classes, is carried through. Even violence may have its etiquette (557/390): scapegoats chosen according to strict rules, violations of everyday limits, incest and even murder carried out according to ritual protocol. Despite his references to revolution, Durkheim sees small danger that most forms of effervescence will break their ritual bounds. He avidly describes the violence in some effervescent events, but maintains that it affirms the vitality of the group; that even transgression can uphold and reproduce the sacred, and that emotive expenditure and excess are somehow necessary to social reproduction. Similarly, Victor Turner refers to ecstatic de-differentiation as *communitas*, not chaos (see also Pickering 1984:416). For Durkheim, the key safeguard appears to be that effervescent assemblies are typified by a balance of two factors: strong collective sentiment, and sentiment *objectified* in symbols (Ono 1996); or as Gane might put it, delirium, and the ritual inscription of a sacred language (see Gane 1983a, 1983b).

For Durkheim, then, differentiation entails totality and necessitates reciprocity. Totality is expressed and reciprocity made possible through a structure of *représentation* in terms of which I and the other with whom I reciprocate are placed in obligation by our common stature as representative members – subjects – of a whole which our reciprocal bond enacts. For Mauss, the importance of reciprocity lies in its obligatory nature: whereas his question in the 'Essai sur le don' is in what sense and under what circumstances is it necessary that a gift given should be reciprocated? This focus on obligation has led to occasional reproaches that Mauss imported the idea of self-interest into an essay that otherwise challenges the very premises of possessive individualism and of *homo oeconomicus*. But, in a Durkheimian reading of Mauss, the obligatory character of the gift could be said to be based, not only in self-interest, which, as Mauss notes, should not always be equated with the modern notion of the self, but also in a need for recognition, in terms of a representational structure through which one sees oneself in the other. In short, Mauss's exchangism can be construed as a model of mutual recognition and as a symbolic structure.[10]

Conclusion: the legacy and future of the concept of effervescence

In a 1936 letter to a Danish colleague, Mauss discussed what he saw as his and Durkheim's failure to anticipate Fascism in the following words:

> Durkheim, and after him, the rest of us are, I believe, those who founded the theory of the authority of the collective *représentation*. One thing that, fundamentally, we never foresaw was how many large modern societies, that have more or less emerged from the Middle Ages in other respects, could be hypnotized like the Australians are by their dances, and set in motion like a child's roundabout ... We also contented ourselves with proving that it was in the collective mind (*dans l'esprit collectif*) that the individual could find the basis and sustenance for his liberty, his dependence, his personality and his criticism (*critique*). Basically, we never allowed for the extraordinary new possibilities.
>
> (Mauss 1936. English translation, Lukes 1973:338–9)

Georges Bataille and Roger Caillois set out to explore this 'new means' in a deliberately 'extraordinary' pedagogical and theoretical experiment and so formed the Collège de Sociologie. Grounded in the thematics of *The Elementary Forms*, and inspired by Mauss, Hertz and Hubert, the attempt reverberates to this day in French cultural theory (Richman 1995, Gane 1988:89). But how are such reverberations to be assessed?

It is generally agreed that *The Elementary Forms* is a great but flawed work: its definition of religion in terms of totemism is seen as problematic, as are the assertions that religion is at the core of social life, and that religious *représentations* lie at the origin of scientific concepts. And like other examples of Durkheim's sociology, *The Elementary Forms* can be said to exhibit what Schmaus (1995) terms an insufficient distinction between functional and causal explanations. Pickering (1984:120–2) notes a difficulty in Durkheim's attempt to relate the categories of the sacred and profane to a 'dichotomous social organization', namely, seasonal oscillations between mundane activities and effervescent assemblies. But Pickering also asserts that Durkheim is 'not concerned with historical origins', and characterizes the relation between *représentations* and social structure as dialectical. In somewhat similar terms,[11] we too would argue that the themes of differentiation and duality explored here, and their consequences when energized by the affective pull of effervescence, may be seen as elements of a dialectical rather than a causal – or indeed even a functional account. It is the extension and modification of this dialectical thematic which, we suggest, links the *The Elementary Forms* to the larger body of Durkheim's work, and to the later efforts of Mauss and Bataille.

While Durkheim, Mauss and Bataille all explored the importance of the sacred and of the gift to the constitution of society, Bataille stressed the centrality to social life of excess, a will to destruction, heterogeneity, *dépense*, in a way that distinguishes his work from the Durkheimian tradition. For Bataille, expenditure and destruction exist alongside and vie with production and order. Expenditure involves a will to transgress the limits of self, self and others, life and death, individual and totality. This will is not a simple matter of personal or antisocial orientation; it is essential to social life (Bataille 1938/t.1988:123–4). But the violence of Bataille's images is pre-figured, however faintly, in the enthusiasm of Durkheim's descriptions of collective effervescence as a violent expenditure of human energy, some-times to the point of death. They have their echoes, too, in Mauss (see Gane 1983b:267n.2). For all three, the differentiated condition of social life occasions tension: a transgressive possibility fuelled by a de-differentiating impulse in moments of heightened emotional intensity. Differentiation, a structure in tension, defined by tension, invokes its own potential collapse.

For Mauss and Durkheim, catastrophe is checked by social balance; apoc-alypse threatens when inequity and injustice reign. It also occurs when individuals or organizations act as if they were autarchic totalities, owing nothing, least of all their identities, to the collective. Both are good Kantians: proposing that duty, honour and respect express and guarantee the neces-sary existence of differentiating social, cognitive and moral categories. But they add to the Kantian scenario both the idea that fundamental cultural and cognitive categories are collective, and that they are infused by will and sentiment: love of duty, of responsibility, and of others who represent to one both oneself and humanity. Such categories are also imbued with an affective nostalgia accompanied by a will to transcend and collapse limits, separation and particularity. But the actual destruction of social distinctions occurs only in limited or revolutionary circumstances, or on occasions in which a society out of balance implodes.[12]

For Bataille, however, a will to death, expenditure, *dépense*, simply *is*. It is fact, not potential. The differential structure of modern social life is also a given, but this 'homogeneous' order is necessarily countered by the energy of heterogeneity. If excess and transgression are denied, they will reappear in other forms.[13] Thus, Bataille shifts emphasis from balance to excess, scarcity to plenitude; from the objectively existing social to the subjective stance of the embodied person confronted by others and by nature. Communication between self and others, as between individuals and totality, takes place not simply in terms of recognition, respect and reciprocity, but also in forms of violation through which real contact with the other is said to be possible. Those who risk excess risk loss of self and subjective disin-tegration – a risk catastrophic in its possible effects but necessary to human being. This is analogous to Durkheim's description of participants in effer-vescent events, but the social totality, for Bataille, no longer serves as the principle of ecstatic merger or the focus of affective dependency. The social is instead an 'acephalic' structure. Bataille plays Nietzsche to Durkheim: the death of God (and of mankind) is the death of the *social* (and of the integrated moral subject). Its energy survives in moments of violation, which for Bataille can be instances of recognition, but as a headless process in perpetual oscillation between energizing violence and the recovery of order. There is no guarantee that the self, offered up in this process, will be given back. This vision of social life without totality, without God or society-as-god, is powerful (see Richman 1982, 1995), though it also invites criticism. Which God is dead? And is violation love? Bataille takes one side of an implicit Durkheimian dialectic of order and excess, makes it explicit, and reconfigures what Durkheim might have termed an anomic pathology as essential to social life, leaving us with the maxim that that life is necessarily transgressive.

Despite its vivid depiction in *The Elementary Forms*, the concept of effervescence attracts criticism. It appears to reveal much and promise more: who could deny the emotion, personal and collective, generated in extra-ordinary gatherings at signal points in time: VE Day, rock concerts, revival meetings – or the Nuremberg rallies? Yet when used in a functionalist sense, it seems to run out of conceptual energy. Its strength appears to lie less in its analytic rigour as part of a theory of social order or solidarity than in the vivacity of its description. In this sense, the tone of Durkheim's own writing challenges its functionalist or integrationist interpretations. Is the will which underwrites the differentiated order of *représentation* and reciprocity tied to an impulse to de-differentiation and excess, and do these two forces meet, with particular intensity, in the phenomenon called effervescence?

Notes

1 An early version of this article was presented at the conference on Durkheim's *The Elementary Forms of Religious Life*, at Oxford, July 1995. I thank participants at that conference, and L. Beaman-Hall and W. S. F. Pickering, for critical comments and encouragement.

2 The fact that these scenarios are structurally similar to those developed by Mauss and Beuchat from studies of Inuit societies, raises fascinating questions about Durkheim's debt to Mauss.

3 Lannoy (1996:71ff.) notes that Durkheim's ethnographic description owes much to evocative passages in Spencer and Gillen, but also that Durkheim 'choisit des expressions françaises plus fortes, supprime certains passages et en regroupe d'autres' deliberately for the desired effect (ibid.:73).

4 As Gane notes (1983b), linked to blood are images of victimization or scape-goating.

5 My use of this term does not imply agreement with Goldenweiser's attribution of a crowd psychology to Durkheim. Durkheim suggested that the affective and cognitive features of effervescence were collective in both origin and effect (see Pickering 1984:396–403). I wish to thank H. T. Wilson for stimulating discussions about these and related issues.

6 Inasmuch as Durkheim treats religion and the social as mutually implicated, social life itself could also be characterized in such terms. But for Durkheim, differentiation is less a functional requisite of social relations than a constitutive and defining fact of both social life and consciousness. The concepts of differentiation and representation are inseparable in practice.

7 See Pearce 1989. Note that the conception of differentiation at work here is less functionalist than it is symbolic, referring to the structure of recognition and consciousness.

8 See Pickering's (1984:385–9) distinction between creative and re-creative effervescence.

9 A synthesis analogous, for Durkheim, to a chemical reaction (see Pickering 1984:415). For contemporary studies of revolutionary and other 'liminal' social events, utilizing elements of a Durkheimian perspective (see articles by Lynn Hunt and others in Alexander (ed.) 1988).

10 And a symbolic theory of the results of reciprocity unbalanced (competitive prestation, unequal exchange), or denied (competitive acquisition, philanthropy as moral superiority). Giving in excess can enforce subordination or enslavement, or, in unstable situations, threaten social equilibrium. Reciprocity denied can lead to war: those whose gifts are not returned are told symbolically that they do not exist; that they are, in effect, dead: they must, in return, kill. Something similar, Mauss implies, animates modern class conflict (Mauss 1925b/t.1990:76–7).

   In discussing the category of the person (1938/t.1985), Mauss claimed that the first forms of personal differentiation were masks (*personae*) representing social roles. Only after a long development have we identified with our masks in terms of a generic category of individual personhood, and has an interior life evolved to accord with that category. (That life bears marks of its origin to the extent that it is given dramatic and narrative forms of meaning.) As a social category, personhood entails reciprocity, and persons exist *per se* only via the gift of recognition. In Durkheimian terms, we are now both sacred (as representatives of humanity), and mundane (in our everyday particularity). But what if we were to take our mundane particularity to be equivalent to a sacred law ('a law to oneself')? By treating our particularity as sacred, would we not profane our sacredness (our representative humanity)? In such inversions, *élan vital* would translate into an instrumentality directly contradicting the social basis and symbolic status of personhood. In turn, this instrumentalism would tempt a return of the repressed: effervescent invocations of absolutist totalities, repressing rather than complementing the particularity of individual personhood. In Victor Turner's words, this excess would be destructively innovative. In pathologically individualistic societies, one might expect oscillations between a culture of self-absorption, and de-differentiating political or religious enthusiasms. For individuals, self-interest as a rule of life might alternate with or suddenly be displaced by an overwhelming desire to merge with others (e.g. in obsessive romantic or religious attachments).

11 However, posing the issue as one of 'relations' between representations and social life implies a causal distinction between ideas and social relations; e.g., treating effervescence as a 'source' of collective representations, motivating the production of ideas or giving them force (see Pickering 1984:412–14). Given Durkheim's maxim that the social be thought of as collective *représentations*, one might ask if such distinctions do full justice to his admittedly somewhat ambiguous position on the subject.

12 Mauss (1925b/t.1990:82; see also 34–43; 117, n.164) refers briefly, via an ethnographic example, to the suddenness with which a people can 'pass from festival to battle'.

13 Caillois observed that war could be analysed as a form of effervescence. For Bataille, the absence of destruction in capitalism (privatized consumption, accelerating production and accumulation) would be pathological. One wonders what he would have made of 'sustainable' models of capitalism, complete with analyses of the economic value of recycling.

12

EFFERVESCENCE AND THE ORIGINS OF HUMAN SOCIETY

N. J. Allen[1]

There are many reasons why one might be interested in *The Elementary Forms*, but mine may not be among the most obvious: I am interested in the origins of human society, and think that the great classic can help us reflect on how society acquired a structure. This does not imply blanket endorsement – I shall also have some criticisms of the work; but my aim is less to identify defects than to look for help in answering unsolved questions about the origins of society.

At first sight it may seem unlikely that the book can be used in this way. Surely, one might think, what Durkheim has to say about social origins must be wholly out of date, both as regards theory and facts? Has not social anthropology long ago rejected the evolutionism that Durkheim took for granted, and do we not nowadays know so much more than he did about prehistory, let alone about Australian Aborigines?

Neither issue, however, is straightforward. Take the matter of theories. It is perfectly true that, within social anthropology, soon after Durkheim's time there was a massive rejection of evolutionism, and that, in spite of protests from Marxists and others, the whole approach remains somewhat out of favour. No doubt Durkheim did indeed underestimate the problems of moving from nineteenth century tribal ethnography to the social history of mankind fifty or more millennia earlier. On the other hand, it is not clear what it means to 'reject evolutionism'. The phrase can merely imply that social anthropologists should get on with their fieldwork and not waste time speculating about the distant past. Such pragmatically-based rejection no doubt served a useful function in the growth of the discipline, and remains a reasonable position for individuals to adopt; but there is no reason why it should still constrain the curiosity of all practitioners. Rejection of evolutionism can also mean avoiding certain vocabulary, words like 'primitive' and 'progress', which sound dated and may be taken to imply unacceptable value judgements; but a rejection based on such politico–moral–aesthetic grounds is quite different from one based on theoretical or epistemological grounds.

In its strictest form this third sort of rejection (the most interesting) would maintain that ethnography is of zero relevance to world history – either because the latter concept is itself incoherent, or because the relevance is too difficult, or even impossible, to establish. Societies simply cannot be allotted to stages allowing systematic comparison between different periods. But an argument along these lines puts one on a slippery slope: carried through consistently, it has to deny that one social group can ever be classified as moving ahead of or falling behind another with respect to any particular feature – an extreme and untenable stance. Like any other approach, evolutionism can be misused; but practised with sufficient skill and caution, it is not an unreasonable way to try to understand society, and the fact that Durkheim was an evolutionist does not in itself render his ideas obsolete.

I turn next to Durkheim's data. Clearly the range of facts on which *The Elementary Forms* draws is very limited. The book is about the origin of religion, and Durkheim holds that most social institutions derive from religion; so he is really dealing with the origin of sociality, of human society as we know it. This situates his undertaking in what would now be called palaeoanthropology. But the latter has become a huge subject drawing on specialities such as primatology, molecular genetics, sociobiology, palaeontology, climatology, ecology, archaeology, psychology and linguistics, not to mention social anthropology (see e.g. Mellars and Stringer 1989). Its biological component covers such matters as bipedalism, encephalization, infantile dependency, reproductive physiology and vocal tract anatomy. But it also deals with technology (use of fire, stone tools, figurines, rock art), and with more sociological topics such as the sexual division of labour (between males who mainly hunt and females who mainly gather), and the use of resources (non-humans tend to consume food where they find it, humans bring it to a base and share it). The picture is enriched by theories of mental evolution, of the development and reabsorption of specialized cognitive domains or modules (Mithan 1996). The topics are interlinked in complex ways and the whole story is given a measure of precision by scientific dating techniques. If one situates *The Elementary Forms* in this context, it does seem unlikely that, after more than eighty years, it should still have something to offer. But unlikely though it be, that is what I argue.

I shall try to show that the Durkheimian notion of effervescence goes some way towards answering one of the fundamental questions about social origins. It is a question that at first sight pertains more to the domain of kinship and social structure than to religion, but for Durkheim the two are not wholly separate. Religion, like so much of human culture, goes back to *clan* assemblies. Such assemblies generate effervescence, a state in which clan members become aware of forces transcending the individual. Responding creatively to these forces, they symbolize them with totemic emblems, thereby originating the category of the sacred. For initiation rituals the tribe as a whole assembles, generating even more transcendent sacred concepts.

My central concern is not with the sacred or with totemic concepts, but with the context in which they supposedly develop, namely with the 'effervescent assembly' (Pickering 1984:Ch.21). Although I do not know the palaeoanthropological literature in any depth, I doubt if it often refers to such assemblies; for instance they do not feature in the work even of someone like Knight (1991, Knight *et al.* 1995), who starts from a social anthropological background. But why do they merit attention? To answer this question, I consider first the simplest ways of organizing a primitive small-scale society, and then ask how such an organization might itself arise.

Truly elementary social structures

Organization implies division into units or categories. Biology provides two obvious bases for division, namely sex and age, but any further division must be based on social rules. All sorts of rules are theoretically conceivable, for instance, a lottery that allocates individuals to groups at some point(s) in their life-span. But in practice societies seldom employ chance for such fundamental purposes, and the general experience of anthropologists strongly suggests that the earliest human socio-structural rules related to kinship and marriage. This is a classical topic for anthropological theorizing and for some years I have been interested in the simplest way of combining the relevant variables. The solution is a type of structure which I call 'tetradic', since it is quadripartite. However, the way in which tetradic structures themselves originated is less clear: it is here that the effervescent assembly comes to the rescue.

I must now summarize certain features of tetradic theory (Allen 1989, forthcoming). It will be few pages before I return explicitly to the assemblies, but I shall be dealing with matters on which Durkheim wrote elsewhere (especially 1898a(ii)) and which are highly relevant to *The Elementary Forms*.

There are several ways of introducing tetradic models. One approach starts with disciplinary history and presents the theory as the logical development of previous attempts in the same direction. A second starts with data on attested societies, chooses the simplest, and tries to simplify yet further. A third works deductively, starting from first principles. In addition one must opt whether to look at the rules of kinship and marriage from outside (how they structure society as a whole) or from inside (how they bear on an individual ego who has relatives to classify). I was led to tetradic theory largely by an inductive and egocentric path, but here (as in Allen 1995) I take a deductive and sociocentric approach.

So let us start from first principles, and envisage society as an enduring and demographically bounded whole, replenishing itself by its own reproductive activity – the 'structureless horde' of Durkheim's earlier writings. This constitutes a totality, 'the category par excellence' as Durkheim calls it (609).[2] The society contains males and females, young and old, but how else could it be structured? The simplest answer is by bisection into two halves or moieties on the basis of generation. If one moiety is A, the other B, we stipulate that each is endogamous: members of A always and only marry other members of A, and their children belong to B. Members of B marry each other, and *their* children belong to A.

In other words the two moieties exchange children: individuals born in the wombs of A are given to B to constitute its membership, and vice versa. If I am in A, my children and parents are in B, my grand-relatives are in A, my great-grand-relatives in B and so on.[3] Since generations are conventionally shown horizontally, one can diagram thus:

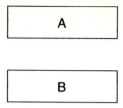

It is important to see that the distribution of ages is the same in each moiety. It is *not* the case that moiety A contains my contemporaries and those of my grand-relatives, moiety B those of my parents and children. The mistake is easily made because of the ambiguity of English *generation*, which means both 'contemporaries' and 'genealogical level'. In fact, moving away from ego to remoter and remoter cousins, one finds within A individuals of all ages, none of them more representative than any other. Generation moieties are not particularly odd, anthropologically speaking. I first met them in a classic essay by Hocart (1970:177) concerning the hill tribes of one of the islands of Fiji: 'the whole population is divided into two alternate generations called *tako* and *lavo*'.

An alternative way of bisecting a society on the basis of rules of kinship and marriage is into descent moieties, which are conventionally shown vertically:

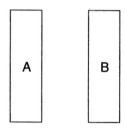

In this case the moieties are *exo*gamous, so that members of A must marry in B and vice versa. In terms of exchange the two units can be thought of as swapping nubile women, not children. However, this marriage rule says nothing about recruitment. Consider a male in A: we need to specify whether his children belong in A or B. The options give respectively patrimoieties and matrimoieties.

We are now in a position to envisage the most obvious tetradic models. They arise if generation moieties are cross-cut by descent moieties. Each generation moiety remains endogamous, but it is subdivided into exogamous 'sections', as they are nowadays called. One diagrams thus:

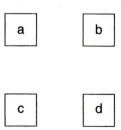

The horizontal relations are easy to envisage, but a slightly more subtle point concerns the vertical dimension. It might seem that the descent moieties need to be specified as either patri- or matri-, but in fact the choice is unnecessary. This is because four entities, whether sections or anything else, can be generated by *two* cross-cutting dichotomies of an initial totality, but they can then be arranged in *three* pairs: ab/cd, ac/bd, ad/bc. So the four sections produced by cross-cutting generation moieties with patrimoieties can be rearranged on the page or in the mind (of native or analyst) as matrimoieties, and vice versa if the cross-cutting is with matrimoieties. Any two of the dichotomies imply the third.

This point is close to Durkheim's interests. Four-section systems are of course extremely widespread in Australia, and he discussed them in *The Elementary Forms* and elsewhere, albeit using different vocabulary – *classe matrimoniale* for 'section' and *phratrie* for 'moiety'. He envisaged them as resulting from primal matrimoieties cross-cut by patrilocal residence, i.e. in effect as the product of the two types of descent moieties. My own emphasis on generation moieties derives from the significance I attach to child exchange, as will become clear at the end of the paper.

So far the tetradic model has been presented in sociocentric terms, as a way of structuring a self-reproducing population. But this gives only a partial view, for the model also needs to be understood egocentrically. This means locating ego in one of the sections and working out the distribution of ego's relatives. Given the built-in rules of marriage and recruitment, it is an easy logical exercise: provided the rules are followed, all possible relatives fall into one or other section. Genealogical distance makes no difference. Whether long dead, or not yet born, all have their place.

In other words, the four sections of society are precisely congruent with four categories of relatives. Society, doubly dichotomized, and the domain of relatives, arranged in four categories, are co-extensive, and use the same dividing lines.[4] The difference consists merely in the point of view, in the way units are identified. Sections can be named in the ordinary sense of the word, whereas categories of relative can only be identified relative to ego, by a kinship term. The four units can be labelled in these two different ways. That is why the analyst can approach tetradic models equally well by a sociocentric or egocentric route.

As I have discussed elsewhere, there are many tetradic structures other than the one just presented, but I should emphasize that all are hypothetical. Four-section systems exist ethnographically, as I mentioned, but the associated classification of relatives is always more complex than in the model. If (to simplify) kinship terminology and classification of relatives are taken as synonymous, one always finds more than four kinship terms – indeed more than the eight that would result from splitting the four by sex. Thus the Kariera of north-west Australia, the textbook example of a four-section system, had around twenty terms. Nevertheless, logically speaking, four would suffice to form a coherent system and one that is not very remote from human practice as we know it.

But why cannot the reduction be carried further? Why would a single dichotomy, accompanied by a binary division of relatives, fail to accord with what is characteristically human? Whichever of the three dichotomies one chose, the classification would simply divide relatives into those of ego's moiety and those of the other. What is wrong with that?

The problem becomes clear when one relates marriage rules to incest. Incest is a fundamental topic, long debated by anthropologists. For many, including Malinowski (1927:179) and Lévi-Strauss, it stands on the border between nature and culture, between non-human and human, and I take it as evidence of Durkheim's penetration that he chose it as the subject for what was both his first original text focusing on tribal societies and the opening article in the first volume of *L'Année sociologique* (1898a(ii)).

Notions of incest are culturally variable, but for analysts the term usually refers simply to the (almost universal) prohibition of sexual intercourse between close relatives, and particularly between primary relatives, i.e. members of the nuclear family. In this minimal sense there are two sorts of incest, intragenerational between brother and sister, and intergenerational between parent and child (either mother–son or father–daughter). Clearly, sexual intercourse, which can be intra- or extra-marital, and marriage, which may or may not involve intercourse, are not synonymous. All the same, marriage can normally be taken to imply intercourse, and the simplest arrangement is for the rules governing marriage also to govern intercourse, so that sex is prohibited outside marriage.

The central point is that a single dichotomy of society cannot rule out incest of both sorts. A division into generation moieties leaves open brother–sister marriage; matrimoieties leave open father–daughter marriage; and patrimoieties leave open mother–son marriage. It might seem that the last two could be avoided by stipulating change of moiety membership on marriage: a woman would join her husband's patrimoiety, and hence (for instance if she were widowed) be ruled out as a legitimate partner for her son. But the problem is merely relocated: a change applying to the mother at *her* marriage must apply to her daughter at *hers*, so that after her marriage the latter becomes a legitimate partner for her own father. To rule out both horizontal and vertical forms of incest one needs two dichotomies.

It is worth translating this sociocentric argument into egocentric terms. It is widely known that tribal peoples tend to group relatives into categories containing indefinite numbers of what to us seem wholly different types of relative. The discovery of 'classificatory' kinship terminologies goes back to Morgan in 1871, and has been described as 'the single most important ethnographic breakthrough of all time' (Barnard 1994:803). So could not the earliest kinship terminologies have consisted of terms grouping all relatives within a moiety? But consider the consequences. Under generation moieties a woman classes in her own moiety her husband and brother; under matrimoieties she classes together in the opposite moiety her husband and father; under patrimoieties her husband and son. In other words she systematically conflates marriageable and unmarriageable: a two-term terminology fails to make the conceptual distinctions needed to avoid marriage within the nuclear family. A four-term terminology does just that:

a woman's father, brother and son are located in three of the categories while the fourth, the source of her husband, contains no primary relatives until she marries into it.

A tetradic terminology, though logically neater and more consistent than any in the ethnographic record, makes no use of principles that are not attested. The classification of all relatives of a given genealogical level under two heads (which may be subdivided by sex and relative age) is commonplace, and the grouping together of relatives from alternate genealogical levels is by no means rare. On a scale leading from empty theoretical simplicity to attested complexity, quadripartition represents a breakthrough, an ethnographic Rubicon.

Australia

Having introduced what I take to be the simplest structuring of society that would look human, I turn to the question of Durkheim's choice of Australia. I have referred twice to Aboriginal data, but this was largely in the hope of retaining the interest of those who find kinship somewhat abstract and dry, and not at all because the argument depended on Australian data. It is a fact of logic that if one tries to model a society in which everyone is related to everyone else, and to do so using rules of kinship and marriage and taking account of the minimal incest prohibitions, then a quadripartite model is the simplest possible model. This would be just as true if measles or some other scourge had wiped out all Aborigines before a line of ethnography had been written on them.

That said, however, it is interesting that Australia offers forms of social organization closer to tetradic models than other areas of the world, insofar as such closeness can be estimated. There is one instance of a four-section system reported from southeastern Peru (Kensinger 1984), and the system has sometimes been postulated as underlying attested forms elsewhere; but Australia remains its *locus classicus* – reports go back at least to the 1850s (Needham 1974:118). The coincidence is interesting because on page 1 of *The Elementary Forms* Durkheim announces that he is seeking societies of maximal organizational simplicity; similarly, he claims later (136/96) that the organization of the Australian tribes is the most primitive and simple that is known. Ironically, however, he mislocates this simplicity: instead of associating it with the four-section systems, he locates it in the organization by clans (ibid). In other words, he overlooks horizontal splitting, based on child exchange, and theorizes solely in terms of vertical splitting; indeed he thinks the clans arise from vertical splitting of the primal matrimoieties, which themselves arise from splitting of the original 'compact and undivided mass' (1898a(ii):63). Perhaps he was influenced by the greater frequency of descent-based constructs throughout the ethnographic world, or by their prominence in the Biblical and classical worlds (the first 'alien' cultures that he knew much about), or by Robertson Smith. But whatever the explanation, he was seeking socio-structural simplicity in the right ethnographic region.

For other reasons too, his choice of Australia is less arbitrary than critics often suppose. He refers briefly to the technology as *rudimentaire* and to the absence of houses or even huts (136/96), also to the 'hunting–fishing' economy (334/233), but there is nowadays more to be said. Australia offers one of the very few large areas of the world where the population continued to rely exclusively on hunting and gathering right up until the time when ethnographers began to describe them; and not only that, but it was populated at an early date (60,000–40,000 BC, tens of millennia before the New World, let alone the Arctic), and thereafter it had little cultural or demographic exchange with the rest of the world. Relative isolation plus conservatism in technology and mode of subsistence does not *necessarily* imply conservatism in other cultural domains such as social structure or religion; but in assessing Durkheim's undertaking, the special position of Australia on the ethnographic world map is worth remembering.

However, if tetradic theory is right, and if one is looking to totemic social structure to explain the earliest forms of religion, then one ought to look, not to totemic *clans* but to totemic *sections*. Durkheim refers to tribes with section totems, notably to the Wakelbura of Queensland (154–5/111–12, with footnotes), but he gives them little weight in *The Elementary Forms*. In 1903 he and Mauss had treated classifications based on four sections (including that of the Wakelbura) before those based on clans. I doubt if this implied some shadowy sense of the evolutionary priority of sections: it was simply that they were moving from binary via quadripartite classifications to ones with larger numbers of units (1903a(i)). In any case, the difference between clan and section merely concerns mode of recruitment: a section contains neither of ego's parents, a clan contains one of them and a caste or endogamous stratum contains both.[5] But the mode of recruitment to a group has no bearing on the idea that, when it assembles, its members become aware of forces transcending the individual, and my criticism of Durkheim's treatment of sections leaves unaffected what he says about effervescence.

Gatherings

Apart from clan versus section, there is another unsatisfying aspect of Durkheim's argument, namely, the weight he gives to clan rituals (the *Intichiuma*) relative to the tribal rituals of initiation. He treats the former first and at greater length, and leaves the reader feeling that they are chronologically prior. No doubt he does this because he regards the totemic emblems as the first sacred symbols, and wants to interpret the high gods such as Baiame and Daramulun, worshipped exclusively at the tribal gatherings, as pointing to higher stages of religious evolution (420/293). But there is a difficulty here. As he realizes (221/155, 335n/233n), totemic organization necessarily implies a degree of co-ordination between clans, if only to prevent them adopting identical totems. But how could such co-ordination be effected except at tribal gatherings? The totemic clan presupposes the tribal assembly, which is therefore logically prior. Should not Durkheim have put the emphasis on tribal ritual rather than on clan ritual?

If he had, this too would leave the concept of effervescence unaffected. The bigger gathering could generate ideas of the sacred as well as or better than the smaller. Indeed the argument would become more characteristically Durkheimian, for in so far as a clan is exogamous, it can never be more than part of a society, while Durkheim usually emphasizes society as a whole – if not as *the* whole. But it does not follow that a tribal gathering would have to generate a unitary sacred concept like a high god. A gathering that emphasized social quadripartition could generate a fourfold idea of the sacred.

In thinking about tribal assemblies among hunter–gatherers (whether ethnographic or prehistoric), I suspect Durkheim was right to emphasize the emotions generated simply by assembling. I have felt something similar, and noted it in others, even in a peasant society. The days pass in the more or less humdrum activities of village life, with social contacts confined to a small circle of relatives and neighbours, and a gathering such as a festival or market does indeed produce excitement. Probably everyone has had similar experiences, and the effect may be greater in hunter–gatherer society, where the population density is typically so low and the membership of the coresidential band so restricted (of the order of twenty-five members).

Let me insert a note on the history of ideas. Pickering observes that Durkheim uses the term *effervescence* in *Suicide* in 1897 and in other writings from around 1900, but suggests that Durkheim was also drawing on the famous 1906 essay by Mauss on the Eskimos (1984:382). This is certainly right, and it merits more attention than it usually receives. Mauss, too, was studying hunter–gatherers, and distinguishing between two phases of social life, dispersed nomadism during the summer, when religious activity is minimal, and concentration in the winter stations, where life is given over to religion and sociability. Mauss actually uses the term *effervescence* in describing the phase when his tribal society is concentrated (1906:125), and a close comparison between the two texts would show that not only vocabulary but also many of the fundamental ideas of *The Elementary Forms* are foreshadowed in 1906. No doubt Mauss in turn was partly drawing on his uncle, but Durkheim's two footnote references to his nephew's paper are scanty acknowledgement.[6]

To return to my main theme. According to Durkheim, gatherings are creative in that they are the social context in which religion originates. But at the same time, under totemism, the relation between religion and social structure is so close that the two are virtually aspects of each other (thus he derives incest prohibitions from the exogamy of totemic clans). So should we envisage both religion and kinship-based social structure arising in the same context?

The main attraction of this idea is the implausibility of alternatives, and in particular the difficulty of imagining how a tetradic structure could arise among hunter–gatherers dispersed in bands over considerable areas of countryside. The classification of ego's relatives, the positive rules of recruitment and marriage, the negative rules against incest, the division of society into units – all are interlinked, and although the package is not complicated (indeed it is logically as simple as one can get), it does presuppose a conception of society as a totality. How could the whole complex originate except when the whole society (or at least its representatives) was assembled in one place?[7]

Palaeoanthropology usually sees matters differently, giving each aspect of primitive society a separate origin story. Thus social structure may be derived from two hordes which meet and decide to exchange females; or the minimal lineages which in chimpanzees link the patrilineal descendants of a patriarch are envisaged as expanding in time and scope so as to cover the descendants of a dead clan founder.[8] As for incest, many (like Fox 1980) start with the avoidance of close kin mating in apes, and envisage it turning into a sanctioned rule and expanding its range until in some societies it becomes the rule of clan exogamy. Similarly the usual approach to the origin of classificatory kinship terminologies, for instance that of Morgan himself, or of Fortes (1983:21, citing Radcliffe-Brown), envisages the terminology starting off with primary relatives and creeping outwards to meet the sociocentric divides. These approaches can be called 'extensionist' in that they take the individual as the starting point for theorising and work outwards. Some writers (such as Gamble forthcoming) explicitly dissociate themselves from Durkheim, who is presented as an outdated functionalist. In contrast, my own approach, which follows both Durkheim and Hocart, aims to be consistently contractionist. No doubt extensionism can be useful for purely synchronic purposes, but I think that the less explored contractionist view is closer to what actually happened and has more insights to offer.

Origins

Returning to effervescent assemblies, one need not regard them as a distinctively human innovation. On the contrary, primatological descriptions of 'chimp carnivals' suggest a pre-human origin, which may indeed go back many millions of years (Reynolds 1967:106f.). What happens is that groups of apes from different areas meet, perhaps at places where food is abundant, and the meeting results in 'social excitement'. Individuals shake branches, fling themselves around in trees, jump up and down, bang the ground or drum on trees (particularly on the thin protrusions that fan out at the base of certain species), vocalize loudly and sometimes rhythmically or in chorus (ibid.:131f., 181). The occasions may stimulate sexual activity (ibid.:107, 123), and Reynolds compares them in passing with the festivities of hunter–gatherers (ibid.:271). So the contrast between periods of social dispersal and concentration seems to have extremely deep roots.

If tetradic structures originated during the gatherings, the dispersed phase of social life might for a while have continued to operate according to older patterns. Instantaneous spread of the innovation from the one social context to the other seems less likely than a transitional period juxtaposing old and new.

Effervescent assemblies, chimp or human, tend to involve sexual behaviour, but it does not follow that the regulation of this behaviour was the original reason for the emergence of a tetradic structure. Apart from sex the assemblies involve other behaviour potentially subject to structuring. Is it not more likely that creativity and experimentation were directed in the first instance to aesthetic or ludic ends, rather than to social engineering? Various possibilities might be considered – chanting, drumming, dancing, ritual role-playing, games or contests. Durkheim himself remarks on the 'recreational' aspects of ritual (542f., 378f.), and there is no need here to be more specific.

However, I have long wondered (Allen 1982) whether the innovation might be related to the notion of rhythm – a topic mentioned in connection with gatherings both by Reynolds, Mauss and Durkheim.[9] Rhythm involves repetitions (of sound, movement or whatever), and can of course be generated by a single individual or a chorus acting in concert. But an alternative is for more than one individual or group to *take turns*. So perhaps the original function of the dichotomies (or an early one) was to structure the 'recreation' by group turn-taking.

Let us then imagine the gathering splitting into four teams or dance groups which pattern the subsequent sexual relations. If the pattern was carried over from one gathering to the next, that might go some way towards explaining the tetradic marriage rules, but it would say nothing about recruitment. New members of society are born (whether from relations during the gatherings or during the phase of dispersal), and they have to be placed somewhere within the quadripartite whole. But how? Does Durkheim offer any hints?

I think he does, though not deliberately. As we noted, he said that the purpose of the tribal gatherings was initiation, but he did not explain why that ritual should occur at tribal rather than clan gatherings, or indeed why it is so salient in Australian and other ethnography (La Fontaine 1985). But initiation and recruitment both concern the continuity of society across the generations, so they could be linked.

My suggestion is that originally initiation was not into the clan of the relevant parent but into the opposite generation moiety, or a section of it. In other words, child exchange took place not at birth but at initiation: what I called a generation moiety actually contained individuals belonging to two generations – initiated members of one, and uninitiated members of the next. Another way of putting it would be to define a generation as stretching, not from birth to childbirth within one lifespan, but from initiation to initiation across two. The idea has various attractions.

(1) Empirically, in tribal ethnography generally birth ritual is much less salient than initiation, which tends to occur shortly before reproductive maturity. Although in the archaeological record initiation is less salient than death ritual, it is not necessarily less ancient or fundamental.

(2) Where perinatal mortality is high, the continuity of society is ensured less by the birth of babies (which is merely the precondition for there being a generation after next) than by their arrival at reproductive maturity. If rites are 'above all the ways by which groups periodically

affirm themselves' (553/387), initiation is the most sensible time in the life-cycle at which to affirm the enduring existence of the group, whether it is society or its sections.

(3) If horizontal marital exchange is dramatized by weddings, it seems that vertical child exchange should have been dramatized no less forcefully; and whatever may be its functions in attested societies, initiation could have served that purpose in a tetradic society. One might go further. If initiation and wedding were once parts of a single ritual complex, then, by dramatizing *both* the fundamental modes of exchange at once, the ritual could have provided a perfect instance of a system of *prestations totales*, better than any that Mauss could have found in the ethnographic literature.

Many issues have been left undiscussed. Assuming tetradic theory is right, did the structure emerge just once, or did it emerge repeatedly at different times and places? Is there any possibility of dating the emergence by relating it to other innovations in the history of humanity? Could a tetradic social structure develop without the use of language (logically, sections could be identified by contrasted body markings as effectively as by names, and egocentric categories by contrasted styles of behaviour as effectively as by kinship terms)? Can one argue that a division into absolutely identified groups preceded one into relatively identified categories, that (to put it crudely) the egocentric derives from the sociocentric; or were the two correlated from the start? Were the rules structuring gatherings the first social rules? Might initiation have been the first ritual?

What I have been trying to do is (as in Allen 1994 and 1995) to show the continuing usefulness of *L'Année sociologique* ideas for thinking about current problems. If I am right, *The Elementary Forms*, together with Mauss's essay on the Eskimos, helps to fill out tetradic theory and make it more relevant to palaeoanthropology. In any case I think Durkheim draws attention to matters which cannot be neglected by those who think seriously about the origins of society.

Notes

1   I should like to thank Dr Nathan Schlanger and Professor Kathleen Gibson for critical comments on an earlier draft.
2   Although I translate the title, page references are to the French.
3   The expression 'child-exchange' can also be applied to the quite different situation where (for instance) *some* members of patriclan or patrimoiety A exchange children on a temporary or permanent basis with patriclan or patrimoiety B. If *all* members of A gave their children to B, children would cease to belong to their father's group and the 'patri-' would become meaningless.
4   The preceding discussion does little more than rephrase the insights of Granet, who was well aware of the significance of *double bipartition* (1939:170f) in the simplest forms of social organization. In the understanding of elementary structures of kinship Granet's priority relative to Lévi-Strauss has been well analysed by Héran (1996).

5 In connection with the world-historical approach to Gender Studies one notes that, at this level of abstraction, sections and classes have in common that ego's place in society depends equally on both parents, while in social structures based on unilineal descent one parent is more significant than the other.

6 It is a pity too that Durkheim could not or did not draw on his nephew's critical observations on the ethnography of Spencer and Gillen (Mauss 1968–9:notes 160, 281).

7 Cf. Lourandos (1988: 150), who argues, with reference to Australia, that 'the context for change' was provided by 'the arena of intergroup relations (for example, feasting, ritual and exchange)'. Although as analyst I used the notion of a bounded totality in constructing the tetradic model, and although I assume that the original inventors did likewise, it does not follow that in reality social boundaries were impermeable.

8 Cf. Quiatt and Reynolds, who rightly see tetradic theory as a challenge to their ideas, in that it is difficult to reconcile with any simply notion of continuity from primate to human patrilineages (1993:286).

9 Not to mention Granet (1939:175–7), who writes of the rhythm of social life and frequently draws on dance in his references to the *chassé-croisé* of domestic life.

13

CHANGE, INNOVATION, CREATION

Durkheim's ambivalence

Dénes Némedi

Sociology in the twentieth century was more interested in social reproduction than in social creation or innovation. However, change and innovation are recurring phenomena of our world. The year 1989 became the symbol for extensive change. There is an obvious discrepancy between the challenge of the contemporary world and the theoretical incapacity of sociology (and of social sciences in general) to provide tools for sufficient understanding of the emergence of new social forms and practices. Attempts to introduce creativity in sociological theory show that the problem cannot be solved by simply adding complementary theorems. The introduction of creativity in the theoretical core of the discipline requires the reconstruction of the whole theoretical infrastructure (Joas 1992).

A possible way to cope with the problem would be a recombination of old traditions. By combining the individualistic Weberian explanation of change with Durkheimian emphasis on group processes and on institutions, Tiryakian arrives at the concept of 'charismatic community' as the agent of change.

> It is that being in and part of the charismatic/effervescent tradition gives the charismatic community a sense of power – power not based on control of physical or material resources, but effective power nonetheless by virtue of being part of a moral community. I am tempted to say that this sentiment of empowerment, which occurs only in certain moments, transforms the group into a charismatic community, transforms, ultimately, social structure into agency.
>
> (Tiryakian 1995:274)

In this paper I set myself rather restricted objectives. I shall try to show how the elements of the rudimentary late Durkheimian theory of innovation are related. I look for the theoretical links between parts of the arguments as well as for rhetorical devices which lend credence to the propositions. By reconstructing the shaky edifice of the Durkheimian theory I show what are the elementary problems a theory of socio-political change has to face.

The argument of the paper will turn on the conceptual difference between institutional processes of innovation on the one hand and the breakdown and re-creation of institutions on the other. This difference is present in the Durkheimian argument itself. Obviously, in the Durkheimian theory in general the institutional aspect is more visible, but there are moments when Durkheim turns his attention to eruptive creative events. In *The Elementary Forms* this aspect is most visible.[1] It remains to be seen whether Durkheim succeeded in synthesizing the institutional and exceptional elements in a single theory and, if he failed, what can be learned from his failure.

I

The aims Durkheim followed while writing *The Elementary Forms* were complex and related to different layers of his theory. Foremost among his preoccupations was a concern with epistemology. In a letter to Xavier Léon in 1908, offering the future introduction of *The Elementary Forms* for publication in the *Revue de métaphysique et morale*, he described his intentions as follows:

> In fact I intend to point out as I proceed with the book several of the social elements which have been used to form certain categories we use ([. . . ?], causality, the notion of force, the notion of personality). This question has preoccupied me for a long time and I do not dare tackle it head on; but I believe it is possible to deal with it obliquely through religious thought.
>
> (1975b, 2:467)

The important points in this statement are that Durkheim maintained a very close link between the theory of religion and epistemology (Pickering 1993) and that he was interested in the 'constitution' of categories. I will come back to the interlacing of different strands of arguments later. Here I would stress the preoccupation with the problems of 'origin', 'source', and 'constitution' of categories. If, as was the case, he was interested in showing the social nature of knowledge, he could have solved the task by proving that the processes leading to the rearrangement of our conceptual apparatus are necessarily social processes. The argument would have involved a network theory of knowledge and would have required special attention to the institutional aspects of knowledge production. However, Durkheim's conception of knowledge was different. His general idea of science and knowledge had a vague similarity with Kantian epistemology. He therefore paid special attention to the categories, which he defined in a rather imprecise manner (113/80) and he believed that the decisive argument should be centred on the question of origins. All that is well known but it has to be mentioned because the general epistemological orientation heavily biased the detour through religious theory and influenced the suggested solution to the problem of the origin of conceptual thinking.

Durkheim mentioned two attributes of categorical thinking that can be explained by the sociological hypothesis. The irreducibility of categories to empirical observations was postulated by the apriorists, he said – the sociologist can explain it. The categories 'are essentially collective *représentations*', whereas the empirical impressions are of an individual nature. 'So between these two sorts of *représentations* there is all the difference which exists between the individual and the social, and one can no more derive the second from the first than one can deduce society from the individual' (22/16).[2] Where the apriorist was blocked was by an insurmountable paradox the sociologist could easily overcome. After all, he was the expert in explaining phenomena which could not be reduced to the individual – or at least Durkheim believed that he was.

Similarly, Durkheim thought that the necessary character of categories became understandable if one accepts the sociological hypothesis.

> Thus society could not abandon the categories to the free choice of the individual without abandoning itself. If it is to live there is not merely need of a sufficient degree of moral conformity, but also there is a minimum of logical conformity below which it cannot safely go.
>
> (24/17)

The basic idea of a sociological epistemology was already present in Durkheim and Mauss' classification essay (1903a(i)). However, the fact that *The Elementary Forms* deals with elementary forms of *religion* introduced crucial differences. First of all, Durkheim related conceptual thinking not to social organization in general but to the 'primal institution' of religion (Pickering 1993:64). In other words, by the simple fact that he became interested in primitive religion, he turned towards institutional facts. In 1903 he tried to prove that the basic human cognitive capacity of classification was of social origin. Now, he was forced by the logic of his investigation to look for special *institutional* practices which can explain the emergence of special human categories. The burden of proof he took upon himself was much heavier than earlier.

The conception he had of religion determined his investigations more concretely. While, in the introductory chapter of *The Elementary Forms*, he spoke of the categories of understanding (space, time, cause, etc.),[3] the social origin of which should and could be shown, later on he lost sight of these general 'categories' and narrowed his attention down to some basic religious ideas. There are three general Durkheimian concepts that can aspire to categorical status: the difference of sacred and profane,[4] the idea of impersonal (religious) force and the idea of soul (*âme*).

The logic of the argument led him away from the investigation of the practices maintaining and reconstructing the sacred–profane divide. In the Durkheimian school, there were already important investigations in related problems. Mauss' research was concentrated on subjects related to this problem (Mauss 1909; Hubert and Mauss 1899, 1904) and Hertz's important essay on the sociology of death can be mentioned too (1907). Durkheim took it for granted that the sacred–profane divide was the important and general fact about religion and looked further for the origin of this divide.

The quest for the origin of religious categorization implied two different, sometimes contradictory approaches. On the one hand, as a student of religion Durkheim directed his attention toward religious *institutions* and institutionalized beliefs as the most observable side of religion. The supposed totemistic religious system was already an elaborated body of beliefs with refined distinctions and complex rituals and he attempted to provide a general theory of totemism. On the other hand, as a student of the origins of religion, Durkheim had to go beyond the established practices, towards the supposed initial state or something reminiscent of absolute beginnings. He had to turn his attention towards events which were not institutionalized, which could be characterized as the source of institutions. The stage was set for the intricate dialectical reasonings Durkheim was fond of and also for circular argument, where established practices, incorrectly recognized as absolute beginnings, were taken as explanations of beliefs and basic thought structures. These in turn supported the same established practices.

The issue was further complicated by Durkheim's unilateral attention to the sacred side of the religious dichotomy. His lack of interest in the profane side of the divide strengthened his preference for *exceptional* practices and social phases. On the one hand, he quite naturally turned towards the institutional aspects of religiosity, and on the other, he selected for analysis religious rituals which appeared to be exceptional, unique, elevated above the dull repetition of everyday life. The exceptional ceremonial practices were regarded as causes of certain epistemic innovations. The idea of an extremely creative, intense social phase was already present in earlier works. Now it became prominent in Durkheim's thought and he more or less voluntarily disregarded the inherently repetitive and institutional aspects of sacred practices.

Important was the fact that the focus on religious categories opened up the possibility of linking social epistemology with *moral and political issues*. This was possible because in the Durkheimian conceptual scheme, religion was the place where the interconnections between different social spheres could be established (cf. Durkheim 1899a(ii)). The reasons for this type of problem-integration are well known. They are related to the specific position occupied by Durkheimian sociology in the French university system. Durkheim saw his sociology as a moral institution with a definite educational vocation and as a scientific institution that had to integrate the social sciences (1900b; letter to Léon mentioned above) and to overcome scientific anomie. Moral and civic renovation and scientific innovation were the twin *raisons d'être* of the Durkheimian sociology.

II

The crucial importance of the shift of perspective was concealed by the fact that the issue of the sacred–profane dichotomy as analysed in Book I, Chapter I, was not connected in any argumentative way with the issue of categories in the introductory chapter. The reason for this break in continuity was perhaps that the introductory philosophical chapter was written and published earlier in 1909 and was taken over without textual alteration (the third, highly provocative part excepted) as an Introduction to the book (1909d). However, the conclusion of the book established the connection missing at the outset. There Durkheim stated explicitly that the roots of logical thinking were to be looked for in religion: 'the fundamental notions of science are of a religious origin' (616/431). According to the Durkheimian conception, the analysis of religion was an exemplary analysis of central issues of social epistemology.

From the point of view of the *origins* of categories and of thought in general, Chapters VI and VII of Book II are the most important. Durkheim there said that he would explain the origins of totemistic beliefs in particular and of religious thought in general. However, as the central idea to be explained was the idea (*représentation*) of an *impersonal force* (mana), the demonstration turned out to be the demonstration of the social origins of categories (or rather the proof of the statement that it is not absurd to suppose that the categories are of social origin).

The idea of force was, according to Durkheim, the central element in totemistic beliefs.

> This is what the totem really consists in: it is only the material form under which the imagination represents this immaterial substance, this energy diffused through all sorts of heterogenous things, which alone is the real object of the cult.

> (270/189)

On the other hand, the idea of impersonal totemistic force was, according to Durkheim, the primitive equivalent of the idea of force as employed in modern sciences.

> What we find at the origin and basis of religious thought are not determined and distinct objects and beings possessing a sacred character of themselves; they are indefinite powers, anonymous forces, more or less numerous in different societies, and sometimes even reduced to a unity, and whose impersonality is strictly comparable to that of the physical forces whose manifestations the sciences of nature study.

> (285–6/200)

As the totemistic force was similar to the forces studied in modern physical sciences the idea that the Australian aborigines made of these forces was the most ancient forerunner of scientific theories. Therefore, by studying the origins of the idea of impersonal force Durkheim observed the emergence of conceptual thought in general.

As it is well known, Durkheim believed that the idea of the impersonal force emerged during collective rituals where individuals were elevated above everyday circumstances. One example studied by Durkheim was the celebration of the serpent *Wollunqua*. There the participants (members of the tribe *Warramunga*) had exceptional experiences.

Feeling himself dominated and carried away by some sort of an external power which makes him think and act differently from normal times, he naturally has the impression of being himself no longer ... everything is just as though he really were transported into a special world, entirely different from the one where he ordinarily lives, and into an environment filled with exceptionally intense forces that take hold of him and metamorphose him (312/218).

The religious form appeared, from this point of view, as a self-evident and practical mode of thought in which these experiences could be formulated. 'Since religious force is nothing other than the collective and anonymous force of the clan, and since this can be represented in the mind only in the form of the totem, the totemic emblem is like the visible body of the god' (316/221).

Of course, Durkheim himself never saw any primitive effervescent gathering. He borrowed his descriptions of the *Wollunqua* festivities from Spencer and Gillen (1904). By comparing this source with Durkheim's short text in *The Elementary Forms* two differences strike the reader's eye.

On the one hand, Durkheim dramatized the event. He created the impression that it was a singularly significant happening. He mentioned cursorily that it 'consists of a series of ceremonies lasting through several days' (310/217), but he said nothing of the ceremonies taking place before and after the effervescent happening. According to Spencer and Gillen (1904:228–48), the *Wollunqua* ceremony was a kind of ritual narration of the story of a mythical being. The participants followed the wandering of the serpent *Wollunqua* through the region, re-enacted the important turning points of his story. The ceremonies terminated with the diving of the serpent into a water-hole, i.e. with his return to the Dreamtime. As Spencer and Gillen relate it, the *Wollunqua* ceremonies were integrated in the complex institutional structure of primitive religion. This was the aspect which was relegated to the background in Durkheim's text.

Durkheim employed rhetorical devices, too, to accentuate the dramatic, exceptional character of the event. His text was a fairly close transcription of Spencer and Gillen's story. Durkheim terminated his description by a phrase which emphasized the exceptional nature of what was going on earlier: 'The fires died away and profound silence reigned again' (311/217). Spencer and Gillen were less dramatic: 'The fires died down, and for a short time [!] there was a silence. Very soon, however, the whole camp was astir, and, just at sunrise, the ceremony of *parra*, or subincision was performed upon the three youths who had recently passed thorough the earlier stages of initiation' (Spencer and Gillen 1904:238).[5]

On the other hand, Durkheim passed over the fact that the effervescent assembly had quite different meaning for different groups of participants and therefore, even if it was effervescent, it could not have created the same basic ideas (the idea of an impersonal and therefore general force). Durkheim mentioned the fact that the ritual was prepared by the phratry *Kingilli* whereas the serpent *Wollunqua* was a sacred being only for the members of the phratry *Uluuru*. Spencer and Gillen dealt extensively with this basic fact (1904:226 ff.). While the division of ritual labour between the phratries could have been interpreted as the reinforcement of the solidarity between them, Durkheim regarded the ritual as the practice which was at the origin of the common conceptual apparatus. He did not face the problem how a ritual which had different meaning for the two participant groups could be the cause of a common system of categories.

The differences between Durkheim's main anthropological source material and his use of it indicate that he turned his attention away from the institutional aspects of innovation (which he himself introduced by putting religion in the centre of research) and toward the exceptional moments of social life.

III

By eclipsing the institutional aspects of innovation he himself introduced earlier, Durkheim disguised the inherent circularity of his argument. That Durkheim's reasoning was faulty from a logical point of view has been observed several times. I quote only Evans-Pritchard: 'The rites create the effervescence, which creates the beliefs, which cause the rites to be performed' (1965:68, see also Lévi-Strauss 1962:102–3: Lukes 1973:30–4). In other words, Durkheim had to admit tacitly that the *Warramungas* were able from the outset to distinguish between the sacred and profane realm. The separation of sacred and profane time was the precondition of the institution of ritual and of exceptional practices. On the other hand, according to Durkheim the emergence of the competence of distinguishing these spheres could be explained only by the sacred practices themselves. Durkheim's ambition was to establish that the competence to order sensual perception in categorical forms was a socially acquired and preformed competence. Durkheim conceived the ritual which supposedly created the idea of an impersonal sacred force as a kind of *experimentum crucis* for sociological epistemology. Therefore, if the argument was logically invalid, the whole edifice of social epistemology was destroyed.

Certainly, perfect logical clarity was not Durkheim's most prominent virtue. However, circular reasoning was a rather elementary fault. Why did not Durkheim see the logical defect that even an undergraduate student could have discerned? How was his text *stabilized*[6] if the argument was obviously, and in an elementary way, faulty?

(1)   The first thing I would like to stress is that there was no logical problem with Durkheim's arguments as far as problems of *social integration* were concerned.[7] The rites and the collective effervescence as analysed fulfilled an integrative function, as Durkheim himself said. They renewed and reinforced collective identities. The periodicity of rites was itself a functional necessity, given the different or contradictory requirements of collective life.

> The rhythm which the religious life follows only expresses the rhythm of the social life, and results from it. Society is able to revivify the sentiment it has of itself only by assembling. But it cannot be assembled all the time. The exigencies of life do not allow it to remain in congregation indefinitely; so it scatters, to assemble anew when it again feels the need of this.
>
> (499/349)[8]

To approach the problem of integration, Durkheim should have followed the path of institutional analysis which he was tacitly abandoning. The effervescent gathering could have been interpreted, in this sense, as a special mechanism of institutional reconstruction/renovation. However, an analysis confining itself to the study of institutional integrative processes was unable to explain the origin of conceptual thought.

(2) Durkheim treated the *Warramunga* rites as *creative and renovative* practices, at one and the same time. However, the tools he developed for the analysis of religious phenomena and institutions were insufficient to deal with this double question. Durkheimian ethnological theory was more apt to deal with the integrative aspects of ritual. Described from the point of view of the ethnologist, the observed collective effervescence had a restorative function but it could not be conceived in the same context as the birthplace of society.

The creative aspects appeared because epistemological problems were introduced.[9] The creative effervescence was indispensable for the sociological explanation of categories. The Durkheimian scheme of explanation required that the origins of the *explanandum* (here of a special symbolic competence) could be shown. Durkheim worked with causal assumptions. The creative effervescence had to be the cause of human symbolic competences. This conception of creativity and causality made the circular argument inevitable. The effervescent ritual as an *integrative* institution required the previous division of the world into sacred and profane halves and this division was explained causally by the same ritual as a *creative* event.

(3) Given that the fatal circularity of the Durkheimian argument in *The Elementary Forms* resulted from a faulty genetic argument where creative functions were assimilated with integrative ones, would it not be possible to separate creativity and integration?[10] Whatever the merits of this solution, Durkheim could not accept it. Quite simply, he did not even consider it. I have shown above that he muddled the difference between routine, recurrent ritual practices and extraordinary, singular events or rather: he knowingly presented routine rituals as extraordinary events. He was forced to do that and consequently his analysis of the *Wollunqua* ritual had to carry the burden of an epistemological proof. His interest in the origins of conceptual thought (conceived as moments of absolute beginnings) forced him to reconstruct observed, recurrent rituals as extraordinary points of creation.

The neglect of the problems resulting from the confusion of integration and creativity was facilitated by Durkheim's tendency to combine philosophical, moral, political and strictly sociological arguments. The combination of philosophical and sociological arguments was the basic idea behind *The Elementary Forms*. I have shown that the problem of creativity emerged because Durkheim expected that he would solve the philosophical paradoxes of his time by sociological analysis. The central sociological argument on the potentialities of the effervescent assembly were 'stabilized' because Durkheim introduced some political considerations.

IV

The political aspects of the Durkheimian theory of effervescence are manifest. In the paragraphs preceding the analysis of collective effervescence, Durkheim considered in general terms the elevating and renovating impact of society. There are periods, he said, when this effect was particularly powerful and effective.

> In the midst of an assembly animated by a common passion, we become capable of acts and sentiments of which we are incapable when reduced to our own forces; and when the assembly is dissolved and when, finding ourselves alone again, we fall back to our ordinary level, we are then able to measure the height to which we have been raised above ourselves.
>
> (299–300/209–10)[11]

The examples Durkheim gave prove that he regarded the mass impact on the individual as beneficial and positive in a political sense: he mentioned the night of the 4th of August 1789, the period of the crusades, the Revolution (300–1/210–11). The conclusion of *The Elementary Forms* contained a compact and pregnant formulation of his conception of politics and morals:

> There can be no society which does not feel the need of upholding and reaffirming at regular intervals the collective sentiments and the collective ideas which make its unity and its personality. Now this moral remaking cannot be achieved except by the means of reunions, assemblies and meetings where the individuals, being closely united to one another, reaffirm in common their common sentiments; hence come ceremonies which do not differ from regular religious ceremonies, either in their object, the results which they produce, or the processes employed to attain these results.
>
> (610/427)

Obviously, the assimilation of integration and creativity characterized Durkheim's moral–political argumentation, as well. Durkheim believed that common beliefs and ideals should be reinforced and restated periodically. He believed in the possibility of a 'civic cult', as many places in his writings prove. According to him, the periodic return of sacred periods helped to confirm civic identities, gave new force to common symbols. The similarity of religious and civic belief systems was to be found in their similar structure. Both had an integrative impact because they assured the periodic return of ceremonial events. They had an integrative force because they rested on pre-existing common beliefs. In this sense he spoke of political gatherings (300/210), of commemorative civic festivities (610/427), of the French revolutionary cult (611/428).

However, he often stressed the necessity of creative events and periods, too. In his own time, he saw moral and political mediocrity, 'moral frost' (froid moral). There was no common faith that could integrate society.

> If we find a little difficulty to-day in imagining what these feasts and ceremonies of the future could consist in, it is because we are going through a stage of transition and moral mediocrity. The great things of the past which filled our fathers with enthusiasm do not excite the same ardour in us . . . but as yet there is nothing to replace them.
>
> (610/427)

The periodic return of ceremonial occasions would not help if there were no common ideals. The social bonds had to be re-created and only critical, effervescent periods could do that. Durkheim did not exclude the possibility that this will be possible.

> A day will come when our societies will know again those hours of creative effervescence, in the course of which new ideas arise and new formulae are found which serve for a while as a guide to humanity; . . . There are no gospels which are immortal, but neither is there any reason for believing that humanity is incapable of inventing new ones.
>
> (611/427–8)

As examples of creative social–political effervescence Durkheim mentioned the medieval Christian crusades, Jeanne d'Arc, the Revolution and particularly the night of the 4th of August (301/210–11).[12]

The creative aspect of Durkheimian political sociology is well known.[13] The transition between creative and commemorative political practices and events was in Durkheim's rudimentary political sociology relatively easy. As the political argument was less elaborated than the religious one, the inherent theoretical difficulty of combining integration and creativity was less visible in this case.

In addition, recent political events made the assumption of creative political innovation more plausible. The issues of the French revolution were still debated, the Republic was still in its youthful phase. Durkheim also lived in the classical period of the workers' movement. He must have been familiar with the innovative/creative rituals of socialism – in fact, he mentioned modern socialism among the examples of creative effervescence.

From Durkheim's not very numerous political writings it can be seen that his understanding of political creativity meant essentially two different things. On the one hand, he demanded the renovation and modernization of institutional forms. His only concrete proposal was that the corporations should be re-established. He did not go into the details of radical institutional innovations. He did not consider who could be the agents of the change, neither did he ask about the possibility of a total remodeling of a modern society. On the other hand, political innovation meant for him the elaboration of new common ideals, something similar to the institution of revolutionary religion. Mathiez's study on the revolutionary cult had a certain influence on him (Tiryakian 1988).

As Durkheim's political conceptions were not elaborated in detail, the integrative/renovative and the creative aspects were not separated clearly. The problem of institutional change and the possibility of the emergence of real innovation were not analysed in any detail. However, even in their rudimentary form, the political arguments contributed to the stabilization of the analysis of religion.

It is important to note the strategical location of political remarks. Chapter VII in Book II constitutes the most important part of the work as far as the problems of integration/creativity are concerned. In the previous chapters, Durkheim described totemistic beliefs. Chapter VII was devoted to the problem of origins. Section II began with a general statement on the quasi-divine nature of society (295/206) and it went on with general sociological considerations on the constraining and empowering character of society. Durkheim was preparing his argument that the notion of force emerged in effervescent gatherings (like the *Wollunqua* ritual). However, the 'strengthening and vivifying action of society' was illustrated by the night of the 4th of August (300/209–10) and not by any Australian example. Durkheim believed that creative social moments can be understood better by taking relatively recent political examples than by the technical analysis of Australian ethnography. The general effect of this procedure was that the sympathetic reader was already convinced of the truth of the Durkheimian idea when he met with the interpretation of the *Wollunqua* ceremony (which was to be the real proof). It is in this sense that the sketchy political arguments stabilize the shaky ethnological reasoning (and the latter stabilizes the belief in political innovation – as the conclusion of *The Elementary Forms* testifies).

V

Essentially, Durkheim's problem was how he could explain the emergence of new, previously unknown *competences*. The categorical ordering of perception, the dividing of the world into sacred and profane halves was something totally new in an evolutionary sense, according to Durkheim. Therefore, he believed that the sacred–profane divide must have been instituted in an unprecedentedly creative gathering. Whether this supposition could have been proved by deeper knowledge of Australian reality and by a more careful analysis of the documents, is doubtful. In any case, the plausibility of the argument rested more on the combination of philosophical, sociological and political ideas than on its factual and logical correctness.

The separation of the epistemological, political and moral aspects of Durkheimian theory is impossible. It remains to be seen whether a better and more convincing combination of these elements is possible. Personally I am convinced that in our time when disciplinary boundaries are breaking down and the identity of the social sciences is becoming questionable, once again the example of theoretical endeavours that combine approaches in an unconventional manner remains essential.

Durkheim's problems with a satisfactory theory of creativity direct our attention to the facilitating or hindering role of religious theory. It was religious theory which made innovation and creativity a problem for Durkheim. It was the study of religion that provided the conceptual frame for the integrated analysis of the perception of the natural world and of the ideas concerning morals and politics. Durkheim believed that by studying religion, the sociological integration of social sciences would be possible (if sociology studies religion and if religion is the most original and central element of society then sociology must be the integrative science (cf. 1899a(ii)). However, the same factor that facilitated the breakthrough toward a novel conception of knowledge blocked its full development.

Toward the end of his career, Durkheim declared that he had become more and more interested in philosophy, but he approached philosophy essentially through a theory of religion (see Lukes 1973:406). Durkheim was not much interested in new developments in philosophy. To him, this neglect was legitimate. If sociology – as sociology of religion – should replace philosophy, there was not much sense in bothering about irrelevant questions. In the analysis of conceptual creativity this neglect of technical philosophical problems was a serious disadvantage.

Religious theory was a well chosen field of research for someone who tried to elaborate the relation between repetitive ritualistic practices, institutional innovation and exceptional events. However, Durkheim did not provide a satisfactory theory of institutional innovation. In fact, he abandoned the study of institutions (institutionalized ritual practices) at the crucial point for a dubious theory of creativity. Therefore, the worst strategy to overcome the difficulties of the Durkheimian theory would be the combination of the idea of creative effervescence with the Weberian idea of charisma – as Tiryakian proposed (1995). In a theoretical sense, it would mean concentrating on the weakest point in Durkheim's theory. In a practical sense, it would mean waiting for the never-coming great communal experience while we depend, all of us, on the innovative and creative capacities of the institutions.

Notes

1 The de-institutionalization and de-structuration inherent in some creative practices was conceptualized by Turner as *communitas* (Turner 1969). Following him, we can contrast highly structured social processes with predefined roles and stable statuses with moments when structure breaks down, and status differences are, at least temporarily, suspended.

2 The citation is taken from the text Durkheim offered in 1908 to Léon for publication in the *Revue de métaphysique et morale*.

3 Durkheim maintained that space and time were categories, not perceptual forms!

4 Sacred and profane are not independent categories in Durkheim's thinking because they mutually define one another. The basic human category, according to him, was the idea of a difference separating two mutually exclusive realms while the objects situated in both were not different in any other way.

5 Durkheim adopted the same dramatizing procedure in the description of the fire ceremony (312/218) which was, too, part of a complex ritual procedure, lasting more than two weeks (Spencer and Gillen 1904:375ff.).

6 By stabilization I mean the process by which a text (a chain of arguments) is established as scientifically 'valid', acceptable. The scientist uses different means to achieve stabilization. Empirical evidence is only one among them. Logic is another, but there are other ones, too. The end-product of stabilization is science as such – and social and natural 'objective' reality, too, as far as they are perceived through science. The stabilization is always the settlement of a dispute (*réglement d'une controverse*) as Latour understands it (Latour 1989: 97–160).

7 Obviously, the ritual collaboration of *Kingilli* and *Uluuru* was an important contribution to *Warramunga* integration.

8 Durkheim was clearly influenced by the essay of Mauss and Beuchat (1906) on the seasonal variation of Eskimo life.

9 The Mauss and Beuchat essay (1906) remained in this respect inside the Durkheimian ethnological theory and was unconcerned by epistemological problems. As far as the integrative aspects of sacred periods were concerned, this essay contained many insights that were utilized freely by Durkheim.

10 This is the solution Lockwood imputes to Durkheim. He introduces a distinction between ordinary, integrative rituals and creative hyper-rituals. 'Just as ordinary rituals serve to bring believers into a moral communion to counteract the force of self-interest, so moments of creativity in the moral life occur when, for some reason, these collective interactions become exceptionally powerful and intense. It might be said, therefore, that the creation of new social values takes place under conditions of *hyper*-ritual.' (Lockwood 1992:34, cf.252). The rituals Durkheim analysed were parts of recurrent, normal rituals (while Durkheim certainly created the faulty impression that they were in a way exceptional). Durkheim certainly believed that there was a simple collective mechanism which transforms every gathering into a potential creative one: 'The very fact of the concentration acts as an exceptionally powerful stimulant. When they are once come together, a sort of electricity is formed by their collecting which quickly transports them to an extraordinary degree of exaltation' (308/215). In this sense every ritual was a hyper-ritual. However, this elementary creativity further aggravates the problem because the spontaneous, primordial creativity threatened even the basic sacred–profane divide. It would imply that people would be able spontaneously to transgress the highly institutionalized boundary between the two realms. Consequently, Durkheim maintained that rituals were part of a recurrent, institutionalized order – and created the impression that they produced something new. He remained inside the circular argument.

11 According to Durkheim, mass events elevated human potentialities. The mass psychology of his day (Tarde, Le Bon) had the opposite opinion.

12 It was a sign of change in French political thought and an indication of Durkheim's ambition of political integration that Jeanne d'Arc and the Revolution were mentioned in the same paragraph and both in a positive sense. In Durkheim's youth Jeanne d'Arc was unequivocally the symbol figure of the anti-republican Right.

13 See e.g.: 'In *The Elementary Forms*, then, "crisis" has become more of a catharsis, therapeutic for societal renovation and regeneration. But that modern society is also subject to the same phenomenon of periodic regeneration in crucial situations, that modern society also needs to and does experience on rare but vital occasions its "moment of truth", is a subtler lesson which it is nevertheless Durkheim's intention to convey' (Tiryakian 1978:223).

14

DURKHEIM ON THE CAUSES AND FUNCTIONS OF THE CATEGORIES

Warren Schmaus

According to Emile Durkheim, our most fundamental categories of thought, including our concepts of space, time, genus, number, cause, substance, and personality, can be attributed to social causes and hence are socially variable.[1] At least since Talcott Parsons, Durkheim's theory of the categories has been interpreted as implying an epistemological relativism according to which a system of categories is valid only for a particular type of society (1937:447). If the categories are regarded as psychological capacities responsible for our ability to perceive the world, the social variability of the categories would imply that people from different types of societies may have radically dissimilar, perhaps even incommensurable experiences. Members of a society operating with one system of categories may not be able to evaluate knowledge claims about experiences generated through other systems of categories.

William Ray Dennes (1924:34–9), Charles Elmer Gehlke (1915:52–3), Edward L. Schaub (1920:337), and more recently, David Bloor (1982:294–5) argue that since Durkheim identified the categories with *représentations collectives*, they are not mere capacities but have actual content. Bloor nevertheless adopts an epistemological relativism, which he tries to support with Durkheim's and Marcel Mauss's primitive classification hypothesis, according to which classifications of things in nature reproduce classifications of people in society.

An analysis of Durkheim's arguments, however, reveals that his theory of the categories does not support epistemological relativism. His arguments trade on an ambiguity in his concept of a category, in which it is identified with its functional role in society as well as with its collective *représentation*. Since the categories appear to play the same functional roles in all societies for Durkheim, all societies seem to have the same categories. Only the *représentations* of the categories are socially variable for Durkheim. Indeed, he does not seem to have had a theory of the social causes of the categories themselves. If different societies merely have distinct *représentations* of the same set of categories, however, there is no reason to think that their respective putative knowledge claims will be incommensurable. If the primitive classification hypothesis merely says that societies have various ways of representing the category of a class, it does not support Bloor's epistemological relativism. Nevertheless, Durkheim's hypothesis that there is a universally shared set of categories that are functionally necessary for society indicates a possibly fruitful direction that empirical research in the sociology of knowledge may take.

The philosophical context for Durkheim's theory of the categories

Many of Durkheim's critics, including E. Benoît-Smullyan (1948:518 n. 67), Steven Collins (1985:46f.), Mary Douglas (1975:xv), Anthony Giddens (1978:111), Terry Godlove (1989:39), Robert Alun Jones (1984:74), Steven Lukes (1973:447), Stjepan Meštrović (1989b:260), William S. F. Pickering (1993:53), and W. Paul Vogt (Jones and Vogt 1984:54), assume that he meant the categories in Immanuel Kant's sense. Some of these critics, however, subscribe to controversial readings of Kant. When Kant said that the categories are the a priori conditions of the possibility of experience, he meant that they bear a purely logical relationship to the contents of experience. To say that the category of quantity is necessary for experience, for instance, is to say that one could not experience objects without their having some quantity or other. Kant was not offering his theory of the categories as an empirical, psychological account of the origin of experience (1783:sec. 21a). Douglas (1975:xv) nevertheless interprets Kant's categories as psychological rather than logical conditions of experience and Collins (1985:51) regards the a priori character of the categories as a matter of their origin, rather than of their justification.

If the categories are understood in Kant's sense, they would be the same everywhere and could not be socially variable. There is no reason to assume, however, that Durkheim had Kant's concept of a category in mind. To make sense of Durkheim's theory of the categories, we would do well to place it in the context of what was happening in philosophy at that time in France. Durkheim's theory of the categories was proposed in response to philosophical traditions that were proposing alternatives to Kant's account of the categories. Spiritualism, the dominant tradition in academic philosophy, derived from the work of Victor Cousin (1860:19–35), who held the foundation of philosophy to be an introspective psychology that was supposed to reveal the existence in the soul of necessary and universal principles of divine origin. Cousin's thought was reflected in Paul Janet's (1879) and Elie Rabier's (1884) manuals of philosophy, which were the standard texts in French lycées when Durkheim taught there as an agrégé in philosophy.[2] These texts continued to treat the categories as part of an introspective yet empirical psychology, adopting Maine de Biran's argument that the categories of substance, cause, unity, finality, etc. could be derived from the individual's inner experience of the self or will (Rabier 1884:277ff.; Janet 1879:110ff.).

Charles Renouvier was an outsider to the academic establishment who was nevertheless an important influence on Durkheim (Lukes 1973:54). He dismissed the spiritualists' Cartesian introspection of the soul as a mere paralogism, a 'mortal leap' from the phenomenon of consciousness to spiritual substance. For Renouvier, the categories are an irreducible set of laws governing the relations among the phenomena that make experience possible and cannot be derived from it (1875:17, 119). He was an inspiration for Louis Liard (1878) and for Octave Hamelin (1907), from whom Durkheim adopted the following argument for including space and time among the categories rather than, like Kant, regarding them as forms of intuition: 'space is not this vague and indeterminate milieu that Kant had imagined: purely and absolutely homogeneous, it would be of no use and would not even offer anything for thought to grasp' (15).[3] Similarly, one could not represent time to oneself without some way of dividing and measuring it, Durkheim thought (14). Others, like Durkheim's philosophy professor, Emile Boutroux, held that the categories are not necessary but contingent, evolving over time. He was influenced by Herbert Spencer's evolutionary hypothesis according to which the categories are acquired characteristics transmitted by heredity (Nye 1979:114; 18n.2).

Where others offered psychological and even biological re-interpretations of Kant, however, Durkheim regarded the categories as social phenomena that are transmitted culturally. In *The Elementary Forms of Religious Life*, he explained that the categories are social in two senses. They are not only the product of society, but express social things. The category of a class, genus, or species was constructed on the model of a human social group, with the entire society providing the archetype for the category of totality, the class that includes all other classes. The prototype for the concept of force associated with the category of causality was the experience of the collective forces that each society imposes upon its members. The category of time was formed from the seasonal and daily rhythms of social life and the category of space was patterned after the spatial distribution of social groups (628–30). He cited evidence from his and Mauss's earlier paper, 'Primitive Classification', that certain tribes conceive space on the model of a circular campsite. In this representation of space, there are as many directions in space as there are clans in the tribe. The name or totem associated with each direction derives from that of the clan that, when the entire tribe gathers, traditionally occupies the part of the campsite that lies in that direction. The Zuñi, for instance, divide space into seven regions since there are seven groups of clans in their tribe (16; cf. Durkheim 1903a(i)/1969c:425–45).

Durkheim's defence of his theory of the categories

Durkheim argued that his theory of the social causes of the categories provides a better explanation than other accounts, whether empiricist or a priori, of their generality, universality, necessity, and variability (18).

According to the empiricist philosophy, the individual human mind constructs the categories from its sensations. Durkheim argued that empiricism could explain neither the universality nor the generality of the categories, nor the necessity with which they impose themselves on our thought. For Durkheim, the generality of the categories consists in their applicability to all objects. By the universality of the categories, he meant that they are independent of individual subjects and serve as 'the common ground where all minds meet' (19). Categories, like concepts generally, are 'communicable to a plurality of minds, and even, in principle, to all minds' (619n.1). The categories then could not have been constructed from sensations, which have the 'diametrically opposed' characteristics of being private, subjective, and particular. Although there is a sense in which sensations, like the categories, also impose themselves on us, we retain more freedom with respect to how sensations are conceived, he argued. Thus, in attempting to derive them from sensations, empiricism renders illusory the universality and necessity of the categories (19–20).

Durkheim also found fault with the a priori philosophy, which he understood as maintaining that:

> the categories are not derived from experience: they are logically anterior to it and condition it. One represents them to oneself as so many simple givens, irreducible, immanent in the human mind in virtue of its native constitution.
>
> (18)

However, to say that the categories are inherent in the nature of the human mind, Durkheim argued, is no explanation of whence the mind possesses this 'surprising prerogative' to go beyond experience and to add things to it that experience does not reveal to us. Transcendental arguments do not solve this problem for him. To say that the categories make experience possible, he thought, is to beg the question as to why experience should depend on conditions that are external and antecedent to it (20). To suggest that the categories 'are necessary because they are indispensable to the functioning of thought' is merely to offer a tautology (23). To attribute a divine cause to the categories, he protested, is to offer an untestable hypothesis.[4] Furthermore, he believed, if the divine mind is immutable, this hypothesis cannot account for the fact that 'the categories . . . are never fixed under a definite form; . . . they change in accordance with places and times' (20–1).[5] One can avoid all the problems faced by empiricism and the a priori philosophy, Durkheim thought, 'if one admits the social origin of the categories' (21).[6] This hypothesis can explain the fact that the generality or extension of these concepts far exceeds the experience of any individual. It can also explain the fact that these concepts are readily communicable from one individual to another. The necessity with which the categories impose themselves upon our thought can be explained in terms of society's need for conformity of thought among its members. Finally, the social origin of the categories can account for their variation from society to society (21–5; 619–20). As Godlove (1989:40) points out, Durkheim was making demands on empiricism that are incompatible with those he made on the a priori philosophy.[7] The same theory cannot be expected to show that the categories are universal and necessary and yet at the same time variable with respect to time and place. For Durkheim's own theory to account for these incompatible characteristics, it would have to proceed from inconsistent premises or commit a paralogism. Durkheim's paralogism results from an ambiguity in his concept of a category.

Pickering (1993) contributes to the clarification of Durkheim's concept of a category in distinguishing what he takes to be the explanatory goals of *The Elementary Forms* from those of 'Primitive Classification'. As Pickering sees it, only the *The Elementary Forms* is concerned with the categories in something like Kant's sense of the term, while the earlier work is concerned with merely our classificatory concepts, including our concepts for classifying the directions of space and the units of time.[8] The classificatory concepts are not the categories themselves, but merely the ways in which various societies represent the categories of space, time, and class. It is only these ways of representing the categories that Durkheim meant when he said that the categories have no fixed form but vary with time and place.

Pickering's distinction between concepts that are universally shared and different ways of representing these shared concepts can then be generalized to include all of the categories and not just the categories of space, time, and class. The category of causality, for instance, is also represented in different ways in different places and times. Even within a single society, Durkheim added, *représentations* of this concept vary with social factors, such as the level of education, and even from one scientific discipline to another (527). All societies may have the categories of space, time, causality, and class, but these concepts may be represented in diverse ways.

Once the notion of a category is distinguished from that of the form in which a category is represented, Durkheim's arguments against the a priori philosophy can be reconciled with his arguments against empiricism. When he claimed that his sociological hypothesis provides a better explanation of the variability of the categories than does the a priori philosophy, he seems to have meant not the categories themselves but their *représentations*. On the other hand, when he argued that his hypothesis provides a better explanation than empiricism of the universality of the categories and of the necessity with which they impose themselves upon our thought, he meant the term 'categories' in the sense of our most fundamental concepts.

We should also keep in mind the distinction between categories and their *représentations* when evaluating the ethnographic evidence adduced by Durkheim. When he showed that totemic systems of social organization are used to classify things in nature (201f.), he may have demonstrated the social origins of totemic classificatory concepts but not of the category of a class. Similarly, he did not necessarily prove the social origins of the categories of space and time by bringing forth evidence that, in Australian and Native American tribes, the units in which time is measured and the number of divisions of space and their names are taken from social life (15–17; cf.1903a(i):425–45).

Although Pickering's distinction between a category and a classificatory concept is important, he may have overstated the difference between

Durkheim and Mauss' 1903 paper and Durkheim's 1912 book. Durkheim represented the earlier work as concerned not merely with classificatory concepts but with the very concept of classification (205). After presenting evidence for the social origins of our concepts of space, time, and class, Durkheim and Mauss suggested that similar sociological accounts could be provided for cause, substance, and the other categories (1903a(i):461). Durkheim attempted to do just that in *The Elementary Forms*. To appreciate these works, perhaps further clarification of Durkheim's concept of a category, beyond distinguishing it from a classificatory concept, is needed.

Durkheim's social functional notion of a category

In both 'Primitive Classification' and *The Elementary Forms*, Durkheim used the metaphor of a framework (*cadre*) to explain what he meant by the category of a class, which he distinguished from a general idea or image of the sort of thing that belongs to that class (1903a(i)/1969c:399; 13, 208–9). He also employed this metaphor of framework and content in *The Elementary Forms* to explain the difference between the category of causation and the individual's experience of regular succession (526). Indeed, he seems to have extended this metaphor to all of the categories. As Durkheim explained, the categories:

> are like the solid framework that encloses thought; it seems we cannot think of objects that are not in time or space, which are not numerable, etc. Other notions are contingent and changeable; we conceive that they may be lacking to a person, a society, an epoch; the former appear to be nearly inseparable from the normal functioning of the mind. They are like the skeleton of the intelligence.
>
> $(13)^9$

For Durkheim, then, the categories appear to constitute a universally shared conceptual framework that makes it possible for us to conceive of objects. However, as Godlove argues, the framework metaphor suggests that the categories organize sensations that are independently given and prior, which should be distinguished from Kant's notion of concepts that are logically presupposed by the very possibility of empirical experience (1989:36–7). Indeed Durkheim, unlike Kant, seems to have thought that experience is possible without the categories. As he explained in a published draft of the introduction to *The Elementary Forms*, for 'the recent disciples of Kant ... the categories preform the real, whereas for us, they recapitulate it' (1909d:757 and n.1). According to Durkheim, the categories make explicit relations that exist only implicitly in individual consciousness. The individual has a sense of time, place, resemblance and regular succession, he believed, without the categories of time, space, class and causality (628–9). For example, the individual does not require the category of causality in order to be able to avoid danger (632). In fact, Durkheim appears to have thought that the categories depended on these psychological capacities. He admitted, for instance, that classification presupposes the ability to recognize resemblances (206).[10]

Furthermore, if Durkheim had meant Kant's concept of the categories, it would not have been appropriate for him to have sought a causal account of their universality and necessity. Kant had argued that we cannot seek in our experience an explanation of why we have the categories that we do, since our categories make experience possible in the first place (1783:sect. 36; 1787: B145). According to Godlove (1986:393f.; 1989:11f.) and Lukes (1973:447), Durkheim refused to accept Kant's restriction and sought to provide an empirical answer to a philosophical question. The most that experience could show us, however, is that these categories *always* impose themselves on experience; it could never show us that they *necessarily* do so. For the categories to be contingent upon causes in the empirical realm would be for them only to *seem* necessary and not to *be* necessary. Also, if the categories were contingent upon causes, alternative sets of categories dependent on other causes would then be possible, and the categories would not be truly universal. Hence, Durkheim's sociological theory of the causes of the categories would appear to be no more successful than the empiricist philosophy in explaining the universality and necessity of the categories.

According to Godlove, Durkheim sought to avoid the problems of both empiricism and the a priori philosophy by ascribing social causes to the categories and then locating society outside the empirical realm of space and time. Only a timeless cause, Durkheim supposedly thought, could account for the universality and necessity of the categories.[11] Once society is relocated in the stream of history, however, the categories would once again be contingent and variable (Godlove 1989:44–5).

> As the unscientific a priorists cannot, [Durkheim] can point to the antecedent cause of our categories, namely, society acting to ensure its own survival. But unlike the hubristic empiricists, he can represent their genesis as timeless, and so, as independent of a constructing subject.
>
> (ibid.:45)

Although Godlove is certainly correct that Parsons, whom he cites, believed that Durkheim in *The Elementary Forms* had transformed society into a timeless entity, I find little to recommend Parsons's interpretation on this point. Parsons seems to have thought that Durkheim's having made society a postulated mental entity that we do not directly experience implies that for Durkheim society is outside space and time (1937:444–5). However, this implication does not follow: making society a mental entity places it outside space, only on the assumption of mind–body dualism, and does not place it outside time at all. There are further difficulties with Godlove's interpretation. Only entities that exist in time can act or need to be concerned with survival. Even if we were to relocate society back in time, Godlove's interpretation would risk ascribing intentions to society, to which Durkheim would have strenuously objected.

A more likely interpretation of Durkheim's theory of the categories says that the necessity with which the categories impose themselves on our thought is a functional necessity. He may be read as having proposed the empirical hypothesis that the categories are functionally necessary for social life in order to replace what he regarded as the question-begging transcendental argument that the categories are logically necessary for thought. In the conclusion to *The Elementary Forms*, Durkheim argued that society is not possible without the categories. For there to be a society, individuals must be organized into groups. Society thus requires the category of a class. Places must be divided among these groups, requiring divisions and directions of space. Convocations to feasts, hunts, and military expeditions require a common way of fixing dates and times. Co-operation with the same end in view requires agreement about means and ends, that is, agreement about a causal relationship (632–3). Because the categories are necessary for social life, they should be found in all societies; that is, they are universal.

Durkheim appears to have conceived the categories as necessary only to our ability to function as social beings. As we saw above, he believed the individual to have a sense of time, place, resemblance, and regular succession that does not depend on the categories. Although he also said that the categories are 'nearly inseparable from the normal functioning of the mind', he would no doubt have agreed that the individual's mental life is fully developed only in society. Even for Durkheim to have said that the categories are necessary for us to conceive of objects is not inconsistent with his social functional sense of a category. The ability to conceive of objects makes the social use of language possible. Without the ability to talk about objects, we would be reduced to reporting on only the subjective, private aspects of our experience.

To give a functional account of the categories, however, it is not enough to show that they are necessary for society. One must also show how the beneficial effects of the categories help to maintain them in existence. Durkheim's arguments suggest a way to construct such a functional explanation. Different societies may develop different ways of dividing space, measuring time, or classifying things in nature. Such systems for measuring and classifying help to preserve the society by helping the members of the society procure the basic necessities of life. The society is then able to transmit these *représentations* of the categories to the next generation as part of its culture. These various systems of measuring and classifying then play the functional roles of the categories in their respective societies. What Durkheim attempted to show with his functional argument is that any society must develop some system or other for representing the categories.

Causal and functional explanations of the categories

To show that the categories have social functions, of course, is not necessarily to show that they have social causes. In *The Rules of Sociological Method* (1895a), Durkheim distinguished causal from functional explanations in sociology, saying that 'when one undertakes to explain a social phenomenon the efficient cause that produces it and the function it fulfils must be investigated separately'. In distinguishing causal from functional explanations,

Durkheim did not intend to proscribe the latter from sociology as long as these are kept distinct from intentional explanations. The term 'function' for Durkheim connotes merely the 'correspondence' between the social fact and 'the general needs of the social organism'. The functions of social facts are to be found among their effects rather than their causes. He added that it is appropriate to investigate the cause of a social fact before we investigate its effects, for indeed sometimes a phenomenon will have the effect of preserving its cause. In such cases, knowing the cause will help us to discover the function more easily (1895a/1901c:117–18). Indeed, one could argue that it was Durkheim's investigation, in the 1903 paper written with Mauss, of the social causes of our classificatory concepts that led to his hypothesis in *The Elementary Forms* regarding the social functions of the categories represented by these concepts.

If the function of the categories is to preserve their cause, and if they have the function of preserving society, Durkheim may have reasoned, then society must be their cause. Other things Durkheim said in *The Rules* about functional explanations, however, indicate that he believed that we could not infer causes from functions so readily. In this work he maintained that the usefulness of some social phenomenon to society, which generally is what allows it to continue to survive, may not be what brought it into existence in the first place (1895a/1901c:119). The cause that gives rise to the existence of some social fact may be independent of the purpose it serves. The same social institution may come to serve a new function, he argued. Alternatively, 'a fact can exist without serving any purpose', either because it never had one, or because it once had a purpose, but no longer does, and continues only through custom (ibid.:112–13).

Durkheim's caution against inferring causes from functions is well taken. Presumably, for a phenomenon to have some function that allows it to continue to survive is for it to have some effect that would in turn be causally responsible for maintaining the phenomenon. But if, as Durkheim seems to have suggested, the cause that maintains some phenomenon in existence could be different from the cause that originally brought it about, there could be a plurality of causes for that phenomenon. Hence, even if the categories are maintained by society because they perform an important social function, it would not follow that they were originally due to social causes. Alternatively, they could have psychological or even biological origins and still perform these social functions.

Elsewhere in *The Rules*, however, Durkheim denied the possibility of a plurality of causes for the same effect (ibid.:156).[12] This denial would seem to conflict with the consequences of his arguments against inferring causes from functions. One way to resolve this difficulty, of course, would be to regard that which is being maintained in existence as a different phenomenon or effect than that which was originally brought about. Thus, the present phenomenon could have a different cause than the original one without assuming a plurality of causes for the same effect. His proscription against inferring causes from functions could then be read as ruling out inferring the cause of the original phenomenon from the function of the present one. In the case of Durkheim's theory of the categories, one could argue that the categories that maintain a society in existence are not the same as those that were originally brought about by such social causes as the structure of society. The social causes of the present set of categories, which have the function of maintaining society, may be their cultural transmission to the next generation, which the use of these categories helped to make possible.

However, as we have seen, Durkheim believed that all societies had the same categories, when these are understood in their functional sense. Only in the representational sense of the categories could those that presently maintain a society be different than those it originally had. That is, the *représentations collectives* of the categories that maintain a society in existence are not the same as those that were originally brought about by and modelled on the structure of that society. This interpretation accords with Durkheim's account of how the concepts representing the categories can be constructed on social models and yet apply to things in nature. He explained that if some artifice enters into the categories because they are constructed concepts, it is an art that approaches nature by degrees. For Durkheim, the categories are comparable to other sorts of tools that societies have improved over time (25–7). He appears to have anticipated an evolutionary epistemology, in which concepts evolve in the direction of more accurate *représentations* of nature and are justified by their adaptive value.

By distinguishing a society's original from its subsequent *représentations* of the categories, we may defend Durkheim and Mauss' primitive classification hypothesis against Rodney Needham's objection that their ethnographic evidence does not establish that such classifications vary with social structure (1963:xi–xxix). On my interpretation, only a society's original system of classification need reflect its social morphology. Of course, if these societies lack a recorded history, the primitive classification hypothesis becomes nearly untestable.

Even if we found some way to make the primitive classification hypothesis testable, however, it provides the social causes of only the *représentations collectives* of the original set of categories. Also, if a society's present is distinguished from its original categories only in the representational sense, cultural transmission would be the social cause only of a society's present *représentations collectives* of the categories. It appears that Durkheim had no account of causes of the categories when these are understood in their social functional sense. Nevertheless, his hypothesis that certain categories may be functionally necessary for social life is an important contribution to the sociology of knowledge that is open to empirical investigation.

A proposal for the empirical investigation of the categories

Durkheim appears to have held that all human societies think in the same way and that this way of thinking requires certain categories. To say that all human beings think alike is not necessarily to say that all human beings adhere to certain 'universal' (Lukes 1970:208) or 'necessary' (Hollis 1970:218) standards of rationality, such as *modus ponens* or the principle of non-contradiction. To make this claim is to create an easy target for one's relativist opponents (e.g. Barnes and Bloor 1982:35f.). When Durkheim said that primitives and moderns think alike he did not try to argue that either always adhere to textbook rationality. He recognized that European scientists as well as Australian tribespeople make logical mistakes, commit *post hoc* fallacies, defend their ideas with *ad hoc* hypotheses, and so on.

In order for the sociology of knowledge to be at all possible, Durkheim argued, we need to assume that all people think alike. He seems to have regarded the alternative assumption as *ad hoc*, rejecting Spencer's and Frazer's theories of the origin of religion, which rely on attributing absurdities to primitives, for just this reason (76–7, 250). In effect, Durkheim believed that to say that others think differently than we do is to offer no explanation of their thought at all. Even evidence that primitives may group human beings and animals together in the same totemic classes did not suffice for Durkheim to show that they think differently than we do. In reply to Lucien Lévy-Bruhl's primitive mentality hypothesis, according to which primitives do not recognize contradictions, Durkheim argued that to identify kangaroos with human beings is no more a contradiction than to identify heat with the motion of molecules or light with electromagnetic vibration (341).[13] For Durkheim, totemic systems of classification function like scientific theories, in the sense that what counts as a contradiction depends on what else one thinks.

To argue that all people in all societies think alike on the grounds that it makes the interpretation of their societies possible is to offer what appears to be a transcendental argument. For Durkheim, however, it seems that transcendental arguments were to be regarded only as ways of reasoning to hypotheses and not as probative demonstrations. In order to test the hypothesis that all societies have a similar mode of thought that functionally requires similar categories, we can draw the test implication that certain categories should be present in all societies. The hypothesis can then be tested against the presence or absence of the categories in various societies.

In our empirical investigations, we should be clear as to whether different societies have genuinely different categories or simply the same categories but with different *représentations collectives* or ways of dividing up or measuring the things in the categories. That is, although ways of classifying and measuring things may vary widely from society to society or even within a society, we may still be able to interpret these systems of classification through their functional roles. For instance, it does not matter that another society divides two-dimensional space into five or seven directions instead of four and then names them after their various clans. By taking into account the way these names are being used, we can distinguish when they are referring to spatial directions and not to clans. To be sure, the concept of space may have different meanings in different societies to the extent that it has different *représentations collectives* in each. However, people from different societies may be able to understand each other's concepts of space just to the extent that they are able to recognize the functional roles being played by each other's ways of dividing space. To the extent that we share many such functionally defined categories, mutual understanding and communication is possible.

Collins (1985:52–3) interprets Mauss as having attempted to establish the alternative, relativist thesis by adducing evidence of variability in the categories. For example, he reports that Mauss argued that certain concepts were formerly categories, including big and small, animate and inanimate, and right and left. These, however, are classificatory concepts rather than categories. Mauss' evidence is consistent with the view that the societies that used these concepts all shared the category of a class. In addition, Mauss suggested that our category of substance may have originated in the concept of food (1950:309–10). However, the very fact that Mauss could trace the category of substance to the concept of food argues for a kind of continuity in our thought.

Categories present in all societies would appear to be necessary for the kind of thinking that social life in general requires. If we were to find evidence of the presence of some categories in some societies but not others, that would call for empirical investigation into the special functions those categories may have in those societies. Such variability in the categories alone, however, would not suffice to demonstrate the existence of incommensurable modes of thought. If it were possible to understand the different functions of these different concepts, that in fact would be evidence that the people who use these concepts think much as we do. We may have evidence for epistemological relativism if we were to find other societies that had *none* of our categories, but this outcome seems highly unlikely.

In accounting for the presence or absence of categories in various societies, we should be careful to distinguish their functional roles from their causes. It is not even clear that we need to concern ourselves with the causes of the categories in their functional sense. That is, we may want to provide causal accounts only for the different *représentations* of these categories in various societies, in which these *représentations* perform the social functions of the categories. Nor is there any reason to assume that the *représentations collectives* that play the same kinds of functional roles in different societies, or even in different parts of the same society, must be produced by the same kinds of social causes.

The categories in Durkheim's functional sense are concepts that social scientists bring to bear upon the interpretation of other societies. If there is a causal story to be told about these concepts, it is perhaps a story about how western social scientists and philosophers arrived at these categories as the appropriate concepts for the interpretation of other societies. The investigation of the social causes of the categories understood in their social functional sense may then belong to the sociology of scientific knowledge rather than to the sociology of primitive peoples.

Notes

1 Following the practice of Kant's translators, I will use the definite article in referring to these specific, fundamental categories as 'the categories', in order to distinguish them from categories in general. The term 'categories', without the definite article, also refers to such classificatory concepts as, for instance, animal, vegetable, and mineral, which would be subsumed under the category of 'substance'.

2 I am indebted to Brooks (1996) for my knowledge of the lycée *programme* in philosophy in the Third Republic.

3 For an analysis of this argument, see Godlove 1996.

4 Collins (1985:51) suggests this interpretation of the a priori theory is due to Hamelin.

5 It seems inconsistent for Durkheim to have argued that the hypothesis of divine origins is untestable and then to have offered evidence that it is false. I read him as having meant that this hypothesis is false only on the assumption of divine immutability, and that there is no way of experimentally corroborating such divine attributes.

6 Durkheim's essentialist model of causal explanation conflated causes with origins. For a detailed account of Durkheim's views on causal explanation, see Chapter 4 of my book, Schmaus 1994.

7 Godlove (1989:165–6 n.4) rejects attempts to reconcile these demands by affirming that a system of categories is necessary and universal merely within a particular society. Indeed, this suggestion is either incoherent or equates 'universality' with 'generality'.

8 According to Pickering, another difference between these two works is that the earlier work explains these concepts in terms of social morphology while the latter explains the categories in terms of religion. However, I am using the concept of social causes in a broader sense that includes not only social morphology but social and religious forces.

9 Durkheim appears to have reversed his position the following year in his lectures on pragmatism, in which he said: 'We can no longer accept a single, invariable system of categories or intellectual frameworks. The frameworks that had a reason to exist in past civilizations do not have it today' (1955a:149). However, since Durkheim in this work identified all concepts, including the categories, with their collective *représentations* (ibid.:202), this passage may be interpreted as concerning variation in the collective representations of the categories.

10 Kant also seems to have allowed for a wholly subjective kind of perception that does not involve the categories (1783:sections 18–20; 1787:B142), and it is not clear that these passages can be made consistent with the rest of his philosophy. However, Durkheim was discussing the views of his contemporaries and not interpreting Kant.

11 Collins also seems to interpret Durkheim as having postulated a timeless cause, grounding the universality and necessity of the categories in 'the nature of human sociability' (1985:63).

12 For an analysis of his arguments for denying the plurality of causes, see Schmaus 1994:69f.

13 For a detailed comparison of Durkheim's and Lévy-Bruhl's views on primitive mentality, see Schmaus 1996.

15

DURKHEIM AND A PRIORI TRUTH

Conformity as a philosophical problem

Terry F. Godlove, Jr.

In *The Elementary Forms of Religious Life*, Durkheim argues that knowledge in general, and logic in particular, is context-dependent, even down to the principle of contradiction. Durkheim's basic proposal is that the force of even what we are used to calling the logical laws must be understood as expressions of the social structure of the communities from which they emerge:

> If society is to live . . . there is a minimum of logical conformity which it cannot do without. For this reason it uses all its authority upon its members to forestall dissidence. Does a mind ostensibly transgress these norms of all thought? Then society no longer considers it a human mind in the full sense of the word, and it treats it accordingly.
> (24/17)

I want to focus not on Durkheim's dark, suggestive coda, but rather on the revolutionary import of his underlying thesis. The classical tradition in epistemology had made the laws of logic a priori, that is, true, independent of experience, since roughly speaking, they arise from the nature of thought itself. By contrast, Durkheim saw a social rather than an epistemic necessity; conformity is required for admission not to the class of thinking beings, but to that of social ones.

Durkheim's reduction of epistemic to social necessity merits scrutiny for both historical and systematic reasons. Historically, it has been decisively influential for such diverse thinkers and movements as Bataille, Baudrillard, Braudel, Foucault, the structuralism of Lévi-Strauss and the so-called Strong Programme in the sociology of knowledge. Philosophically, the steady shrinkage of what we are prepared to call a priori marks a defining trend in twentieth-century Anglo-American thought. This trend is, of course, an emblem of American pragmatism, and is perhaps best exemplified in Quine's willingness to revise 'even the logical law of the excluded middle', just as 'Kepler superseded Ptolemy, or Einstein Newton, or Darwin Aristotle' (Quine 1953:51).

Recently, however, the traditional conception of a priori truth as arising from the nature of thought has come in for renewed scrutiny at the hands of Michael Dummett, John McDowell, Hilary Putnam, Manley Thompson, and others. If I judge the matter correctly, the issue is again becoming unsettled, as it was in Durkheim's day.

The history of (non)conformity

In advocating a thoroughly context-dependent logic, Durkheim was rejecting the two main philosophical options available to him, the Aristotelian and the Kantian. In *Metaphysics* IV, Aristotle gives the principle of contradiction as, 'the same attribute cannot at the same time belong and not belong to the same subject and in the same respect'. While he calls it, 'the most certain principle', Aristotle does not see it as self-supporting. Rather, he argues that 'there must be something which signifies substance', and that 'if this is so it has been shown that contradictories cannot be predicated at the same time'. Aristotle's argument takes the form of an 'elenctic demonstration', the refutation of someone who denies a principle (Aristotle 1927:1006a 10–12). Thus, the interlocutor must agree that his utterance has a definite meaning, that it means p and not at the same time and in the same respect not-p. But, for Aristotle, this consideration does not by itself vindicate the principle of contradiction, for he also holds that objective reference – reference to objects as they truly are rather than by the sensations they produce in us – makes definite meaning possible. Reference to objects-as-they-appear will not suffice, for an object may appear to be p to me and not-p to someone else; we will then be unable to say what it is that appears as p and not-p. That ability would itself presuppose objective reference. The result is that Aristotle defends the principle of contradiction by appealing to an ontological classification. Having tied meaning to signification of substance, we must then admit the notion of an accident – place, time, quality, quantity, relation and so on – a kind of being which cannot exist without substance. For Aristotle, anyone who claims to have asserted anything must admit an ontological distinction between substance and accident. We cannot reject the principle of contradiction and the distinction between substance and accident without, as Terrence Irwin has put it, 'self-refutation or self-defeating silence and failure to speak significantly' (Irwin 1977:222).

In the modern period, Leibniz sees no need to go beyond the first stage of Aristotle's defence of the principle of contradiction, the elenctic demonstration. Thus, in a fragment from the early 1680s, Leibniz writes that it is sufficient to prove a metaphysical or arithmetic or geometrical point to show that the contrary implies a contradiction (Leibniz 1989:19). And more than thirty years later, in his fifth and last paper for Clarke, Leibniz is still confident that 'reasonable and impartial men will grant me that having forced an adversary to deny that principle is reducing him *ad absurdum*' (Leibniz 1989:346). For Kant, too, the principle of contradiction needs no defending. Kant questioned Aristotle's condition of objectivity – the distinction between substance and accident – but never argued for the certainty of the principle of contradiction.

It is, as Kant remarks in the *Critique of Pure Reason*, 'the universal and completely sufficient principle of all analytic knowledge'. Since 'no knowledge can be contrary to it without self-nullification', the principle of contradiction is 'inviolable' (Kant 1963:A151–2/B191).[1] Thus, while Leibniz and Kant depart from Aristotle in seeking no defence of the principle, so to speak, outside itself, they too see it as admitting no exception. Durkheim thinks otherwise:

> The hold that the notion of contradiction has had over thought has varied with times and societies. Today the principle [of contradiction][2] dominates scientific thought; but there are vast systems of *représentations* ... where it is frequently ignored: these are the mythologies, from the crudest up to the most learned. There, we are continually coming upon beings who have the most contradictory attributes at the same time, which are at the same time one and many, material and spiritual. These historical variations of the rule that seems to govern our present logic show that ... [it] depends at least in part upon factors that are historical, hence social.
>
> (17–8/12–3)

We might call this the argument from the history of mythology (after Putnam's remark that Quine argues for revising the law of the excluded middle 'from the history of science' (Putnam 1983:129)). Durkheim is representing himself as commenting on someone else's violation of Aristotle's principle of contradiction – someone who holds that materiality at the same time belongs and does not belong to the same subject and in the same respect (ibid.:271). While modern 'scientific thought' conforms to the principle of contradiction to a greater extent than does 'religious thought', Durkheim adds, in a footnote apparently aimed at Lévy-Bruhl, that even 'science cannot escape violating it' (17 n.3/12 n.4).

What, then, would it be for the principle of contradiction to lapse? Let us consider one of Durkheim's examples, the thought of a religious being who is 'at the same time one and many'. Here it is important to emphasize that Durkheim does not contemplate someone who is merely ambivalent, or someone who uses 'one' and 'many' in different senses. Rather, when Durkheim imagines the violation of the principle of contradiction, he is imagining someone who thinks that god is one and that god is many (notone) in the same sense at the same time. He thinks both p and not-p.

I want to make two points about Durkheim's thought experiment. First, while it may be possible to think a contradiction – to think or mean or intend p and not-p – in so doing we must rely on none other than the principle of contradiction. That is, if Durkheim's religious person is to think p and not-p, he cannot intend by that its negation: neither p nor not-p. But if he is to violate genuinely the principle of contradiction he must mean to say p and not-p and its negation, neither p nor not-p. A moment's thought shows that, under these conditions, he has said nothing at all, for whenever we give his thoughts some definite content, he must quickly assure us that he meant the negation of that content, and so on and on.

So, to Durkheim's claim that the principle of contradiction has lapsed and, to a lesser extent, continues to lapse, we must say – you'll forgive me – yes and no. Yes, we have seen no reason why a person could not think a contradiction (and I know of no such reason). But in so doing, he must rely on the principle of contradiction and so the alleged nonconformity is not absolute. From my reading of *The Elementary Forms of Religious Life*, Durkheim is countenancing an absolute nonconformity, a genuine lapse. This point must count heavily against him.

Second, you will have noticed that I have been playing fast and loose with the pronouns. Officially, I have followed Durkheim's lead in fashioning my own thought experiment in the third person. Officially, we have been asking how conformity to the principle of contradiction affects someone else's ability to mean anything by his thoughts or words. This third person stance is essential to Durkheim's or any 'social scientific' approach to epistemology – a point I shall return to at the end.[3] But though our remarks have been cast in third-person terms, in fact their character is, as Thompson has stressed, radically first personal. In trying to picture Durkheim's religious man failing to conform to the principle of contradiction, I of course cannot intend to picture the negation of that enterprise. That is, in all this third-person picturing I am forced to conform to the principle whose status I am representing myself as considering. But, then, in concluding, as I have, that he cannot exempt himself from conformity to the principle, I must admit that I am basing my conclusions on the unavoidability of my own conformity (cf., Thompson 1981:161).

Let me restate these two points and suggest a preliminary moral. The first point is that Durkheim was wrong to think that, *qua* sociologist or anthropologist, he could meaningfully inquire into a religious person's – or anyone's – failure to conform to the principle of contradiction. We cannot make sense of religious persons doing any such thing (though, as I have said, I am not going to insist that we cannot imagine someone thinking a contradiction). Second, behind Durkheim's failure is his own unavoidable reliance on the principle, a result we in turn establish based on – what else? – our own unavoidable reliance upon it. What we want, then, is a way of expressing this point that makes it independent of whether we are targeting our own thinking or someone else's. As a first approximation, these two points suggest that conformity to the principle of contradiction is a condition of thinking, intending, or meaning *überhaupt*, as Kant might say – that it is presupposed by and makes possible the activity of thinking *per se*. If we then take experience to be the application of thought to what the world forces on us, the principle of contradiction will be a priori in the radical, Kantian sense – true absolutely, independent of all experience.

A dialectical weapon

I have been criticizing Durkheim for failing to see that conformity to the principle of contradiction is not optional for thinking beings, that its presuppositional status places it beyond the reach of sociological analysis. I shall return to press this claim in a moment. But first I want to note that Durkheim himself comes close to this view in a well-known series of lectures delivered in 1913, just a year after the initial publication of *The Elementary Forms of Religious Life,* and known to English readers under the title, *Pragmatism and Sociology* (1955a). Most commentators have rightly emphasized the continuity of thought between the two works. But regarding our present topic – Durkheim's treatment of the principle of contradiction – we find him striking out on a rather different line.

In the Twentieth Lecture, Durkheim uses the principle of contradiction as a potent dialectical weapon against proponents of pragmatism.

> Pragmatism itself rests on reasoning which involves concepts, and which is based on the principle of contradiction. Denying this principle would mean denying the possibility of any intellectual relationship. We cannot make a judgment or understand anything at all if we do not first agree that it is this object and not another that is at issue.
>
> (1955a/t.1983a:94)

My interest here is not in the issues that may or may not divide Durkheim and the pragmatists, but rather in the use Durkheim makes of the principle of contradiction. While he is frustratingly brief, it is possible to see Durkheim in this passage as pressing the same sort of point against the pragmatists that I am urging against *The Elementary Forms of Religious Life.* Thus, when Durkheim writes that the one who denies the principle of contradiction undermines, 'the possibility of any intellectual relationship', I should like to read him as pointing out that such a person would have to both intend and not intend the same thought at the same time. This person – I am happy to let Durkheim express it – 'cannot make a judgment'.

I do not want to dwell on the apparent transformation of Durkheim's treatment of the principle of contradiction from 1912 to 1913, mainly because, even reading this passage in the way that I should like to, I think the transformation is only skin deep. My feeling is that, even in 1913, Durkheim saw the principle of contradiction merely as a convenient debater's tool to be discarded after use. In this he joins a distinguished line stretching back at least to Plato's *Theaetetus.*[4]

More precisely, I doubt whether Durkheim appreciated the deeper point that we presuppose conformity to the principle of contradiction in all our thinking. I doubt this because, in the pages following the passage I have just quoted, he explains that the objectivity of the principle is based on, 'the realities of social life' (1995a/t.1983a:97). And in insisting on grounding the principle of contradiction in an external subject matter, one outside the activity of thinking itself, as in the requirements of social life, Durkheim shows his continuing allegiance to the main line of argument in *The Elementary Forms of Religious Life.* In it Durkheim insists that the universality and necessity of the categories must be 'accounted for' in sociological terms, as required for the linguistic exchange that makes possible human social interaction (e.g. 24/17; 526/368; 625–6/438–9). But we need not have the details to know that this cannot be right. For, in thinking whether the principle of contradiction is somehow grounded in society, we realize this very activity is already constrained by the principle about which we claim to be theorizing. Thus, our unavoidable conformity does not show something about the nature of society nor, as Thompson remarks, does it even show something about the nature of thought (Thompson 1981:462–3). When we take either of these as an external subject matter, as something whose nature is open to investigation, whose nature is as it is whether we like it or not,[5] then we must remind ourselves again that, in even that investigation, we presuppose the objectivity of the principle of contradiction. Its objectivity consists in making it possible for us to investigate the nature of any subject matter at all, including the nature of society or indeed of thought itself.

Explaining conformity

I have been taking Durkheim to task for insisting that the principle of contradiction must be grounded in the nature of some external subject matter. To sharpen this point and to bring out how seductive it is, I shall look briefly at three thinkers who succumbed to the same temptation – two in Durkheim's day, one in ours.

The point comes out clearly in one of Durkheim's teachers, in Emile Boutroux's *Natural Law in Science and Philosophy* (1895). 'The human mind', writes Boutroux, 'bears within itself the principles of pure logic; but since the matter offered to it does not seem to conform exactly with these principles, it endeavors to adapt logic to things so as to interpret the latter in a way that approaches perfect intelligibility as nearly as possible' (1914:27). Thus, Boutroux explains the unavoidability of the principle of contradiction by tracing it back to the nature of 'the human mind'. But, in taking the human mind as an objective subject matter to be investigated, Boutroux invites yet further investigation into why our minds have come to be constituted as they are. It is this, his teacher's question, that Durkheim's sociological theory of the categories is meant to answer (ibid.:27; and see chapter by R. A. Jones here). In response, we must distinguish between an explanation of the fact that we presuppose the principle of contradiction from an explanation of the principle itself as yielding a priori truths about the activity of thinking (cf. Thompson 1981:474). Following Thompson, I have been urging that no inquiry into any external subject matter can explain why we must presuppose the principle of contradiction.

Russell makes a parallel mistake in *The Problems of Philosophy* published, as was the *The Elementary Forms*, in 1912. Russell argues against the apriority of the principle of contradiction that 'nothing can at once have and not have a given quality', by urging that it is not a 'law of thought'.

> The belief in the law of contradiction is a belief about things, not only about thoughts. It is not, for example, the belief that if we think a certain tree is a beech, we cannot at the same time think

that it is not a beech; it is the belief that if the tree is a beech, it cannot at the same time be not a beech. Thus, the law of contradiction is about things, and not merely about thoughts.

(Russell 1978:88–9)

Russell's comments are effective against positions such as Boutroux's: we do want to say that a beech, no less than the thought of a beech, has just the nature that it has and not some other. Russell thinks positions such as Boutroux's go wrong in too narrowly restricting what the principle of contradiction is about. They convey the illusion of apriority by arbitrarily confining the principle to the realm of thought. But, in fact, Russell's emphasis on what belief in the principle of contradiction is about completely by-passes the question of its apriority. To expose the principle's apriority we have to see it as unavoidably presupposed in all our thinking, and not as a fact about thoughts or things. Thus, when Russell thinks that the principle of contradiction is about things and not only thoughts he cannot thereby mean the negation of that thought. Russell is quietly conforming to the principle even as he represents the principle as being about a subject matter independent of his activity.

In our own day, the question of explaining our reliance on the principle of contradiction lies at the heart of the continuing controversy between proponents of the Strong Programme in the sociology of knowledge, such as David Bloor and Barry Barnes, and on the other hand, critics such as Martin Hollis and Steven Lukes. As I understand them, Hollis and Lukes have maintained that the principle of contradiction is among the 'common core' shared by all cultures; it helps serve as the 'rational bridgehead' which makes linguistic communication possible (Hollis 1982:75ff.; Lukes 1982:266ff). By way of response, Bloor and Barnes insist that Hollis and Lukes have not produced 'context-independent criteria of truth and rationality' sufficient to demonstrate the principle's universality and necessity, and that, in any case, field linguists meet with as much failure as they do success (Bloor and Barnes 1982:35). It is important for my purposes to see that both sides in this debate are presupposing, or conforming to, the principle of contradiction in a way that undermines their positions. Hollis and Lukes want to give the principle of contradiction a privileged place in any acceptable theory of linguistic interpretation. Perhaps they are right. But whether right or wrong, any inquiry into the nature of linguistic interpretation will have to employ the principle it seeks to place.[6]

Perhaps Bloor and Barnes are right that 'all beliefs are on a par with one another with respect to the causes of their credibility' (ibid.:23). This is what they call their 'equivalence postulate', that is, they want to place 'all beliefs on a par with one another for the purposes of explanation' (ibid.:25). As I understand the idea, it is very plausible. Thus, in my own case, I believe that the principle of contradiction is strongly a priori, and I believe that I believe this for the reasons I am now relating. Of course my self-assessment might be mistaken. With Bloor and Barnes, we may ask after the unnoticed influence of authority. And of course there is always the possibility of self-deception. So long as we take the equivalence postulate to be about the explanation of belief (of someone's attitude of holding true some proposition), nothing I have to say in this paper can put it in jeopardy.

But Barnes and Bloor do not always confine it to the explanation of belief. They also want to deny 'the idea that some standards or beliefs are really rational as distinct from merely locally accepted as such'. There are, they think, 'no context-free or super-cultural norms of rationality' (27). From the point of view I am developing, the key phrase is 'they think'. To think or mean that there are no context-free or super-cultural norms is to deny that there are such norms. As before, I recognize that I am not making a point about what Barnes and Bloor can or cannot think or mean; nor on this point can there be any question of external coercion or self-deception. Rather, what is in view is my inability to think or mean anything in the absence of conformity to the principle of contradiction. In that sense, the formal conditions of thought are indeed context-free and super-cultural.

Let us take stock. Our present theme is the uselessness of trying to explain why we must conform to the principle of contradiction. Boutroux appealed to the nature of thought, Russell to the nature of things, Durkheim to the requirements of social life, and Hollis and Lukes to the foundations of linguistic communication. All are representing themselves as able to isolate the subject matter that enforces our conformity (what I have been calling an 'external' subject matter) and that strategy cannot succeed. It cannot succeed because it tries to stand outside the activity of thinking in a way that must fail. Of course a great deal more remains to be said both in explication and in defence. But for the purposes of the remainder of this essay, I am going to take it as granted that we cannot do what Durkheim and many others have tried to do, namely, to explain why we must presuppose the formal conditions that make thought possible.

Justification, resignation, exculpation

Supposing, then, that it is so, how ought we to react to the fact that we cannot explain our reliance on the principle of contradiction? In this section I shall canvass three influential reactions.

Justification

One reaction would be to proclaim the joyous news that we have established at least one a priori truth, one whose legitimacy is owed not merely to convention or stipulation but 'to an objective necessity that arises from the nature of thought itself' (Thompson 1981:480). Adopting this line, we might then go on to inquire whether thought and experience are constrained a priori in other ways as well. On the epistemological side, a positive finding would then rule out the possibility that any human knowledge could fail to meet these conditions. On the metaphysical side, it would bring with it a distinction between objects of experience and things considered apart from our possible cognition of them. This, of course, is one way to view the basic thrust of Kant's transcendental idealism. Kant's idea was to give up explaining our necessary reliance on the principle of contradiction (and much else!) in favour of justifying that reliance as a condition of experience. (I shall return to the Kantian strategy at the end.)

In *The Elementary Forms of Religious Life*, Durkheim explicitly rejects Kant's reaction to the realization that our cognitive activity is necessarily bound by the principle of contradiction in a way that we cannot explain. This rejection is of course consistent with Durkheim's conviction that our necessary conformity could be explained by the new discipline of sociology. Although we have already put Durkheim's proposal behind us, the details of his objection to Kant's reaction are of independent interest. Durkheim alleges a circularity problem. In the Introduction to *The Elementary Forms of Religious Life*, Durkheim voices doubt that Kant's appeal to the conditions of experience has even 'changed the problem' (27). And in the Conclusion he complains that, in appealing to the conditions of experience, Kant has 'merely repeated the question in slightly different terms' (494). Durkheim's point, as I understand it, is that we cannot justify our reliance on a given rule or principle by appealing to that same rule or principle. Durkheim is not at this point denying that Kant's categories are inescapable – rather, he is denying that their inescapability precludes our adopting a genuinely explanatory strategy toward them.

To repeat: while I have already rejected Durkheim's own strategy for the purposes of this paper, his charge of circularity has prompted a different, influential reaction, to which I now turn.

Resignation

Bloor and Barnes have also advanced a circularity objection against those who wish to justify our conformity to the principle of contradiction. But they do not follow Durkheim in advancing their own explanation. Instead, their reaction is resignation. They see no way around the circularity, for they think that any justification or explanation of our reliance on the principle of contradiction is going to have to appeal to that principle. So they give up the project of justifying our 'basic modes of reasoning' in favour of a frank relativism in which all justification is 'local' (1982:40). (Their proposal does preserve a strong Durkheimian flavour, since the search for the causes of credibility will in many – perhaps all – instances, be a sociological undertaking. But they are happy to leave Durkheim's justificatory ambitions behind.) I think we must admit that, if any attempt at justifying or explaining our necessary conformity to the principle of contradiction must be guilty of the fallacy of circular reasoning, then, for those seeking its justification, resignation would indeed be the appropriate reaction.

What, then, is it to argue in a circle? Ordinarily, we bring charges of circularity when someone appeals to the very principle that he is trying to establish in the course of trying to establish it. But this is clearly not our case. We are not trying to defend or ground the principle of contradiction by appealing to the principle of contradiction; rather, our motivating insight has been that, in thinking the principle of contradiction (or anything) we must have presupposed it. The point is that the principle has been in force before any question of an appeal can arise. The larger issue raised by the charge of circularity brought by Durkheim and by Bloor and Barnes is how to regard logic as a subject matter. On this point all are quite clear. Bloor and Barnes write that:

> Logic, as it is systematized in textbooks, monographs or research papers, is a learned body of scholarly lore, growing and varying over time. It is a mass of conventional routines, decisions, expedient restrictions, dicta, maxims, and *ad hoc* rules.
>
> (ibid.:45)

In historicizing logic they follow Durkheim's own emphasis on 'the different characteristics which logic presents at different periods in history; it develops like the societies themselves' (626–7/438–9) (see also 17–18/12–13 and 341–2/238–9). Following this line of thought, we are to place the circularity involved in trying to justify the principle of contradiction in a textbook chapter together with such other logical fallacies as inconsistency, prejudice and irrelevance. On this view, a logical truth can only be justified, to use Barnes and Bloor's term, 'locally', that is, relative to the current textbook, to the definitions, maxims and the like that comprise the formal system within which we are presently working. The key to Barnes and Bloor's relativism is to recognize that any such system of definitions and maxims may itself be regarded as one among many possible alternatives.

No doubt large portions of logic can be fruitfully regarded in this way, as one subject matter among many. But I do want to insist that this view of logic must be compatible with the claim I brought earlier against Durkheim's attempt to make logic a topic for sociological inquiry – that we must presuppose the truth of the principle of contradiction whenever we think at all, regardless of subject matter. Then, to countenance a genuine alternative to the principle of contradiction would be to contemplate the impossibility of thought.

We may take the following moral from Durkheim's and Bloor and Barnes' circularity objection. To the extent that it, and the resignation it prompts in Bloor and Barnes, depends upon viewing logic as a subject matter with a nature independent enough of the activity of thinking to be held up for inspection, revision, codification, and so on, to that extent it loses sight of the very apriority to which it is reacting.

Exculpation

Let us take Hilary Putnam as representative of a third and final reaction to our inability to explain why we must conform to the principle of contradiction. Putnam agrees with Leibniz, Kant and Bloor and Barnes that we cannot explain our necessary conformity to the principle of contradiction (for those keeping score, this puts him at odds with Aristotle, Boutroux, Durkheim and Russell). And he agrees with Leibniz, Kant and Durkheim that this inability should not make us doubt its objectivity. (Bloor and Barnes disagree). But, rather than follow Kant in search of justification, Putnam is content to substitute exculpation.[7]

That is how I understand his comment that 'even with respect to the part of logic ... that is a priori, it seems to me that the apriority tells us something about the nature of rationality, not something about the nature of logic'. By rationality in this context Putnam means our powers of explanation. Thus, he continues: 'some truths of logic are so basic that the notion of explanation collapses when we try to "explain" why they are true' (1983:137-8). Putnam insists that it is not 'that there is something "unexplainable" here'; rather, the point is that 'there is simply no room for an explanation of what is presupposed by every explanatory activity'. Here Putnam is with Durkheim in refusing to leave the truths of logic ungrounded in the sense of requiring, but lacking, an explanation. However, rather than follow Durkheim in providing an explanation for their truth, Putnam suggests that the nature of rationality in the form of the presuppositions of explanation, stands in the way. His point is that we can not be blamed for the fact that the nature of rationality is what it is. I want to portray this as a half-way measure. Putnam gives up explaining why the principle of contradiction is true, but justifies his giving up and our use of the principle, by appealing to yet another external subject matter, namely, the nature of rationality. This is where the sense of exculpation comes into play. The presuppositions of rationality are simply given to us as underlying all of our explanatory activity. We are to take it as a basic fact about ourselves, as something fundamentally contingent and inexplicable, that human rationality has just these and no other presuppositions. We cannot be expected to explain how just these presuppositions have come to be in force because any such explanation is going to have to be derived from them.

At this point, it is instructive to see Putnam and Boutroux as vulnerable in the same way. We have noted that Boutroux tried to build the principle of contradiction into 'the nature of the human mind', to which Durkheim understandably levelled the charge of dogmatism, that is, how did it come to be thus? Similarly, Putnam is trying to build the principle into the nature of rationality. When the issue is posed in this way, by resting the matter on a contingent fact about ourselves, I think we should take our cue from Durkheim and ask why we may not inquire further. Not surprisingly, in his recent book titled, *The Nature of Rationality*, Robert Nozick does precisely that. He argues that adherence to the principle of contradiction has been forced upon us by the blind (non-teleological) mechanisms of evolutionary biology (Nozick 1993:110-11). Perhaps Nozick is right. But, then, in resting our explanation on a subject matter that has a place in the world, we lose contact with our original insight that conformity to the principle of contradiction makes possible the thought of any subject matter whatever. Putnam's attempt at exculpation is an invitation to change the subject.[8] It is once again to lose sight of the apriority that had just come into view.

Let me sum up this section. I think that recent discussion about the status of the principle of contradiction has tended to oscillate between the second and third unsatisfying positions I have just sketched, though to redeem this claim would require a far more detailed survey than I can provide here. Before I sketch the oscillation let us recall its motive. Its motive is the double realization that we must conform to the principle and that that necessary conformity cannot itself be explained by appealing to the nature of any further subject matter. The oscillation, then, is between on the one hand, an attempt at exculpation which invites us to quietly change the subject, and on the other, a relativism which threatens to make thought impossible.

How, then, to end the oscillation? That is, how ought we to react to the realization that our necessary conformity to the principle of contradiction cannot be explained?

Conclusion

Let me say finally something about the source of our dissatisfaction with the two poles of the oscillation as I have sketched it. I hope that this will lead to some insight into the form of any acceptable view. The first thing to notice about the two positions is that each one reacts to the realization of our necessary conformity by tracing that necessity to the nature of an external subject matter – logic for Barnes and Bloor, rationality for Putnam. And of course before them, Durkheim had traced it to the nature of society. By 'external subject matter' I have meant putative truths about something other than (external to) the activity of thinking. But the preliminary moral drawn from the first section, reinforced by what has followed, was that the apriority of the principle of contradiction only comes into focus when we take it as applied to our own activity of thought. My suggestion is that the views we have been considering go wrong in refusing to keep to the first-person point of view. Why was there a turning away from thought in the first place? What made it seem necessary to stand outside thought (on the nature of logic, on the presuppositions of rationality, on the requirements of social life) was the desire to explain – or at least comment on – the nature of thought. But if we stop taking the nature of thought as a further subject matter to be explained or commented upon, that motive will have lost its force. Why should we stop taking it as such? Because the necessity of presupposing the principle of contradiction in all of our thinking prevents our adopting an external point of view on that necessity. There simply is no subject matter to be explained or commented upon.

At that point, as Thompson in commenting on Putnam puts it, 'what collapses . . . is not so much the notion of explanation as the distinction between subjectivity and objectivity' (1981:477). Certainly I do think, but I am not able to convert the necessary formal conditions of that activity into a subject matter to be investigated. Yet those conditions are objective, in that they attach not to my thought in particular but to every thinking creature, to the very notion of a thinking subject. Viewed in this way, the principle of contradiction limits a priori our thinking, and, by extension, our knowledge of the world that imposes itself on our thinking. And with the notion of an objective a priori limit comes the characteristically double-edged force of a Kantian-style transcendental argument: the restriction of knowledge claims to the field of possible experience, coupled with the claim that, so restricted, our a priori principles serve as formal conditions of empirical truth.

Such claims are of course well beyond what we currently have in view.[9] Our reflections on the status of the principle of contradiction have led us to the distinction between the theory of knowledge, which, in the sense that I have been taking it, must maintain a radically first-person perspective, and what are often still today called the social sciences – sociology, anthropology, psychology, economics and the like – which rightfully take the activity of human thought as one subject matter among others. Durkheim refused to recognize this distinction, and the strongest currents of twentieth-century thought have sided with him. It seems, rather, to be an open question.[10]

Notes

1 Two paragraphs earlier Kant gives the principle as 'no predicate contradictory of a thing can belong to it'. Thus, Kant removes the temporal reference from Aristotle's formula 'at the same time'. Kant is drawing on his discussion of time in the Transcendental Aesthetic, according to which it is not a concept, but rather a pure intuition; a temporal reference would then remove the principle from the domain of logic.

2 Durkheim has 'identity', but, as the context makes clear, he is treating the two as equivalent.

3 I have urged this point against Durkheim's larger approach to categories in Godlove (1996) and (1989).

4 Plato 1980:182c–183b, 179a10–b9, 170c2–171c7; see also the discussion in Irwin 1977:223ff.

5 That society has its own nature is one of the bedrock theses of the The Elementary Forms; see, for example, 28–9, 237, 257, 426, 492, 493.

6 Thus, my concerns are orthogonal to the debate between followers of Davidson, including, in this respect, Hollis and Lukes, and their critics over the status of the principle of contradiction in the theory of interpretation. Davidson has long argued that attitude-attribution requires the interpreter to find a large degree of consistency amongst the beliefs, desires, and actions of those she interprets. And in a well-known note to 'Radical Interpretation', he remarks that his method 'probably does not leave room for indeterminacy of logical form' (1984:136). But the Davidsonian context is that of an interpreter out to 'optimize' her on-going understanding of others' sounds and movements; it assumes the empirical context of interpretation, i.e. a speaker, an interpreter and their physical environment. By contrast, I have been urging that the apriority of the principle of contradiction comes into view only when the interpreter reflects on the necessary conditions of her own activity of thinking. The two contexts are thus quite different. While Davidson has never, to my knowledge, said otherwise, nor said anything which would prevent him from saying otherwise, enthusiastic readers have occasionally claimed to find support in his work for the 'flexibility' of the principle of contradiction, for example, Malpas 1992:20, 80.

7 I have taken the language of exculpation and the image of oscillation (below) from John McDowell 1984:9ff. The philosophical contexts are unrelated.

8 Putnam has been a moving target on this issue. I take his recent, repeated rejections of a 'God's-eye' or 'Archimedian' point of view in epistemology to be congenial to the stance I am developing here. We cannot, he writes, 'survey

others as if they were not ourselves, survey them as if we were, so to speak, outside our own skins' (Putnam 1990:17). I am accusing Putnam of representing himself as able to comment on the theory of rationality as if he were outside his own skin. I make no attempt here to characterize the development within Putnam's views.

9 Even granting, for example, that the principle of contradiction is an a priori truth, Irwin has asked whether it may be the only one of its kind (1977:224ff.). I take up this question in Godlove 1996.

10 An earlier draft of this paper benefited from comments at the July 1995 Oxford conference on *The Elementary Forms*. For helpful criticism I wish to thank my colleagues in the philosophy department at Hofstra University, and Tony Dardis in particular. My debt to Manley Thompson's work on a priori truth is large indeed.

BIBLIOGRAPHY

(The dating-enumeration for works by Durkheim is that found in Lukes 1973/ 1992. Where 't.' is followed by a date, the t. refers to the date of an English translation. See Explanatory note for other technical points. Further details of any items by Durkheim mentioned below can be found in Lukes ibid.)

Ackerman, R. (1975) 'Frazer on Myth and Ritual', *Journal of the History of Ideas*, 36:115–34.
Ackerman, R. (1987) *Frazer: His Life and Work*, Cambridge: Cambridge University Press.
Alexander, J. C. (ed.) (1988) *Durkheimian Sociology: Cultural Studies*, Cambridge: Cambridge University Press.
Allen, N. J. (1982) 'A dance of relatives', *Journal of the Anthropological Society of Oxford*, 13:139–46.
Allen, N. J. (1989) 'The evolution of kinship terminologies', *Lingua* 77:173–85.
Allen, N. J. (1994) '*Primitive classification*: the argument and its validity', in W. S. F. Pickering and H. Martins (eds) *Debating Durkheim*, London: Routledge.
Allen, N. J. (1995) '*The Division of Labour* and the notion of primitive society: a Maussian perspective', *Social Anthropology*, 3:49–59.
Allen, N. J. (forthcoming) 'The prehistory of Dravidian-type terminologies', in T. Trautmann, M. Godelier and F. Tjon Sie Fat (eds) *Transformations of Kinship Systems: Dravidian, Australian, Iroquois and Crow-Omaha*, Washington: Smithsonian.
Althusser, L. (1971) *Lenin and Philosophy and Other Essays*, t. by B. Brewster, London: New Left Books.
Aristotle (1927) *Metaphysics*, t. by W. D. Ross, Oxford: Oxford University Press.
Asad, T. (1993) *Genealogies of Religion*, Baltimore: Johns Hopkins University Press.
Barnard, A. (1994) 'Rules and prohibitions: the form and content of human kinship', in T. Ingold (ed.) *Companion Encyclopaedia of Anthropology: Humanity, Culture and Social Life*, London: Routledge.
Barnes, B. and Bloor, D. (1982) 'Relativism, rationalism, and the sociology of knowledge', in M. Hollis and S. Lukes (eds) *Rationality and Relativism*, Cambridge: MIT Press.
Barthes, R. (1967) *Elements of Semiology*, London: Cape.
Barthes, R. (1972) *Mythologies*, London: Cape.
Bastide, R. (1965) 'La pensée obscure et confuse', *Le Monde non-chrétien*, 75–6; 137–56 (reprinted in *Bastidiana* 7–8, July–Dec. 1994:123ff.
Bataille, G. (1938) 'Attraction and repulsion I: tropisms, sexuality, laughter and tears,' t. 1988 by B. Wing, in D. Hollier (ed) *The College of Sociology (1937–9)*, Minneapolis: University of Minnesota Press.
Baudrillard, J. (1976) *Symbolic Exchange and Death*, t.1993. Thousand Oaks: Sage.
Beattie, J. (1964) *Other Cultures*, London: Cohen and West.
Beattie, J. (1966) 'Ritual and social change', *Man* (n.s.) 1:60–74.

Beattie, J. (1970) 'On understanding ritual', in B. R. Wilson (ed.) *Rationality*, Oxford: Blackwell.

Beck L. W. (1966) *A Commentary on Kant's Critique of Practical Reason*, Chicago: University of Chicago Press.

Bellah, R. N. (1973) *Emile Durkheim on Morality and Society*, Chicago: University of Chicago Press.

Belot, G. (1913) 'Une théorie nouvelle de la religion', *Revue philosophique*, LXXV, 4:329–69.

Benoît-Smullyan, E. (1948) 'The Sociologism of Emile Durkheim and his School', in H. E. Barnes (ed.) *An Introduction to the History of Sociology*, Chicago: University of Chicago Press.

Bloor, D. (1982) 'Durkheim and Mauss revisited: classification and the sociology of knowledge', *Studies in History and Philosophy of Science* 13, 4:267–97.

Bloor, D. and Barnes, B. (1982) 'Relativism, rationalism and the sociology of knowledge', in M. Hollis and S. Lukes (eds) *Rationality and Relativism*, Cambridge, Mass.: MIT University Press.

Borlandi, M. (1995) 'Les faits sociaux comme produits de l'association des individus', in M. Borlandi and L. Mucchielli (eds) *La Sociologie et sa méthode. Les Règles de Durkheim un siècle après*, Paris: L'Harmattan.

Boudon, R. (1990) *L'Art de se persuader des idées fausses, fragiles ou douteuses*, Paris: Fayard.

Boudon, R. (ed.) (1992) *Traité de sociologie*, Paris: Presses Universitaires de France.

Boudon, R. (1995) *Le juste et le vrai. Etudes sur l'objectivité des valeurs et de la connaissance*, Paris: Fayard.

Bouglé, C. (1908) *Essais sur le régime des castes*, Paris: Alcan.

Bouglé, C. (1922) *Leçons de sociologie sur l'évolution des valeurs*, Paris: Armand Colin. (2nd ed. 1929)

Boutroux, E. (1909a) *Science and Religion in Contemporary Philosophy*, t. by J. Nield, Port Washington, New York and London: Kennikat Press.

Boutroux, E. (1909b) 'Contribution to discussion: "Science et religion"', *Bulletin de la Société française de philosophie*, 9:19–39; 53–6; 60–2, 71–4.

Boutroux, E. (1914) *Natural Law in Science and Philosophy*, t. by Fred Rothwell, London: David Nutt.

Boutroux, E. (1916) *The Contingency of the Laws of Nature*, t. by Fred Rothwell, Chicago: Open Court.

Boutroux, E. (1926) *La philosophie de Kant. Cours professé à la Sorbonne en 1896–1897*, Paris: Vrin, (1st ed. 1896).

Bréhier, E. (1949) 'Originalité de Lévy-Bruhl', *Revue philosophique*, CXXXIX, 4:385–8.

Brooks, J. I., III. (1996) 'The definition of sociology and the sociology of definition: Durkheim's *Rules of Sociological Method* and high school philosophy in France', *Journal of the History of the Behavioral Sciences* 32, 4:379–407.

Collins, S. (1985) 'Categories, concepts, or predicaments? Remarks on Mauss' use of Philosophical Terminology', in M. Carrithers, S. Collins and S. Lukes (eds) *The Category of the Person: Anthropology, Philosophy, History*, Cambridge: Cambridge University Press.

Copleston, F. (1977) *A History of Philosophy*, Vol. IX, New York: Doubleday.

Cousin, V. (1860) *Du Vrai, du beau et du bien*, Paris: Didier.

Davidson, D. (1984) *Truth and Interpretation*, New York: Oxford University Press.

Delbos, V. (1905) *La philosophie pratique de Kant*, Paris: Presses Universitaires de France. (Republished 1969)

Dennes, W. R. (1924) 'The methods and presuppositions of group psychology', *University of California Publications in Philosophy*, 6, 1:1–182.

Deploige, S. (1905–7) 'Le Conflit de la morale et de la sociologie', *Revue néo-scolastique*, 12:405–17; 13:49–79, 135–63; 281–313; 14:329–54, 355–92.

Douglas, M. (1966) *Purity and Danger*, London: Routledge & Kegan Paul.

Douglas, M. (1975) *Implicit Meanings*, London: Routledge & Kegan Paul.

Durkheim, E. (1886a) Review. 'Herbert Spencer, *Ecclesiastical Institutions*, part VI of *Principles of Sociology, Revue Philosophique*, XXII:61–9;
(t.1975a) by J. Redding and W. S. F. Pickering, in W. S. F. Pickering (ed.) *Durkheim on Religion. A Selection of Readings with Bibliographies and Introductory Remarks*, London and Boston: Routledge & Kegan Paul.

—— (1887b) Review. 'Guyau. *L'Irréligion de l'avenir*', *Revue philosophique*, XXIII: 299–311;
(t.1975a) by J. Redding and W. S. F. Pickering in W. S. F. Pickering (ed.) *Durkheim on Religion. A Selection of Readings with Bibliographies and Introductory Remarks*, London and Boston: Routledge & Kegan Paul.

—— (1887c) 'La Science positive de la morale en Allemagne', *Revue philosophique*, XXIV:33–58, 113–42, 275–84.

—— (1888a) 'Cours de science sociale: leçon d'ouverture', *Revue de l'enseignement*, XV: 23–48;
(t.1978a) by M. Traugott, in M. Traugott (ed.) *Emile Durkheim on Institutional Analysis*, Chicago and London: University of Chicago Press.

—— (1890a) 'Les Principes de 1789 et la sociologie', *Revue internationale de l'enseignement*, XIX: 450–6.

—— (1893b) *De la Division du travail social: Etude sur l'organisation des sociétés supérieures*, Paris: Alcan;
(1902b) 2nd edition by Durkheim.
(t.1933b) by G. Simpson with preface, *The Division of Labor in Society*, New York: Macmillan.
(t.1984a) by W. D. Halls, *The Division of Labour in Society*, with an introduction by L. Coser, London and Basingstoke: Macmillan.

—— (1895a) *Les Règles de la méthode sociologique*, Paris: Alcan; (1901c) 2nd ed. by Durkheim.
(t.1938b) by S. A. Solovay and J. H. Mueller, *The Rules of Sociological Method*, edited, with an introduction by G. E. G. Catlin, Chicago: University of Chicago Press, and (1950) Chicago: Free Press.
(t.1982a) by W. D. Walls, *The Rules of Sociological Method*, London: Macmillan.

—— (1897a) *Le Suicide: Etude de sociologie*, Paris: Alcan.
(t.1951a) by J. A. Spaulding and G. Simpson, *Suicide: A Study in Sociology*, edited, with an introduction by G. Simpson, Chicago: Free Press, and (1952) London: Routledge & Kegan Paul.

—— (1898a(ii)) 'La Prohibition de l'inceste et ses origines', *L'Année sociologique*, I:1–70.
(t.1963a) with an introduction by E. Sagarin, *Incest. The Nature and Origin of the Taboo by Emile Durkheim*, New York: Lyle Stuart.

—— (1898b) 'Représentations individuelles et représentations collectives,' *Revue métaphysique et de morale*, VI:273–302. Reproduced in 1924a.

—— (1898c) 'L'Individualisme et les intellectuals', *Revue bleue*, 4e série, X:7–13.

—— (1899a(i)) Préface, *L'Année Sociologique*, II:i–vi.

—— (1899a(ii)) 'De la Définition des phénomènes religieux', *L'Année sociologique*, II:1–28.
(t.1975a) by J. Redding and W. S. F. Pickering, in W. S. F. Pickering (ed.) *Durkheim on Religion. A Selection of Readings with Bibliographies and Introductory Remarks*, London and Boston: Routledge & Kegan Paul.

—— (1900b) 'La Sociologie en France au XIXe siècle', *Revue bleue*, 4e série, XII: 609–13, 647–52.

—— (1900c) 'La sociologia ed il suo dominio scientifico', *Revista italiana di sociologia*, IV:127–48.

—— (1901a(i)) 'Deux Lois de l'évolution pénale', *L'Année sociologique*, IV:65–95.
(t.1973b) by T. A. Jones and A. T. Scull, 'Two laws of penal evolution', with an introduction, *Economy and Society*, 2:278–308.

—— (1902a(i)) 'Sur le totémisme', *L'Année sociologique*, V:82–121.

—— (1903a(i)) (with M. Mauss) 'De quelques Formes primitives de classification: contribution à l'étude des représentations collectives', *L'Année sociologique*, VI: 1–72.

(t.1963b) by R. Needham, *Primitive Classification*, with an introduction by R. Needham, London: Cohen and West.

—— (1903a(ii)(2)) 'Organization sociale', *L'Année sociologique*, VI:316.

—— (1903c) (with P. Fauconnet) 'Sociologie et sciences sociales', *Revue philosophique*, LV:465–97.

(t.1982a) by W. D. Walls, *The Rules of Sociological Method*, London: Macmillan.

—— (1906a(8)) Review. 'Ribot, T., *La Logique des sentiments*', *L'Année sociologique*, IX:156–8.

—— (1906b) 'La Détermination du fait social', *Bulletin de la Société française de philosophie*, 1906:169–212. Reproduced in 1924a.

—— (1906c) 'L'Evolution et la rôle de l'enseignement secondaire en France', *Revue bleue*, 5e série:70–7. Reproduced in 1922a.

—— (1906e) Summary by A. Lalande of a lecture by Durkheim on religion and morality, delivered at the Ecole des Hautes Etudes in 1905–6, *Philosophical Review*, XV:255–7.

—— (1907b) 'Lettres au Directeur de la *Revue néo-scolastique*, *Revue néo-scolastique*', 14:606–7, 612–14.

—— (1907f) 'Cours d'Emile Durkheim à la Sorbonne', *Revue de philosophie*, VII, 5:528–39; 7:92–114; 12:620–38. Summary by P. Fontana of 1906–7 lecture course, 'La Religion: les origines'.

—— (1909a(1)) Contribution to discussion of 'Science et religion', *Bulletin de la Société française de philosophie*, IX:56–60.

—— (1909d) 'Sociologie religieuse et théorie de la connaissance', *Revue de métaphysique et de morale*, XVII:733–58.

—— (1912a) *Les Formes élémentaires de la vie religieuse. Le système totémique en Australie*, Paris: Alcan.

(t.1915d) by J. W. Swain, *The Elementary Forms of the Religious Life: A Study in Religious Sociology*, London: Allen and Unwin, New York: Macmillan.

(t.1995c) by K. E. Fields, *The Elementary Forms of Religious Life*, with a translator's introduction, New York: Free Press.

—— (1913a(ii)(6) and (7)) Review. 'Lévy-Bruhl – *Les Fonctions mentales dans les sociétés inférieures*, Paris, 1910'. 'Durkheim (Emile) – *Les Formes élémentaires de la vie religieuse. Le Système totémique en Australie*, Paris, 1912', *L'Année sociologique*, XII:33–7.

—— (1913a(ii)(11) and (12)) Review with M. Mauss. 'Frazer – *Totemism and Exogamy*. vol. IV' and 'Durkheim – *Les Formes élémentaires de la vie religieuse. Le Système totémique en Australie*', *L'Année sociologique*, XII:91–8.

—— (1913a(ii)(15)) Review. 'Deploige, Simon, *Le Conflit de la morale et de la sociologie*', *L'Année sociologique*, XII:326–8.

—— (1913a(ii)(31)) Review. 'Frazer, *Totemism and Exogamy*', *L'Année sociologique*, XII:429–32.

—— (1913b) Contribution to discussion of: 'Le Problème religieux et la dualité de la nature humaine', séance de 4 fevrier 1913, in *Bulletin de la Société française de philosophie*, XIII:63–75, 80–7, 90–100, 108–11.

(t.1984b) by R. A. Jones and P. W. Vogt, 'The Problem of Religion and the Duality of Human Nature', *Knowledge and Society*, 5:1–44.

—— (1914a) 'Le Dualisme de la nature humaine et ses conditions sociales', *Scientia*, XV:206–21.

(t.1960c) by C. Blend in K. H. Wolff (ed.), *Emile Durkheim 1858–1917*, Ohio: Ohio State University Press.

—— (1919b) Contribution to F. Abauzit *et al. Le Sentiment religieux à l'heure actuelle*, Paris: Vrin, 97–105; 142–3.

—— (1922a) *Education et sociologie*, Paris: Alcan.

—— (1924a) *Sociologie et philosophie*, preface by C. Bouglé, Paris: Alcan.

(t.1953b) by D. F. Pocock, *Sociology and Philosophy*, introduction by J. G. Peristiany, London: Cohen and West.

—— (1925a) *L'Education morale*, introduction by Paul Fauconnet, Paris: Alcan.

(t.1961a) by E. K. Wilson and H. Schnurer, *Moral Education: A Study in the Theory and Application of the Sociology of Education*, edited, with an introduction, by E. K. Wilson, New York: Free Press.

—— (1950a) *Leçons de sociologie: physique des moeurs et du droit*, forward by H. N. Kubali, introduction by G. Davy, Istanbul: L'Université d'Istanbul. Paris: Presses Universitaires de France.

(t.1957a) by C. Brookfield, *Professional Ethics and Civic Morals*, London: Routledge & Kegan Paul.

—— (1955a) *Pragmatisme et sociologie. Cours inédit prononcé la Sorbonne en 1913–14 par Armand Cuvillier d'après des notes d'étudiants*, Paris: Vrin.

(t.1983a) by J.C. Whitehouse, *Pragmatism and Sociology*, edited, with an introduction by J. B. Allcock, Cambridge: Cambridge University Press.

—— (1968c) 'La morale'. Notes made by G. Davy, probably of 1908–9 lecture course. In Lukes 1968, 2:248–60.

—— (1969c) *Journal sociologique*, with an introduction and notes by J. Duvignaud (Selection of Durkheim's articles), Paris: Presses Universitaires de France.

—— (1970a) *La Science sociale et l'action*, introduction and presentation by J.-C. Filloux, (selection of Durkheim's articles), Paris: Presses Universitaires de France.

—— (1975b) *Durkheim, E., Textes*, 3 vols, edited with introduction by V. Karady (collection of articles, reviews, notes, letters), Paris: Les Editions de Minuit.

Düsseldorfer Stadt-Nachrichten, Beilage der Düsseldorfer Nachrichten of 13 August 1938.

Erikson, K. (1966) *Wayward Puritans*, New York: Wiley.

Evans-Pritchard, E. E. (1934) 'Lévy-Bruhl's theory of primitive mentality', *Bulletin of the Faculty of Arts*, Cairo, 2, 2:1–26. Reproduced in the *Journal of the Anthropological Society of Oxford*, 1970, 1, 2:39–60.

Evans-Pritchard, E. E. (1956) *Nuer Religion*, Oxford: Clarendon Press.

Evans-Pritchard, E. E. (1960) Introduction to *Death and the Right Hand*, by R. Hertz, t. by R. and C. Needham, London: Cohen & West.

Evans-Pritchard, E. E. (1962) *Essays in Social Anthropology*, London: Faber & Faber.

Evans-Pritchard, E. E. (1965) *Theories of Primitive Religion*, Oxford: Clarendon Press.

Evans-Pritchard, E. E. (1970) Comment on Littlejohn, 'Twins, birds, etc.', *Bijdragen tot de taal-, land- en volkenkunde* 126, 1:109–112.

Fauconnet, P. (1921) *La responsabilité. Etude de sociologie*, Paris: Alcan. (2nd ed., 1928)

Ferrero, G. (1893) *I simboli, in rapporto alla storia e filosofia del diritto, alla psicologia e alla sociologia*, Torino: Bocca.

Fields, K. (1995) Translator's introduction to *The Elementary Forms of Religious Life*, New York: Free Press.

Fields, K. (1996) 'Durkheim and the idea of soul', *Theory and Society*, 25:193–203.

Firth, R. (1973) *Symbols, Public and Private*, London: Allen & Unwin.

Fison, L. and Howitt, A. W. (1880) *Kamilaroi and Kurnai*, Melbourne: George Robertson.

Fortes, M. (1983) *Rules and the Emergence of Society*, Royal Anthropological Institute, Occasional Paper 390, London: Royal Anthropological Institute.

Fournier, M. and de Langle, Christine, 'Autour du sacrifice: lettres d'Emile Durkheim, J. G. Frazer, M. Mauss et E. B. Tylor', *Etudes durkheimiennes/Durkheim Studies*, 3, 1991:2–9.

Fox, R. (1980) *The Red Lamp of Incest*, London: Hutchinson.

Friedländer, S. and Seligman, A. (1994) 'Das Gedenken an die Schoa in Israel. Symbole Rituale und ideologische Polarisierung', in J. E. Young (ed.) *Mahnmale des Holocaust. Motive, Rituale und Stätten des Gedenkens*, München: Prestel.

Fustel de Coulanges, N. D. (1864) *La cité antique*, Paris. (Reprinted in 1903)

Gamble, C. (forthcoming) *The Palaeolithic Societies of Europe*, Cambridge: Cambridge University Press.

Gane, M. (1983a) 'Durkheim: the sacred language', *Economy and Society*, 12, 1:1–47.

Gane, M., (1983b) 'Durkheim: woman as outsider', *Economy and Society*, 12, 2:227–70.

Gane, M., (1988) *On Durkheim's Rules of Sociological Method*, London and New York: Routledge.

Gane, M. (1992) 'Introduction: Emile Durkheim, Marcel Mauss and the sociological project', in M. Gane (ed.) *The Radical Sociology of Durkheim and Mauss*, London: Routledge.

Garfinkel, H. (1956) 'Conditions of successful degradation ceremonies', *American Journal of Sociology*, 61:420–4.

Gehlke, C. E. (1915) *Emile Durkheim's Contributions to Sociological Theory*, New York: Columbia University Press.

Gellner, E. (1970) 'Concepts and society', in B. R. Wilson (ed.) *Rationality*, Oxford: Basil Blackwell.

Gephart, W. (1990a) *Strafe und Verbrechen. Die Theorie Emile Durkheims*, Opladen: Leske & Budrich.

Gephart, W. (1990b) 'Mythen, Klischees und differenzierte Wirklichkeiten der Gesellschaft im Nationalsozialismus', *Soziologische Revue* 1990:279–87.

Gephart, W. (1991) 'Einleitung', in W. Gephart and H. P. Schreiner (eds), *Stadt und Kultur. Symposion aus Anlaß des 700 jährigen Bestehens der Stadt Düsseldorf*, Opladen: Leske & Budrich.

Gephart, W. (1992) 'Juristic Origins in the Conceptual World of Max Weber – Or: How Juristic Terms Have Sociological Meaning Instilled In Them', (unpublished paper).

Gephart, W. (1993) *Gesellschaftstheorie und Recht. Das Recht im soziologischen Diskurs der Moderne*, Frankfurt am Main: Suhrkamp.

Gephart, W. (1995) *The realm of normativity. Durkheim and Foucault*, Durkheim–Foucault Conference at Oxford 1995.

Giddens, A. (1978) *Durkheim*, London: Fontana.

Girard, R. (1978) *Things Hidden since the Foundation of the World*, Stanford: Stanford University Press.

Godlove, T. F., Jr. (1986) 'Epistemology in Durkheim's *Elementary Forms of Religious Life*', *Journal of the History of Philosophy*, 24, 3:385–401.

Godlove, T. F., Jr. (1989) *Religion, Interpretation, and Diversity of Belief: The Framework Model from Kant to Durkheim to Davidson*, New York: Cambridge University Press.

Godlove, T. F., Jr. (1996) 'Is space a concept?: spatial representation in Kant, French neo-Kantianism and Beyond', *Journal of the History of the Behavioral Sciences*, 32, 4:441–55.

Goffman, E. (1963) *Stigma*, Englewood Cliffs: Prentice Hall.

Goldenweiser, A. (1915) Review of *The Elementary Forms of the Religious Life*, *American Anthropologist* 17:719–35.

Granet, M. (1939) 'Catégories matrimoniales et relations de proximité dans la Chine ancienne', *Annales sociologiques*, 1–254.

Halbwachs, M. (1925) *Les cadres sociaux de la mémoire*, Paris: Albin Michel.

Hall, S. (1992) 'The question of cultural identity' in S. Hall, D. Held and T. McGrew (eds) *Modernity and its Futures*, Cambridge: Polity Press.

Hamelin, O. (1907) *Essai sur les éléments principaux de la représentation*, Paris: Alcan.

Heald, S. (1989) *Controlling Anger: The Sociology of Gisu Violence*, Manchester: Manchester University Press.

Hebdige, D. (1979) *Subcultures: The Meaning of Style*, London: Methuen.

Hebdige, D. (1989) 'After the masses' in S. Hall and M. Jacques (eds) *New Times*, London: Lawrence and Wishart.

Héran, F. (1996) *Figures et légendes de la parenté*, Thèse de doctorat d'état, Université de Paris V.

Hertz, R. (1907) 'Contribution à une étude sur la représentation collective de la mort', *L'Année sociologique*, X:48–137. Reproduced in Robert Hertz, *Sociologie religieuse et folklore*, Paris: Presses Universitaires de France, 1928. (2nd ed. 1970)

Hiatt, L. R. (1996) *Arguments about Aborigines*, Cambridge: Cambridge University Press.

Hocart, A. M. (1937/1970) 'Kinship systems', in R. Needham (ed.) *The Life-Giving Myth*, London: Tavistock.

Hollis, M. (1967) 'Reason and ritual', *Philosophy* 43:231–47.

Hollis, M. (1970) 'The limits of irrationality', in B. Wilson (ed.) *Rationality*, Oxford: Blackwell.

Hollis, M. (1982) 'The social destruction of reality', in Hollis and S. Lukes (eds) *Rationality and Relativism*, Cambridge, Mass.: MIT Press.

Horton, R. (1973) 'Lévy-Bruhl, Durkheim and the scientific revolution', in R. Horton and R. Finnegan (eds) 1973.

Horton R. and Finnegan R. (eds) (1973) *Modes of Thought. Essays on Thinking in Western and Non-Western Societies*, London: Faber & Faber.

Hubert, H. (1909) Review, 'Salomon Reinach, *Orpheus*', *L'Anthropologie*, 20:594.

Hubert, H. and Mauss, M. (1899) 'Essai sur la nature et la fonction du sacrifice, *L'Année sociologique*, II:29–138. t. 1964 by W. D. Halls, London: Cohen & West.

Hubert, H. and Mauss, M. (1904) 'Esquisse d'une théorie générale de la magie', *L'Année sociologique*, VII:1–146. Reproduced in M. Mauss, *Sociologie et anthropologie*, 1950, Paris: Presses Universitaire de France.

Irwin, T. H. (1977) 'Aristotle's discovery of metaphysics', *Review of Metaphysics*, 31:210–29.

Isambert, F. -A. (1976) 'L'élaboration de la notion du sacré dans l'école durkheimienne', *Archives des sciences sociales des religions*, 42, 2:35–56.

James, W. (1902) *The Varieties of Religious Experience*, New York: New American Library.

James, W. (1907) *The Will to Believe*, London: Longman.

Janet, P. (1879) *Traité élémentaire de philosophie*, Paris: Delagrave.

Joas, H. (1992) *Die Kreativität des Handelns*, Frankfurt am Main: Suhrkamp.

Jones, R. A. (1981) 'Robertson Smith, Durkheim and sacrifice: an historical context for *The Elementary Forms*', *Journal of the History of the Behavioral Sciences*, 17:184–205.

Jones, R. A. (1984) 'Demythologizing Durkheim: a reply to Gerstein', *Knowledge and Society*, 5:63–83.

Jones, R. A. and Vogt, W. P. (1984) 'Durkheim's defense of *Les Formes élémentaires de la vie religieuse*', *Knowledge and Society*, 5:45–62.

Kant, I. (1783) *Prolegomena to Any Future Metaphysics*, t. by P. Carus, revised 1977 by J. W. Ellington, Indianapolis: Hackett Publishing.

Kant, I. (1785/1911) *Grundlegung zur Metaphysik der Sitten*, in *Kant's gesammelte Schriften*, 4, Berlin: Reimer.

Kant, I. (1787) *Critique of Pure Reason*, t. by N. K. Smith, New York: St Martin's Press, 1929.

Kant, I. (1788/1913) *Kritik der praktischen Vernunft*, in *Kant's gesammelte Schriften*, 5, Berlin: Reimer.

Kant, I. (1790/1913) *Kritik der Urtheilschaft*, in *Kant's gesammelte Schriften*, 5, Berlin: Reimer.

Kant, I. (1963) *Critique of Pure Reason*, t. by Kemp Smith, London: Macmillan.

Kensinger, K. M. (1984) 'An emic model of Cashinahua marriage', in K. M. Kensinger (ed.) *Marriage Practices in Lowland South America*, Urbana: University of Illinois Press.

Knight, C. (1991) *Blood Relations: Menstruation and the Origins of Culture*, New Haven and London: Yale University Press.

Knight, C., Power C. and Watts I. (1995) 'The human symbolic revolution: a Darwinian account', *Cambridge Archaeological Journal*, 5:75–114.

Kohlhammer, S. (1994) 'Anathema. Der Holocaust und das Bilderverbot', *Merkur* 48:501–9.

Kugelmass, J. (1994) 'Weshalb wir nach Polen reisen. Holocaust-Tourismus als säkulares Ritual', in J. E. Young (ed.), *Mahnmale des Holocaust. Motive, Rituale und Stätten des Gedenkens*, München: Prestel.

Kuklick, H. (1991) *The Savage Within: the Social History of British Anthropology 1885–1945*, Cambridge: Cambridge University Press.

Kuper, A. (ed.) (1977) *The Social Anthropology of Radcliffe-Brown*, London: Routledge & Kegan Paul.

Kuper, A. (1988) *The Invention of Primitive Society: Transformations of an Illusion*, London: Routledge.

La Fontaine, J. S. (1985) *Initiation: Ritual Drama and Secret Knowledge Across the World*, Harmondsworth: Penguin.

Langham, I. (1981) *The Building of British Social Anthropology: W. H. R. Rivers and his Cambridge Disciples in the Development of Kinship Studies*, Dortrecht: D. Reidel.

Lannoy, J. de. (1996) 'Le Style des *Formes élémentaires de la vie religieuse* d'Emile Durkheim', *Durkheimian Studies / Etudes durkheimiennes*, n.s. 2:61–78.

Latour, B. (1989) *La science en action*, Paris: Editions La Découverte.

Latour, B. (1991) *Nous n'avons jamais été modernes. Essai d'anthropologie symétrique*, Paris: Editions La Découverte.

Lavabre, M.-C. (1994) 'Usages du passé, usages de la mémoire', *Revue française de science politique* 44:480–93.

Le Roy, E. (1913) Contribution to discussion of 'Le Problème religieux et la dualité de la nature humaine', *Bulletin de la Société française de philosophie*, XIII:45–47.

Leach, E. R. (1957) 'The epistemological background to Malinowski's empiricism', in R. Firth (ed.) *Man and Culture: an Evaluation of the Work of Bronislaw Malinowski*, London: Routledge & Kegan Paul.

Leach. E. R. (1966) 'Ritualization in man in relation to conceptual and social development', *Philosophical Transactions of the Royal Society of London*, Series B, No.772, 251:403–8.

Lehmann, J. (1993) *Deconstructing Durkheim*, London: Routledge.

Leibniz, G. W. (1989) 'On freedom and possibility', in R. Ariew and D. Garber, *G. W. Leibniz: Philosophical Essays*, Indianapolis: Hackett.

Lessa, W. A. and Vogt, E. Z. (1979) *Reader in Comparative Religion*, (4th ed.), New York: Harper & Row.

Lévi, S. (1892) 'La Science des religions et les religions de l'Inde', *Bulletin de l'Ecole Pratique des Hautes Etudes, Sciences religieuses*, Paris: Impr. nationale.

Lévi, S. (1898) *La Doctrine du sacrifice dans les Brâhmanas*, Paris: Leroux.

Lévi-Strauss, C. (1962) *Le Totémisme aujourd'hui*, Paris: Presses Universitaires de France.

Lévy-Bruhl, L. (1903) *La morale et la science des moeurs*, Paris: Alcan.

Lévy-Bruhl, L. (1910) *Les fonctions mentales dans les sociétés inférieures*, Paris: Alcan.

Lévy-Bruhl, L. (1931a) *Le Surnaturel et la nature dans la mentalité primitive*, Paris: Alcan.

Lévy-Bruhl, L. (1931b) *La mentalité primitive*. The Herbert Spencer Lecture delivered at Oxford 29 May 1931, Oxford: Clarendon Press.

Lévy-Bruhl, L. (1935) *La mythologie primitive. Le monde mythique des Australiens et des Papous*, Paris: Alcan.

Lévy-Bruhl, L. (1957) Letter 14 November 1934 to E. E. Evans-Pritchard, 'Une lettre de Lucien Lévy-Bruhl, au Professeur Evans-Pritchard', *Revue philosophique*, CXLVII, 4:407–413.

Liard, L. (1878) *La Science positive et la métaphysique*, Paris: Alcan. (4th ed. 1898)

Lienhardt, G. (1961) *Divinity and Experience*, Oxford: Clarendon Press.

Lindholme, C. (1990) *Charisma*, Oxford: Blackwell.

Littlejohn, J. (1970) 'Twins, birds, etc.', *Bijdragen tot de taal-, land- en volkenkunde* 126, 1:91–109.

Livingston, J. C. (1971) *Modern Christian Thought: From the Enlightenment to Vatican II*, New York and London: Macmillan.

Lockwood, D. (1992) *Solidarity and Schism. 'The Problem of Disorder' in Durkheimian and Marxist Sociology*, Oxford: Clarendon Press.

Lourandos, H. (1988) 'Palaeopolitics: resource intensification in Aboriginal Australia and Papua New Guinea', in T. Ingold, D. Riches and J. Woodburn (eds) *Hunters and Gatherers 1: History, Evolution and Social Change*, Oxford: Berg.

Lukes, S. (1968) *Emile Durkheim: An Intellectual Biography*, 2 vols, D.Phil. thesis, Oxford University.

Lukes, S. (1970) 'Some problems about rationality', in B. Wilson (ed.) Rationality, Oxford: Basil Blackwell.

Lukes, S. (1973) *Emile Durkheim: His Life and Work: A Historical and Critical Study*, London: Allen Lane. (Reprinted and bibliography updated 1992, London: Penguin)

Lukes, S. (1982) 'Relativism in its place,' in M. Hollis and S. Lukes (eds) *Rationality and Relativism*, Cambridge, Mass.: MIT Press.

MacIntyre, A. (1970) 'Is understanding religion compatible with believing?', in B. R. Wilson (ed.), *Rationality*, London: Blackwell.

Maddock, K. (1991) 'Metamorphosing the sacred in Australia', *The Australian Journal of Anthropology*, Special Issue, Reconsidering Aboriginality, 2:213–32.

Malinowski, B. (1913) Review of Baldwin Spencer and F. J. Gillen's *Across Australia*, *Folklore*, XXIV:278–9.

Malinowski, B. (1927) *Sex and Repression in Savage Society*, London: Routledge.

Malpas, J. E. (1992) *Donald Davidson and the Mirror of Meaning: Holism, Truth, Interpretation*, New York: Cambridge University Press.

Marett, R. R. and Penniman, T. K. (1932) *Spencer's Scientific Correspondence*, Oxford: Oxford University Press.

Mathiez, A. (1904) *Les Origines des cultes révolutionnaires (1789–1792)*, Paris: Bellais.

Mauss, M. (1899) see Hubert and Mauss 1899.

Mauss, M. (1900a) Review. 'B. Spencer et F. Gillen, *The Native Tribes of Central Australia*', *L'Année sociologique*, III:205–15.

Mauss, M. (1900b) Review. 'Sylvain Lévi, *La Doctrine du sacrifice dans les Brâhmanas*', *L'Année sociologique*, III:293–5.

Mauss, M. (1904) Review. 'K. Girgenssohn, *Die Religion, ihre psychischen Formen und ihre Zentralidee*', in Mauss 1968–9, 1:95–7.

Mauss, M. (1905) Review. 'A. Mathiez, *Les Origines des cultes révolutionnaires*', *L'Année sociologique*, VIII:295–8.

Mauss, M. (with H. Beuchat) (1906) 'Essai sur les variations saisonnières des sociétés eskimos: étude de morphologie sociale', *L'Année sociologique*, 9:39–132.

Mauss, M. (1909) 'La Prière', in Mauss 1968–9, 1:357–477.

Mauss, M. (1913) See Durkheim 1913a(ii)(31).

Mauss, M. (1925) 'Essai sur le don. Formes de l'échange dans les sociétés archaïques', *L'Année sociologique*, n.s. 1:30–186. t. by W. D. Halls, 1990, London: Routledge.

Mauss, M. (1935) 'Sylvain Lévi' in Mauss 1968–9, 3:537.

Mauss, M. (1936) Letter to S. Ranulf, in M. Gane (ed.) (1992) *The Radical Sociology of Durkheim and Mauss*, London: Routledge.

Mauss, M. (1938) 'Une Catégorie de l'esprit humain: la notion de personne, celle de "moi"', *Journal of the Royal Anthropological Institute*, 68:263–81. t. by W. D. Halls, in M. Carrithers, S. Collins and S. Lukes, (eds) (1985) *The Category of the Person: Anthropology, Philosophy, History*, Cambridge: Cambridge University Press.

Mauss, M. (1950) *Sociologie et anthropologie*, Paris: Presses Universitaires de France.

Mauss, M. (1968–9) V. Karady (ed.) *Marcel Mauss: Oeuvres*, 3 vols, Paris: Editions du Minuet.

Mayer, A. (1994) 'Memory and history. On poverty and remembering and forgetting the Judaeocide', in R. Steiniger (ed.), *Der Umgang mit dem Holocaust. Europa, USA, Israel*, Wien, Köln, Weimar: Böhlau.

McDowell, J. (1984) *Mind and World*, Cambridge, Mass.: Harvard University Press.

Mellars, P. and Stringer, C. (eds) (1989) *The Human Revolution: Behavioural and Biological Perspectives on the Origins of Modern Humans*, Edinburgh: Edinburgh University Press.

Melucci, A. (1989) *Nomads of the Present*, J. Keane and P. Mier (eds), London: Hutchinson Radius.

Melucci, A. (1996) *Challenging Codes: Collective Action in the Information Age*, Cambridge: Cambridge University Press.

Mergy, J. (1996) 'Totems et drapeaux: le symbolisme collectif chez Durkheim', *Durkheimiam Studies/Etudes durkheimiennes*, 2, n.s.: 99–121.

Merllié, D. (1989) 'Lévy-Bruhl et Durkheim. Notes biographiques en marge d'une correspondance', *Revue philosophique*, 114, 4:493–514.

Meštrović, S. G. (1988) *Emile Durkheim and the Reformation of Sociology*, Totawa, New Jersey: Rowman and Littlefield.

Meštrović, S. G. (1989a) 'Moral theory based on the heart versus the mind: Schopenhauer's and Durkheim's Critiques of Kantian Ethics', *Sociological Review*, 4, 38:431–57.

Meštrović, S. G. (1989b) 'Reappraising Durkheim's *Elementary Forms of the Religious Life* in the context of Schopenhauer's philosophy', *Journal for the Scientific Study of Religion*, 28, 3:255–72.

Meštrović, S. G. (1991) *The Coming* Fin de Siècle: *An Application of Durkheim's Sociology to Modernity and Postmodernism*, London: Routledge.

Michelet, J. (1967) *History of the French Revolution*, Gordon Wright (ed.), tr. Charles Cocks, Chicago: University of Chicago Press.

Mithan, S. (1996) *The Prehistory of Mind: A Search for the Origins of Art, Religion and Science*, London: Thames and Hudson.

Morphy, H. (1988) 'The original Australians and the evolution of anthropology', in H. Morphy and E. Edwards (eds), *Australia in Oxford*, Oxford: Pitt Rivers Museum.

Morphy, H. (1995) 'Empiricism to metaphysics: in defense of the concept of the dreamtime', in Tim Bonyhady and Tom Griffiths (eds) *Prehistory to Politics: John Mulvaney, the Humanities and the Public Intellectual*, Melbourne: Melbourne University Press, pp.163–89.

Morphy, H., Mulvaney, D. J., and Petch, A. (1997) *Dear Spencer: The Letters of F. J. Gillen to Baldwin Spencer*, Melbourne: Hyland Press.

Mulvaney, J. D. and Calaby, J. H. (1985) *'So Much That is New': Baldwin Spencer 1960–1929*, Melbourne: Melbourne University Press.

Mürmel, H. (1994) 'Bemerkungen zum Problem des Einflusses von William Robertson Smith auf die Durkheimgruppe' in *Gnosisforschung und Religionsgeschichte*, Marburg: Diagonal Verlag.

Myers, J. (1992) 'Nonmainstream body modification: genital piercing, branding, burning, and cutting', *Journal of Contemporary Ethnography*, 21, 3:267–306.

Needham, R. (1963) 'Introduction' to E. Durkheim and M. Mauss, *Primitive Classification*, London: Cohen and West.

Needham, R. (1972) *Belief, Language and Experience*, Oxford: Blackwell.

Needham, R. (1974) *Remarks and Inventions: Skeptical Essays about Kinship*, London: Tavistock.

Nora, P. (ed.) (1984–1992) *Les lieux de mémoire*, 3 vols, Paris: Gallimard.

Nozick, R. (1993) *The Nature of Rationality*, Princeton, New York: Princeton University Press.

Nugteren, A. (1995) 'Rituals around the bodhi-tree in Bodhgaya, India', in J. Platvoet and K. van der Toorn (eds) *Pluralism and Identity: Studies in Ritual Behaviour*, Leiden: E. J. Brill.

Nye, M. J. (1979) 'The Boutroux circle and Poincaré's conventionalism', *Journal of the History of Ideas*, 40:107–20.

O'Neill, O. (1992) 'Autonomy, coherence and independence', in D. Milligan and W. Watts Miller (eds), *Liberalism, Citizenship and Autonomy*, London: Avebury.

O'Neill, O. (1996) 'Interpretation within the limits of reason', draft 6 of 2nd lecture, Tanner Lectures, University of Harvard.

Ono, M. (1996) 'Collective effervescence and symbolism', *Durkheimian Studies/Etudes durkheimiennes*, n.s., 2:79–98.

Ophir, A. (1987) 'On sanctifying the Holocaust. An anti-theological treatise', *Tikkun* 2.

Ory, P. (1992) *Une Nation pour mémoire 1889, 1939, 1989 trois jubilés révolutionnaires*, Paris.

Parsons, T. (1937) *The Structure of Social Action*, New York: Free Press.

Pearce, F. (1989) *The Radical Durkheim*, London: Unwin Hyman.

Peterson, N. (1970) 'Buluwandi: a Central Australian ceremony for the resolution of conflict', in R. M. Berndt (ed.) *Australian Aboriginal Anthropology*, Nedlinds: University of Western Australia Press.

Philonenko, A. (1993) *L'Oeuvre de Kant*, 2 vols, Paris: Vrin.

Pickering, W. S. F. (1984) *Durkheim's Sociology of Religion*, London: Routledge & Kegan Paul.

Pickering, W. S. F. (1993) 'The origins of conceptual thinking in Durkheim: social or religious?' in S. P. Turner (ed.) *Emile Durkheim: Sociologist and Moralist*, London: Routledge.

Pikler, J. and Somló, F. (1900) *Der Ursprung des Totemismus; ein Beitrag zur materialistischen Geschichtstheorie*, Berlin.

Plato (1980) *Theaetetus*, in E. Hamilton and H. Cairns (eds) *The Collected Dialogues of Plato*, Princeton: Princeton University Press.

Platvoet, J. (1995) 'Rituals of confrontation: the Ayodhya conflict', in J. Platvoet and K. van der Toorn (eds) *Pluralism and Identity: Studies in Ritual Behaviour*, Leiden: Brill.

Polhemus, T. (ed.) (1978) *The Body Reader*, New York: Pantheon.

Prades, J. A. (1987) *Persistance et métamorphose du sacré*, Paris: Presses Universitaires de France.

Putnam, H. (1981) *Reason, Truth and History*, Cambridge: Cambridge University Press.

Putnam, H. (1983) 'Analyticity and apriority: beyond Wittgenstein and Quine,' in *Realism and Reason: Philosophical Papers*, Vol.3, New York: Cambridge University Press.

Putnam, H. (1990) *Realism with a Human Face*, James Conant (ed.) Cambridge, Mass.: Harvard University Press.

Quiatt, D. and Reynolds, V. (1993) *Primate Behaviour: Information, Social Knowledge and the Evolution of Culture*, Cambridge: Cambridge University Press.

Quine, W. V. (1953) *From a Logical Point of View*, Cambridge, Mass.: Harvard University Press.

Rabier, E. (1884) *Leçons de Philosophie. I. Psychologie*, Paris: Hachette. (4th ed. 1893)

Radcliffe-Brown, A. R. (1933) *The Andaman Islanders*, reprinted with additions, Cambridge: Cambridge University Press.

Radcliffe-Brown, A. R. (1938) *The Social Organisation of Australian Tribes, Oceania Monographs, 1*, Sydney: Oceania Monographs.

Renouvier. C. (1859) *Deuxième Essai de Critique Générale*, Paris: Librairie Philosophique de Ladrange.

Renouvier, C. (1864) *Quatrième Essai de Critique Générale*, Paris: Librairie Philosophique de Ladrange.

Renouvier, C. (1875) *Essais de critique générale. Premier essai. Traité de logique générale et de logique formelle*, 3 vols, (2nd ed.), Paris: Colin.

Renouvier, C. (1908) *Science de Morale*, 2 vols, Paris: Alcan.

Reynolds, V. (1967) *The Apes, the Gorilla, Chimpanzee, Orangutan and Gibbon: Their History and Their World*, London: Cassell.

Ribot, Th. (1896) *La Psychologie des sentiments*, Paris: Alcan.

Richman, M. (1982) *Reading Georges Bataille: Beyond the Gift*, Baltimore, Maryland: Johns Hopkins University Press.

Richman, M. (1995) 'The sacred group: a Durkheimian perspective on the Collège de Sociologie', in C. B. Gill (ed.) *Bataille: Writing the Sacred*, London: Routledge.

Rivaud, A. (1950) 'Notice sur la vie et l'oeuvre de L. Lévy-Bruhl', Paris: Institut des Sciences morales et politiques.

Rorty, R. (1979) *Philosophy and the Mirror of Nature*, Princeton: Princeton University Press.

Rorty, R. (1984) 'The historiography of philosophy: four genres', in R. Rorty, J. Schneewind, and Q. Skinner (eds), *Philosophy in History*, Cambridge: Cambridge University Press.

Russell, B. (1978) *The Problems of Philosophy*, Oxford: Oxford University Press.

Russell, B. (1989) *The Analysis of Mind*, London: Unwin.

Sanders, C. R. (1988) 'Marks of mischief: becoming and being tattooed', *Journal of Contemporary Ethnography* 16, 4:395–432.

Schaub, E. L. (1920) 'A sociological theory of knowledge', *Philosophical Review*, 29:319–39.

Schmaus, W. (1994) *Durkheim's Philosophy of Science and the Sociology of Knowledge: Creating an Intellectual Niche*, Chicago: University of Chicago Press.

Schmaus, W. (1995) 'Explanation and essence in *The Rules of Sociological Method* and *The Division of Labour in Society*', *Sociological Perspectives*, 38, 1.

Schmaus, W. (1996) 'Lévy-Bruhl, Durkheim, and the positivist roots of the sociology of knowledge', *Journal of the History of the Behavioral Sciences*, 32, 4:424–440.

Schmidt-Wulffen, S. (1994), 'Ein Mahnmal versinkt. Ein Gespräch mit Esther und Jochen Gerz', in J. E. Young (ed.), *Mahnmale des Holocaust. Motive, Rituale und Stätten des Gedenkens*, München: Prestel.

Seger, I. (1957) *Durkheim and his Critics on the Sociology of Religion*, New York: Bureau of Applied Social Research, Columbia University.

Seth, J. (1894) *A Study of Ethical Principles*, Edinburgh: Blackwood. (10th ed. 1908)

Simiand, F. (1934) 'La Monnaie, réalité social', *Annales sociologiques*, ser. D:1–86.

Skinner, Q. (1988) 'A reply to my critics', in J. Tully (ed.) *Meaning and Context: Quentin Skinner and His Critics*, Princeton: Princeton University Press.

Smart, J. J. C. (1967) 'Religion and science', in P. Edwards (ed.) *The Encyclopedia of Philosophy*, New York: Macmillan.

Smith, C. (1967a) 'Boutroux, Emile', in P. Edwards (ed.) *The Encyclopedia of Philosophy*, New York: Macmillan.

Smith, C. (1967b) 'Le Roy, Edouard', in P. Edwards (ed.), *The Encyclopedia of Philosophy*, New York: Macmillan.

Smith, W. Robertson. (1889) *The Religion of the Semites: The Fundamental Institutions*. (Republished 1972, New York: Schocken.)

Spencer, H. (1862) *First Principles*, London: Williams and Norgate.

Spencer, W. B. (1912) *Across Australia*, London: Macmillan.

Spencer, W. B. and Gillen, F. J. (1899) *The Native Tribes of Central Australia*, London: Macmillan.

Spencer, W. B. and Gillen, F. J. (1904) *The Northern Tribes of Central Australia*, London: Macmillan.

Sperber, D. (1975) *Rethinking Symbolism*, t. by A. L. Morton, Cambridge: Cambridge University Press.

Stanner, W. E. H. (1966) *On Aboriginal Religion*, Oceania Monographs, 11, Sydney: University of Sydney.

Stanner, W. E. H. (1967) 'Reflections on Durkheim and Aboriginal religion', in M. Freedman (ed.) *Social Organization; Essays Presented to Raymond Firth*, London: Frank Cass.

Stocking, G. (1968) *Race, Culture and Evolution*, New York: Free Press.

Stocking, G. (1995) *After Tylor: British Social Anthropology 1888–1951*, Madison: University of Wisconsin Press.

Strawbridge, S. (1982) 'Althusser's Theory of Ideology and Durkheim's Account of Religion: an examination of some striking parallels', *Sociological Review*, 30, 1:125–140.

Strawson, P. F. (1989) 'Sensibility, understanding, and the doctrine of synthesis: comments on Henrich and Guyer', in E. Forster (ed.) *Kant's Transcendental Deductions: The Three Critiques and the Opus Postumum*, Stanford: Stanford University Press.

Strenski, I. (1997) *Durkheim and the Jews of France*, Chicago: University of Chicago Press.

Thompson, K. (1986) *Beliefs and Ideology*, London: Routledge.

Thompson, K. (1990) 'Secularization and sacralization', in J. C. Alexander and P. Sztompka (eds) *Rethinking Progress*, London: Unwin Hyman.

Thompson, M. (1981) 'On a priori truth', *Journal of Philosophy*, 78, 8:458–82.

Thompson, M. (1983) 'Philosophical approaches to categories', *The Monist*, 66, 3:336–52.

Tiryakian, E. A. (1978) 'Emile Durkheim', in T. Bottomore and R. Nisbet (eds): *A History of Sociological Analysis*, New York: Basic Books.

Tiryakian, E. A. (1979) 'L'Ecole durkheimienne à la recherche de la société perdue: la sociologie naissante et son milieu culturel', *Cahiers internationaux de sociologie*, LXVI:97–114.

Tiryakian, E. A. (1988) 'From Durkheim to Managua: revolutions as religious revivals', in J. C. Alexander (ed.) *Durkheimian Sociology: Cultural Studies*, Cambridge: Cambridge University Press.

Tiryakian, E. A. (1995) 'Collective effervescence, social change and charisma: Durkheim, Weber and 1989', *International Sociology*, 10, 3:269–281.

Traugott, M. (ed.) *Emile Durkheim on Institutional Analysis*, Chicago: University of Chicago Press.

Turner, B. S. (1991) 'Recent developments in the theory of the body', in M. Featherstone, M. Hepworth and B. Turner (eds) *The Body, Social Process and Cultural Theory*, London: Sage.

Turner, V. (1957) *Schism and Continuity in an African Society*, Manchester: University Press.

Turner, V. (1962) *Chihamba the White Spirit: A Ritual Drama of the Ndembu*, Rhodes-Livingstone Paper, 31.

Turner, V. (1967) *The Forest of Symbols*, Ithaca: Cornell University Press.

Turner, V. (1968) *The Drums of Affliction*, Oxford: Clarendon Press.

Turner, V. (1969) *The Ritual Process. Structure and Anti-structure*, London: Routledge & Kegan Paul.

Turner, V. (1974) *Dramas, Fields and Metaphors: Symbolic Action in Human Society*, Ithaca: Cornell University Press.

Turner, V. (1975) *Revelation and Divination in Ndembu Ritual*, Ithaca: Cornell University Press.

Turner, V. (1985) *On the Edge of the Bush: Anthropology as Experience*, Tucson, Arizona: University of Arizona Press.

Urry, J. (1993) *Before Social Anthropology: Essays on the History of British Social Anthropology*, Chur: Harwood Academic Publishers.

Van Gennep, A. (1920) *L'Etat actuel du problème totémique*, Paris: Leroux.

Watts Miller, W. (1996) *Durkheim, Morals and Modernity*, London: UCL Press.

White, A. D. (1896) *History of the Warfare of Science with Theology in Christendom*, New York: Appleton.

Wolfe, P. (1991) 'On being woken up: the Dreaming in anthropology and Australian settler culture', *Comparative Studies in Culture and History*, 33, 2:197–224.

Wolff, K. (ed.) (1960) *Emile Durkheim (1858–1917): A Collection of Essays, with translations and a bibliography*, Columbus, Ohio: Ohio State University Press.

AUTHOR INDEX

SUBJECT INDEX